# Also available at all good book stores

9781785318405

9781785319952

9781785318252

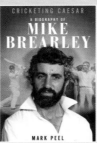
9781785316623

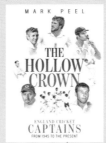
9781785316630

9781785314377

9781785317798

9781785319860

9781785318511

# NEVER SURRENDER

# NEVER SURRENDER

## THE LIFE OF DOUGLAS JARDINE

MARK PEEL

First published by Pitch Publishing, 2021

Pitch Publishing
A2 Yeoman Gate
Yeoman Way
Worthing
Sussex
BN13 3QZ
www.pitchpublishing.co.uk
info@pitchpublishing.co.uk

ISBN 978 1 78531 992 1

Typesetting and origination by Pitch Publishing
Printed and bound in India by Replika Press Pvt. Ltd.

# CONTENTS

# ACKNOWLEDGEMENTS

I'D LIKE to thank the following who provided me with information and advice during my research of Douglas Jardine: Richard Jefferson, Magnus Linklater, Gavin Lloyd, Nigel Hancock, the late Charles Randall, David Frith, Ivo Tennant and Tom Tennant.

I'm extremely grateful to Neil Robinson, the Curator of Collections at Lord's and MCC, for all his help and for permission to quote from the MCC Archives; and to Robert Curphey, the Archive and Library Manager at Lord's, for his many efforts on my behalf.

I'm also indebted to Julie Crocker, the Senior Archivist, The Royal Archives, Windsor Castle, and I acknowledge the permission of HM Elizabeth II for the use of the material; Suzanne Foster, the Archivist, Winchester College, and for permission to quote from its archive; Felix Beardmore-Gray, the Archivist, Horris Hill School; Bill Gordon, the Librarian, Surrey CC, Craig Marshall, the Archivist, Fettes College; Dr Christopher Skelton-Foord, the Librarian, New College, Oxford, Jennifer Thorp, Archivist, New College, Oxford and the staff at the National Library of Scotland.

Last but by no means least, I'd like to express my gratitude to my agent Andrew Lownie; to Richard Whitehead for his highly professional copy-edit; and to Jane Camillin and Alex Daley at Pitch, along with Duncan Olner, Dean Rockett and Graham Hales for all their efforts on the design, proofing and typeset.

# INTRODUCTION

FEW CRICKETERS have been stigmatised as much as Douglas Jardine, the imperious captain of England, who subjected Australia to Bodyline, a form of intimidatory bowling directed at the batsman's head and upper body, on MCC's tour in 1932/33. The Australian opener, Jack Fingleton, who played in the series, wrote in his book *Cricket Crisis* that Jardine was the most hated sportsman ever to come to Australia; the broadcaster, Alan McGilvray, called Jardine the most notorious Englishman since Jack the Ripper; and, more recently, the Australian cricket writer, Gideon Haigh, rated him the most reviled character in sport. It wasn't just Australians who held this view. Pelham (Plum) Warner, manager of the 1932/33 tour, complained in a letter home that 'one simply cannot like him',[1] and Gubby Allen, the one England fast bowler who refused to bowl Bodyline, informed his father that 'Jardine is loathed and, between you and me, rightly more than any German who fought in any war.'[2]

Allen was being unduly personal, but throughout his career Jardine proved a highly divisive figure. Born into a Scottish colonial family in Bombay in 1900, he experienced a solitary upbringing which shaped his austere character. A product of wartime Winchester College, where spartan values were much in vogue, he emerged as a brilliant sportsman, an intense competitor and a leader of iron resolve. A classical batsman of courage and style, he forged a reputation at Oxford and Surrey as one of the leading amateurs in the country, and following a successful Test debut against West Indies in 1928, he was picked to tour Australia that winter. He began with three successive centuries against state sides, and made a valuable contribution to England's retention of the Ashes, but his exposure to Australia and Australians left him distinctly underwhelmed.

Reserved and unbending, he failed to respond to their breezy informality and voluble humour. More pertinently, his icy contempt for the crowds who jeered him for slow scoring added to their impression of him as a snooty colonial lacking the common touch. 'As he strode out to bat, a tall, angular, acidulated and seemingly aloof Englishman, with a gaudy cap rampant and a silk handkerchief knotted around his throat,' wrote Fingleton, 'he walked into the vision of many Australians as the very personification of the old school tie.'[3]

Enigmatic personality aside, Jardine's magisterial batting and powers of leadership won him the England captaincy in 1931 and he immediately set about stamping his authority. The Australian leg-spinner turned journalist Bill O'Reilly regarded him as a modern-day Hannibal, who could have escorted a troop of elephants across the Alps without great difficulties. 'He led his team like an army, demanding absolute obedience, and with rigid on-field discipline.'[4] In his first Test as captain – against New Zealand at Lord's – he confused the names of two debutants, Fred Bakewell and John Arnold, but no one dared contradict him. In the same match, he addressed the 44-year-old Frank Woolley, one of the titans of the English game, as if he were a novice, berated leg-spinner Ian Peebles for getting out to a loose shot as nightwatchman and admonished Peebles's fellow leg-spinner Walter Robins for his juvenile humour. When official business removed him temporarily from the field in the Gentlemen v Players fixture at Lord's in 1932, the atmosphere visibly relaxed as the slip cordon began exchanging pleasantries, only for it to vanish the moment he returned.

With his antipathy towards Australians and his determination to cut their idol, Don Bradman, down to size, Jardine's appointment as MCC captain for the 1932/33 tour – his tactical expertise notwithstanding – was a huge diplomatic gamble. When his former cricket master at Winchester, Rockley Wilson, who had toured Australia in 1920/21, heard of his appointment, he predicted that 'We shall win the Ashes but we may very well lose a Dominion', a prophecy that came to haunt Warner. 'D.R.J. is a very difficult fellow,' he wrote to his wife early in the tour … hates Australians and his special hate is now Bradman!'[5] Shocked by Jardine's crude language, especially towards Bradman, Warner took great exception to his captain's ill-judged remark when they were inspecting the newly opened Sydney Harbour Bridge. As aircraft of the Royal Australian Air Force flew over, Jardine turned to him and said, 'I wish they were Japs. I wish they would bomb the bridge into their harbour.' (The Japanese had recently provoked international outrage by their indiscriminate bombing of Manchuria.)

At a time of severe economic depression and political turmoil, Australia viewed the visit of MCC as a welcome distraction from personal hardship and an opportunity to advance its national identity away from the shadow of the mother country.

The tourists were given a warm welcome when they arrived, but the good cheer soon faded when they unveiled tactics that flouted the spirit of the game. The main exponents of the Bodyline plan were the Nottinghamshire bowlers Harold Larwood and Bill Voce, both quick by any standards, but its author was Jardine. 'Jardine preached a policy of competitive "hate",' wrote Duncan Hamilton, Larwood's biographer. 'You had to hate the Australians on the field to beat them … For his part, Larwood would never waver from his belief that he was of use to his captain, but never used by him. "You know," he said, "I think Mr Jardine would have made a famous soldier."'[6]

In that spirit Jardine forbade his players from exchanging pleasantries with the opposition on the field, and discouraged any fraternising with them off it. He also clamped down on all those who succumbed too easily to local hospitality. Shortly before the second Test at Melbourne, Larwood and Tommy Mitchell, the Derbyshire leg-spinner, spent an afternoon up town and, after meeting a group of actors from a pantomime, returned to the hotel very inebriated. Consequently, Jardine had Larwood tailed the following evening and when he ended up at the same theatre he was called to the phone by his captain, who ordered him home. Larwood told Mitchell that he would be back at half past ten, or eleven o'clock, but come the promised hour there was no sign of Larwood. Jardine's word was law.

A top-class batsman who sold his wicket dearly, Jardine was the man for a crisis, not least against raw pace, which he played with resilience, even when the blows rained down on his body. It was the same in the field. A specialist gully, the mystery of why he missed two difficult catches in that position in the Adelaide Test of January 1933 was only revealed when he was seen bathing a badly bruised hand in his bedroom afterwards. He hated sympathy and expected his team to display similar resolve. In the vital fourth Test of the series, he hauled Eddie Paynter out of hospital where he was suffering from tonsillitis to stave off an England batting collapse and Paynter responded with a fighting 83, which went a long way to securing his side victory.

With England winning the first Test at Sydney and Australia triumphing in the second at Melbourne on a docile pitch which rendered Bodyline ineffective, a lot hinged on the third Test at Adelaide. Jardine's insistence that England's final pre-match practice take place behind closed doors after he'd been heckled by some of the large crowd of onlookers only added to the tension. With its pastoral charm and picturesque view of St Peter's Anglican Cathedral, Jardine wasn't alone in ranking the Adelaide Oval the most beautiful ground in the world, but it was about to play host to the most bruising Test in history.

Following England's first-innings dismissal for 341 on the second afternoon, attention now switched to Larwood, then at the height of his powers. Working up a fearsome pace, he struck the Australian captain Bill Woodfull a vicious blow over the heart with the final ball of his second over. As Woodfull doubled up in agony and 50,000 Australians vented their spleen, Jardine sidled up to Larwood and, in earshot of Bradman, the non-striker, shouted, 'Well bowled, Harold!' The outrage at Woodfull's injury was nothing compared to the blind fury when Jardine stopped Larwood in his run-up at the beginning of his next over and switched the slips to the leg side. His decision was viewed as a serious error of judgement which, given the emotions in the ground, could well have brought the crowd on to the pitch and led to potential casualties.

As Larwood, in company with Allen, worked his way through the Australian upper order, including Bradman caught at short leg, he and Jardine were subjected to repeated taunts, the politest of which decried their sportsmanship. 'This was an astonishingly bad piece of misbehaviour in Adelaide, which admits to being the most respectable city in Australia,' recollected Robert Menzies, later prime minister of Australia. 'But Jardine had, in the homely phase, "bought it". In every step, in every gesture, in every tilt of the head, he showed his contempt for the crowd. He was a cricketing Coriolanus.'[7]

When Warner paid a courtesy visit to the Australian dressing-room to inquire after Woodfull's condition, the Australian captain sent him on his way with a devastating rebuff. 'I don't want to speak to you, Mr Warner. There are two sides out there; one is playing cricket, the other isn't.'

Despite the uproar unleashed by his team's hard-nosed approach, Jardine wasn't to be deterred when the game resumed after a Sunday rest day. A brief fightback from Australia, orchestrated by their popular wicketkeeper Bertie Oldfield, nearly ended in tragedy when he attempted to pull a ball from Larwood. Playing a shade too soon, he edged it on to his forehead, just below the hairline. As Oldfield staggered away before collapsing, the crowd erupted in pandemonium, shaking their fists and hurling vitriol at Jardine and Larwood. While the ground authorities appealed for police reinforcements, Jardine drew further abuse from the terraces when he opened England's second innings in his trademark silk scarf and Harlequin cap. Ignoring the rising chorus of hate, he batted through to the close, his laboured half-century helping to set up an overwhelming win.

Yet victory on the field was superseded by events off it. Appalled by the ferocity of Bodyline – although Larwood wasn't bowling it when Woodfull and Oldfield were hit – the Australian Board of Control conveyed their grave reservations by cable to MCC, accusing their team of unsportsmanlike behaviour and warning that the continuation of such tactics threatened Anglo–Australian relations.

Unwilling to accept that Bodyline – or leg theory, as he termed it – was unsportsmanlike, Jardine risked further opprobrium by continuing to employ it in the remaining two Tests. After winning the series 4-1, he returned to England a national hero, the man who wrested back the Ashes from a nation deemed to be bad losers. Yet Jardine's spell in the sun was brief, since the British public, shielded from the worst effects of Bodyline by a partisan press, now witnessed it with their own eyes the following summer, not least from the West Indian pace bowlers, Manny Martindale and Learie Constantine. With Australia refusing to tour England in 1934 unless intimidatory bowling directed at the batsman was outlawed, MCC began to have second thoughts. By agreeing to Australian demands, they disowned Jardine, precipitating his immediate retirement from the game. He repaired to the press box where he continued to defend the legitimacy of Bodyline, chided MCC for their lack of resolve and denounced the rowdiness of Australian crowds. Ostracised by the cricket establishment, he retreated into the shadows, so that when he died prematurely in June 1958, his passing occasioned regret rather than a great outpouring of grief.

For years afterwards, Jardine continued to be the *enfant terrible* of international cricket, especially among Australians. These sentiments were amply expressed in the 1984 Australian drama-documentary *Bodyline*. Avoiding any attempt at balance and accuracy, the scriptwriters depicted Jardine as a loathsome English toff and Larwood as his doltish accomplice, a portrayal that led to the latter, by then an Australian resident of over 30 years, receiving abusive telephone calls. Yet as the embers of Bodyline were being stoked once again, the changing nature of cricket gave it a more understanding feel. In a more market-driven era, with its win-at-all costs ethos, the tendency towards gamesmanship became ever more pronounced. Nothing better encapsulated these changing values than the preponderance of intimidatory bowling.

Ever since the game began, sides with real speed merchants weren't slow at using them to assault the opposition. England had taken a pounding from Australia's Jack Gregory and Ted McDonald in 1920/21 in Australia and 1921 in England and they saw Bodyline to some extent as an attempt to get even. Jardine always used to say that Bodyline would have raised few ripples had Australia been able to retaliate or they'd won the series. Certainly, once Bradman had the necessary firepower in Ray Lindwall and Keith Miller after the Second World War, he wasn't slow in targeting the England batsmen. According to Fingleton, Lindwall and Miller bowled more bouncers in 1946/47 than Larwood and Voce did in 1932/33, although they weren't directed at the body. After one particularly bruising session in the Trent Bridge Test of 1948 when England's Len Hutton and Denis Compton had endured a withering assault from Miller, Compton, irked by Bradman's evident pleasure at their discomfort, reminded him of his previous statement that this wasn't the right way to play cricket. Forced on to the defensive, an uncomfortable-looking Bradman stuck to his guns. 'You've got a bat in your hand, haven't you,' he retorted. 'You should be able to get out of the way of them anyway – I used to love it when I played against bouncers. I used to hook them.'

With the rise of Australia's Dennis Lillee and Jeff Thomson in the 1970s, along with the long line of West Indian fast bowlers, intimidatory bowling entered a new, more chilling era. At the Melbourne Centenary Test in 1977, Larwood began counting the bouncers Lillee bowled. After a while he turned to his former new-ball partner Bill Bowes and remarked, 'You know, Bill, these fellows have bowled more bouncers in this match than I ever bowled in a season.' Why, he wondered, had Bodyline been singled out for such obloquy when bowlers before and since had bowled with similar aggression? Horrific though the injuries to Woodfull and Oldfield were, the former was able to carry on batting, while the latter was back playing Test cricket within weeks. The England batsmen injured by the West Indian pace quartet in 1984 weren't quite so fortunate. Debutant Andy Lloyd, hit on the head by Malcolm Marshall at Edgbaston, spent a week in hospital and never played Test cricket again; nor did Paul Terry, who had his arm broken by Winston Davis at Old Trafford. Such was the change in ethos by then that lower-order batsmen, once afforded protection from the short ball, now ran the gauntlet like everyone else – although they were at least better equipped with helmets and armguards. Having watched England nightwatchman Pat Pocock face bouncer after bouncer from Marshall in the final Test of that series, *Wisden* editor John Woodcock called it 'a woeful piece of cricket, entirely lacking in chivalry … Perhaps, when the International Cricket Conference do no more than pay lip service to the problem, it is not surprising that umpires are so compliant.'[8]

After reporting on England's 5-0 loss in the Caribbean in 1985/86, Robin Marlar of the *Sunday Times* wrote that current West Indian cricket had become 'a missile out of control which will kill cricket, all cricket, including their own. Even protected, the England players bore bruises which would horrify the toughest among us, and bring tears to their maiden aunts.'[9]

Three years later in Australia, West Indies won convincingly, but, once again, their style of cricket left some critics cold. According to Woodcock, their pace attack in the Melbourne Test was as hostile as anything he'd ever seen, and their failure to register any concern for batsmen who were hit, he found thoroughly unedifying. He also reported that Leo O'Brien, who played for Australia in the Bodyline series, contended that the West Indian bowling was worse than Bodyline because their attack was relentless and many more batsmen were hit. His view was endorsed by the noted cricket historian David Frith. He wrote: 'Bodyline created a sense of betrayal that may never die. But it was nothing compared to the 1980s when the West Indians offered nothing but fast bowling all day with none of it pitched in the batsman's half. With the injuries and stultifying progress of play, that was the most unattractive cricket man has ever had to watch.'[10]

None of this is to excuse Bodyline, but seen in the light of more recent events we can view it with greater objectivity. In 2007, in a series of articles commemorating the 75th anniversary of Bodyline, *The Times* reported that in a poll of 21 present and past captains, seven of whom captained England, two-thirds of them approved of Jardine's tactics. 'Jardine obviously found a tactic that was successful and if it was in the laws of the game then it was fair enough,' said Clive Lloyd, who led the West Indies through some controversial times.[11]

Jardine's rehabilitation continued with the publication of Christopher Douglas's sympathetic biography in 1984, David Frith's weighty *Bodyline Autopsy* in 2002, which made a case for clemency, and Surrey's decision in 2014 to rename a conference centre at the Oval, the Jardine Suite. More astounding was the endorsement he received from Shane Warne, Australia's leg-spinner. In his book, *No Spin*, published in 2018, he wrote that Jardine was one of the best captains ever to play the game for what he achieved against Bradman and for having the courage to change the game's parameters, praise which contrasted with the criticism he levelled against Steve Waugh, one of his former captains.

Beneath Jardine's iron fist there lay a velvet glove, evident to those who became better acquainted with him, or who encountered him away from the cricket field. Raised as an only child and separated from his parents at an early age, his patrician self-confidence concealed a shy, highly strung personality who chewed his nails to the quick, not least when waiting to bat. 'Douglas had no time for trivia,' recalled his cousin Alex Jardine, a renowned artist, 'and though the corner of his lip could occasionally lift in a half smile he had a very dry, dour Scottish humour.'[12] 'He was a typical Scot in his rather dour sense of humour,' concurred Mark Patten, a team-mate of Jardine's at Winchester and Oxford, 'but I found him a delightful companion and a highly intelligent captain.'[13] Although a somewhat hesitant orator in his playing days, he could inject a lighter touch to proceedings. Alluding to the traditional rivalry between Australia's two great cities during the Bodyline tour, he told a Sydney audience that when MCC were down in Melbourne he said they had reached the bullseye of cricket. 'Now we are in Sydney I am inclined to think the target is a moving one.' The renowned broadcaster John Arlott's anxiety about meeting him for the first time soon dissolved when he found a person much more relaxed than he'd anticipated. 'But in his first sentence he made a few jokes and everything was all right. He had a dry sense of humour. He was very funny and could paralyse you with laughter.'[14] He also made a great impression on Lady Game, the wife of Air Vice-Marshal Sir Philip Game, the Governor of New South Wales, when he sat next to her at an official lunch on the 1932/33 tour, and he proved a highly popular guest at two boys' schools he visited. According to the England leg-spinner Ian Peebles, Jardine, beneath his chilly exterior, was a considerable man and one of extremely kind heart, not least to those who sought his advice in times of trouble. Never one to skimp on a round of drinks, he was quick to reciprocate a good deed with a grateful note of thanks and on the 1932/33 tour he not only sent Christmas presents to his players' families, he also gave each player an inscribed silver ashtray at the end of it.

In private, he was a dedicated family man and a committed philanthropist, not least his work for Eton Manor Boys' Club – set up to provide sporting opportunities for deprived youngsters in London's East End. Having seen him buying cricket bats for a number of these youngsters, the South African batsman Herbie Taylor called him a fine fellow. 'A man who will do such things and keep it to himself must be pretty good inside – he is liked by the amateurs and respected by the professionals.'[15]

During the war Jardine served his country in uniform in a number of capacities, proving a popular and unassuming colleague; then afterwards he won renown as a witty after-dinner speaker, a self-effacing team-mate on the village green, a committed president of the newly-formed Umpires' Association and loyal supporter of Oxford University cricket. More surprisingly, as he mellowed he befriended a number of Australian cricketers, Bradman aside, compelling many a former adversary to view him in a new light.

While Bodyline continues to occupy a leading place in cricketing history, it is perhaps only now, in a less chivalrous age, that we can provide a more rounded portrait of its leading protagonist, a man who, whatever his other failings, was a born leader destined to leave his mark on the game.

**Endnotes:**

1   Gerald Howat, *Plum Warner*, p113
2   Brian Rendell, *Gubby Allen: Bad Boy of Cricket?* p37
3   Jack Fingleton, *Cricket Crisis*, p78
4   Alan Hill, *Herbert Sutcliffe: Cricket Maestro*, p190
5   Howat, *Plum Warner*, p113
6   Duncan Hamilton, *Harold Larwood*, p131
7   *The Cricketer Spring Annual* 1968, p50
8   *Wisden Cricketers' Almanack* 1985, p48
9   *The Sunday Times*, 20 April 1986
10  *The Guardian*, 21 October 2002
11  *The Times*, 3 December 2007
12  *The Cricketer,* July 1983, p19
13  Ibid
14  Philip Derriman, *Bodyline*, p12
15  *Daily Telegraph* (Sydney), 13 July 1932

CHAPTER 1

# BORN TO RULE

DOUGLAS ROBERT Jardine was born in Bombay on 23 October 1900 into a Scottish colonial family. The Jardines originally hailed from France and came over to Britain with William the Conqueror and the Normans in 1066. The chief branch of the family settled in Dumfriesshire in south-west Scotland in the 14th century and engaged in many a bloody skirmish over disputed territory with their English rivals across the Border. According to the Scottish writer Alex Massie, the Border bred hard men, quick to resort to violence and slow to forget. 'The Jardine family motto, "Cave Adsum", means "Beware, I am here." It is a statement of fact, a warning and a threat. It seems appropriate for the author of Bodyline's greatest hour.'[1]

In the 19th century the Jardine clan began to migrate to different parts of the world. Douglas Jardine was distantly related to William Jardine who co-founded Jardine-Matheson, the Hong Kong-based trading company in 1832, and to Frank and Alec Jardine, the Cape York pioneers who established a cattle station on the north-east peninsula of Australia in the 1860s. They were also a family of lawyers. Douglas Jardine's paternal grandfather, William Jardine, a Cambridge scholar, graduated from a law professorship at Karachi to a judge of the High Court at Allahabad within six years, and his brother John was a senior member of the Indian Civil Service, a judge on the Bombay High Court and, on his return home, a Liberal MP. In 1873 tragedy struck when William Jardine died of cholera, aged 32, leaving his widow Elinor Georgiana to bring up their three boys, William Ellis, Malcolm – Douglas's father – and Hugh. A woman of formidable character and intellect, she dedicated her long life to her family, ensuring they received a first-rate education at Fettes College, an Edinburgh boarding school, founded in 1870.

The fact that the college quickly established a reputation as the premier school in Scotland was down to the enlightened leadership of its first headmaster, Dr Alexander Potts. Formerly a classics master at Rugby School under its renowned headmaster Dr Thomas Arnold, Potts brought much of Arnold's reforming zeal to Fettes. A man of noble bearing, his inspirational teaching, broad educational vision and warmth of character left a lasting impression on his charges, helping to cement the school's reputation for both scholarship and success on the games field, especially at rugby. In this challenging but essentially benign environment, Malcolm Jardine flourished, excelling at fives, gymnastics and athletics, in addition to rugby and cricket, exploits that won him the Challenge Clock, awarded annually to the school's best all-round sportsman. In four years in the cricket XI, he overcame a dismally wet season in 1888 to average 77 with the bat and 6.3 with the ball. 'A brilliant all-round cricketer, excelling alike as batsman, bowler (fast) and field,' reported *The Fettesian*, the school magazine. 'Has been this season's most effective bowler in the XI, having a tendency to curl in the air, and being difficult to see. Quick and safe in the field, and may with practice have a future as a wicketkeeper. His average with the bat speaks for itself. His strongest point is back play, which is very hard and, as far as we have seen, unerring; cuts beautifully, and places judiciously to leg, forward play, though much improved, is still his weak point, having a tendency to go across his wicket. To these capabilities he combines an absence of nerve and great judgement as captain; he has been the one constant factor of the XI.'[2] Sir Hamilton Grant, head boy of Fettes in 1889/90 and later a distinguished diplomat in the Indian Civil Service, recalled that Jardine was perhaps the most conspicuous personality of his era at school – 'a great cricketer, a fine all-round athlete, a first-class brain full of character and charm'.[3]

At Balliol College, Oxford, Jardine missed out on a rugby Blue because of injury – he proved a valuable centre for London Scottish and played in a trial for Scotland – but represented the cricket XI for four years, captaining them in 1891. In his first year, he made a pair in the Varsity Match at Lord's when Oxford were destroyed by Sammy Woods, already an Australian Test bowler. Woods also proved their nemesis in the subsequent two years, when Cambridge again proved victorious, but Oxford had their revenge in 1892. Cambridge, under Stanley Jackson, a future captain of England, began as clear favourites, a situation seemingly confirmed when they took the first two Oxford wickets without a run on the board. It was at this point that Jardine and the freshman C.B. Fry, later one of England's greatest cricketers, counter-attacked in style by putting on 75 for the third wicket. After Fry was out for 44, Jardine continued to bat imperiously, not least the way he kept hitting Jackson, who was bowling to an overwhelming off-side field, to leg to make a faultless 140, the second-highest innings in Varsity Match history.

After making 365, Oxford bowled Cambridge out for 160, forcing them to follow on, and although Cambridge fought back valiantly, Jardine's assured 39 in their second innings helped his side to a five-wicket victory. According to Fry, Jardine was a beautiful batsman with a perfect late cut and neat off-drive, in addition to being a brilliant fielder, an assessment reinforced by his illustrious England team-mate, Kumar Shri Ranjitsinhji, who rated his fielding in that year's Varsity Match the best he'd ever seen. Had Jardine remained in county cricket, Fry reckoned he would have represented his country, but, aside from a few matches for Middlesex in 1892, and for MCC in 1897, his career in India meant that he was lost to English cricket.

After he was called to the Bar by the Middle Temple in 1893, Jardine returned to India to practise at the Bombay Bar at a time when advocates of British birth still had a large and lucrative share in the legal practice in the Indian High Courts.

Appointed Perry Professor of Jurisprudence and Roman Law of the Government Law School in 1898 and Principal in 1903, he was Clerk to the Crown in the High Court for 12 years before becoming Advocate-General of Bombay in 1915. In 1910 he acted as prosecutor in the Nasik Conspiracy Case in which the militant Indian nationalist Vinayak Savarkar was convicted and sentenced to transportation for life to the Andaman Islands on two charges: for abetment to the murder of a British district magistrate in India and for conspiracy against the King-Emperor.

Jardine also continued to shine at cricket, playing for both Bombay Gymkhana and the Byculla Club, which he captained, and standing out as the leading European player in the annual

Presidency matches against the Parsees staged in Bombay and Poona.

In addition to his cricket, Jardine was an accomplished golfer. A member of the prestigious Royal & Ancient club at St Andrews, he met Alison Moir during one of his visits there and they were married in some style at St Andrew's Episcopal Church in St Andrews in April 1898. Alison was the second daughter of Dr Robert Moir, a pillar of the local church and the Conservative Party, and granddaughter of David Macbeth Moir, an eminent physician and poet who frequently contributed, under the signature of Delta, to *Blackwood's Magazine*. After Indian Army Medical Service, Moir went into practice with his brother, John Wilson Moir, in St Andrews, where their expertise and compassion towards the poor won them the esteem of the whole community. Inheriting her parents' warmth and commitment to social outreach, Alison quickly integrated into the social life of Bombay's colonial elite, winning much respect for her charitable work, especially for the Young Women's Christian Association (YWCA).

In common with many Europeans, the Jardines settled in Malabar Hill, the most exclusive residential location in Bombay with its lush vegetation, cooling sea breezes and stunning views over Back Bay and the city skyline to the north. It was there on 23 October 1900, in the middle of Diwali, the Hindu festival of lights, celebrated with fireworks, that their son Douglas was born. The year is significant because three years after the celebrations surrounding the Diamond Jubilee of Queen Victoria, a British resurgence in the Boer War in South Africa had been the occasion for further national rejoicing. Brought up amid the finery of the Raj, Douglas was steeped in the values of the British Empire, then at its zenith, and the role that sport, especially cricket, could play in cementing imperial solidarity.

As an only child he was his parents' pride and joy and the deep bonds he formed with them in childhood never deserted him. Inheriting his father's love of cricket, Douglas spent many an hour with him learning the rudiments of the game and when he wasn't there to bowl at him, he roped in his family's beloved bearer Lalla Sebastian to perform instead. Douglas benefited greatly from his father's knowledge and coaching expertise, and showed promise as a talented all-rounder. His sophisticated batting technique, which proved the bedrock of his later success, was already evident.

Entranced by its majestic public buildings, its bustling streets and its golden sands and never happier than playing sport at the exclusive Bombay Gymkhana Club, then out of bounds to non-whites, Jardine developed a deep attachment to the city of his birth. It was an attachment he shared with another native of Bombay, the poet Rudyard Kipling, whose works he often quoted. In these circumstances it must have been a terrible wrench when, aged nine, he was packed off to boarding school in England, only returning for a brief holiday each summer, given that it took three weeks to reach India by steamer. The long absences must have been as heart-rending for his parents, and so Malcolm's premature retirement from practice in 1916, caused by throat trouble, had its blessings, since it allowed them to return home. 'The retirement owing to ill health of Mr M.R. Jardine, the Advocate General, Bombay, will be regretted by all who knew him,' wrote *The Times of India*. 'Though he took little part in the public life of the city, he had a wide circle of friends and was everywhere respected and liked. By his colleagues at the Bar, he has been regarded as a sound lawyer well worthy of the high position which he had filled for a little over two years after being Clerk of the Crown for 12 years ... For many years he was one of the chief props of the Presidency side, and there must be many among our readers who can recall a great stand he made for the first wicket with Major Greig. He also helped on many occasions to bring victory to the Byculla Club in their annual match with the Gymkhana, his fielding being particularly brilliant. With Mr Jardine, who sailed for England yesterday, there has gone Mrs Jardine, a lady who will be much missed in Bombay where her many admirable qualities and unostentatious acts of kindness and charity have been much appreciated. The Y.W.C.A in particular loses in her a very good friend.[4]

During his first few years at boarding school, Douglas spent his Christmas and Easter holidays with his maiden aunt Kitty at her rather forbidding mansion outside St Andrews. Devoted though she was to him, the long separations from his parents and his lack of siblings very probably contributed to his singular character. 'As a boy we could never understand Douglas,' his father later told the Australian leg-spinner turned journalist Arthur Mailey. 'He seemed so distant and lonely. He seldom played with other boys.'[5]

While based in St Andrews he did find a mentor in Andrew Lang, the Scottish novelist and essayist who was a friend of the family. Lang, a cricket romantic from Selkirk, not only heaped kindness on him, but also talked to him like an adult as he discoursed on cricket, Scottish history and literature, instilling in him a great love of A.A. Milne, the author who created Winnie-the-Pooh. He also introduced him to golf on St Andrews' famous courses and gave him a lifelong passion for fishing.

In May 1910, Douglas entered Horris Hill Preparatory School, near Newbury, a feeder school for Winchester, renowned for its cricket. Given his parents' Scottish heritage and his father's outstanding career at Fettes, it might seem slightly surprising that he wasn't educated there. Aside from the indifferent weather in Scotland, a real impediment for an aspiring cricketer, the main reason probably lies in their social circle. Malcolm's friend Frederic Thesiger, captain of the Oxford XI of 1890 and later 1st Viscount Chelmsford and Viceroy of India, was a Wykehamist and related to Julia Thesiger, mother of Victoria Ashton, a friend of the Jardines in India. The Ashtons had earmarked Winchester for their brilliant sons – Percy, Gilbert, Hubert and Claude – and another good friend, Ernest Raikes, a Bombay legal advocate who played cricket with Malcolm Jardine, had also opted to send his son Tom to Horris Hill and Winchester.

Founded by Alfred Henry Evans, a double Oxford Blue at rugby and cricket and Winchester schoolmaster, in 1888, Horris Hill was fortunate to have as its first headmaster a man of exceptional ability and charm. A natural leader and born teacher who got the best out of his charges, not least the less able, Evans quickly established the school as a beacon of academic and sporting excellence.

Thrust into this strange new universe, the shy, austere Jardine struggled at first to relate to the other boys, but his aptitude at cricket soon won him their respect. He forced his way into the first XI as a ten-year-old on account of his bowling and made his debut against Twyford on 11 July 1911, bowling two overs for seven runs. Batting for the first time in the next match against Winton House, he failed to score, but the next year he became the talk of the circuit by averaging 42 with the bat and taking 24 wickets at 6.67, including 6-19 against arch rivals Summer Fields.

That year he saved up five shillings out of his pocket money to purchase the former England captain C.B. Fry's classic book *Batsmanship,* which had a profound influence on him. Refuting the accepted convention of keeping the right foot anchored inside the crease and outside the line of leg stump, Fry encouraged his readers to use their feet more freely, advice which Jardine eagerly followed. Admonished by his cricket master for altering his technique, he refused to give ground, justifying his unorthodoxy by quoting from Fry's text.

In July 1913, Jardine hit his first fifty at Twyford – the boys in those days used to travel to away games by horse and cart and train – and in 1914 he carried all before him as captain, averaging 39.5 with the bat and taking 32 wickets at 4.5. Against West Downs, he took 8-39, including four wickets in four balls, all bowled, but his most memorable performance came in the clash against Summer Fields in late June. With both sides unbeaten, there was more hinging on the game than normal, so much so that 'Bear' Allington, Summer Fields' cricket master, vowed to do whatever it took to deny Horris Hill victory. Consequently, after Jardine elected to field first, Summer Fields batted almost the whole afternoon, leaving their opponents a mere 20 minutes to bat. According to Summer Fields' prosaic account of the match: 'Horris Hill won the toss, put us in, but on account of the bowling, and the difficulty of moving the ball on a slow surface, nine wickets fell for only 112 before the innings could be closed; in the time which remained two wickets fell for 19 runs … Jardine took seven wickets for 30 runs; he bowled with great command over the ball and variety of pace; his swerve also induced three batsmen to stop the ball with their pads.'[6] One of these victims was Allen II, better known as Gubby Allen, the beginning of a lifelong love-hate relationship which, prep schools aside, incorporated Winchester and Eton, Oxford and Cambridge and Surrey and Middlesex.

For some time afterwards relations between the two schools remained distinctly frosty and Jardine bore a grudge against Allington for the rest of his days. 'If the school can be criticised, it can be criticised for a great concentration on results,' recalled the writer and politician Christopher Hollis, who made a stodgy 17 for Summer Fields. 'Mr Allington had little hope that we would beat Horris Hill. Therefore … he made us bat all day, so we were able to make a draw of it.'[7]

A striking example of Jardine's maturity came in one of his final matches at Horris Hill when the headmaster's son, Alfred John Evans, an old Blue who played for Hampshire, raised a side to play against both the masters and boys. Failing to ruffle Jardine with his aggressive bowling, a frustrated Evans resorted to something more intimidating, but the more intemperate he became, the further Jardine dispatched him.

In September 1914 Jardine entered Winchester. Founded in 1382 by William of Wykeham, the Bishop of Winchester, the college is one of the oldest and most prestigious of British public schools, its iconic medieval buildings adding to its mystique. In common with all boarding schools at that time, it provided a thorough grounding in leadership for the sons of the elite, espousing the values of militarism, imperialism and muscular Christianity. In a strictly hierarchical society, which gave unfettered power to the prefects, school life, especially for the junior men, as Wykehamists were known, was unremittingly harsh as they were chivvied and harried from dawn to dusk. It wasn't simply the freezing dormitories, the cold showers, the unappetising food and the military parades that grated. Those like Jardine whose time at Winchester coincided with the First World War became inured to the greater restrictions, the depleted staff, the Wykehamist casualty lists – just over 500 died in the conflict – and the fatalism of the senior men as they prepared for life in the trenches.

Entering this monastic all-male environment, new boys were acquainted with the traditions, rituals and private vocabulary, known as Notions, that shaped the life of the school and defined their lives thereafter. A school predominantly for the professional middle class, Winchester differed from its rivals with the emphasis it placed on intellectual rigour, so that even during the austerity of the war years its cultural life abounded with vigorous activity. Many a Wykehamist gravitated to a life of eminence in the law, civil service and diplomatic corps, their intellectual self-confidence and strong sense of public service tempered by a certain priggishness. The playwright Ben Travers wrote: 'Whenever you sit next to a stranger at a club or dinner party, who proves to be excellent company, but whose opinions are superior to yours and somebody tells you that he was at Winchester, your immediate reaction is, "Ah, that accounts for it".'[8] Aside from the 70 scholars who were housed in College, Wykehamists were divided into ten boarding houses of about 40 where they ate, slept, and studied, their lack of privacy a constant bane to those who felt stifled by the communal ethos and rigid discipline. Alongside the severe beatings and fagging – the system whereby a junior man performed menial tasks for a prefect – there was periodic bullying directed primarily towards the weak and vulnerable, as opposed to the physically mature and talented sportsmen who normally escaped such ordeals.

When Jardine arrived at Winchester, he was placed in Du Boulay's, named after its founder, the Rev. J.T.H. Du Boulay, whose daughter married Alfred Henry Evans, and informally known as Cook's after its second housemaster A.K. Cook. His housemaster Charles Little was an aloof academic who played little part in the day-to-day running of the house, but did perform a valuable role in helping to run the cricket during the war. 'The work of R.L.G. Irving and C.W. Little during these difficult years deserves grateful remembrance,' wrote Canon John Firth, who took all ten wickets against Eton in 1917. 'Little's death in 1922, while still in his prime, took from us one who "touched nothing" which he did not adorn.'[9]

According to Hubert Ashton, a sporting prodigy several years his senior, Jardine's reputation as a cricketer preceded him. 'But in addition to this he had a somewhat unusual air about him. He was mature, tall and determined; clearly a new man that must be treated with respect.

'On first acquaintance it might be thought that he was a trifle austere and brusque; I must confess that on occasions he gave me that impression. However, as is so often the case, I have no doubt that this was due to shyness or a lack of self-confidence; perhaps the better and truer word is humility.'[10]

Although no scholar, he kept his end up academically while reserving his real energy for the sports field. Although the cult of athleticism was less important at Winchester than many such institutions, it still played a prominent part in school life. Organised sport – introduced originally in the 1850s as a form of social control to prevent unruly pupils from engaging in disreputable activities such as blood sports – soon began to be perceived as a way of imparting moral virtues such as character and team spirit. The social historian Richard Holt wrote: 'Gradually sport ceased to be a means to a disciplinary end and became an end in itself. The culture of athleticism steadily came to dominate the whole system of elite education.'[11] Games were soon made compulsory and were played with an evangelical fervour, especially prestigious fixtures against rival schools and inter-house competitions. Those that excelled at football and cricket – known as the bloods – not only won recognition through a series of colours – striped blazers, scarves and caps – they also assumed a heroic place in school folklore, which often proved the passport to advancement in later life.

Yet behind the ethos of chivalry and good sportsmanship, glamorised in verse and song, there lay a more ruthless streak to the games cult that reflected the intense one-upmanship of the Victorian public school. Consequently, not every blood absorbed the amateur code in its entirety, as Jardine's career was to demonstrate. 'When I was at school, there were two benches inscribed with mottoes,' he told the boys of Melbourne High School in Australia in 1932/33. 'One of these was "Play up, play up, and play the game" and the other, "Love the game beyond the prize". I think they are two splendid mottoes for cricketers to follow.' Arguably, he followed the second rather more avidly than the first.

Owing to the shortage of senior men because of the war, Jardine found himself playing in the Senior House football and cricket competitions, both of which were keenly contested, from his second year. With his quick reflexes, his safe pair of hands and boundless courage, he proved a most competent goalkeeper for Cook's, before making that position his own for two years in the school 1st XI. With Claude Ashton, a future captain of the England football team, devastating in attack, this was a golden era for Winchester football and their dominance against all-comers kept Jardine relatively underemployed. When called on to perform, he proved himself a reliable last line of defence, his only error coming against Charterhouse in his final year when throwing the ball out he lost control and threw it straight to one of their forwards.

Although no natural athlete, Jardine took to Winchester's other main winter sport, their own code of football, commonly known as Winkies. It is an arcane game, similar to rugby, except there is no picking up the ball or passing, just plenty of punting and kicking. Played in a long narrow pitch with roughly ten-foot-high nets down each side and two waist-high ropes strung between posts the length of the pitch, a yard inside each net, the object was to get the ball into 'worms' – over the opponents' back line, by kicking it in open play and/or manoeuvring down the ropes. Played with teams of either 15 or six players, the game relies more on brute strength than natural skill, especially to those like Jardine who played in the scrum, known as the 'hot'.

In addition to the inter-house competitions, the annual games of Fifteens and Sixes between College, Old Tutors' Houses (OTH) and Commoners (the other half of the school houses) were major school occasions, when Wykehamists thronged the touchline to cheer on their heroes. Representing OTH in Fifteens, Jardine was forced to miss the defeat against Commoners, but made his presence felt in his side's 9-4 win against College by scoring twice.

In the Sixes, a more open game requiring speed and stamina, he scored twice against College in OTH's convincing 21-3 win and although dropped for the match against Commoners, he still was on the Roll, meaning he was awarded his colours.

Jardine also excelled at rackets, a ball game played singles or doubles in an enclosed court with four walls and a ceiling. First pair for two years and captain in his final year, he and his partner, Richard Hill, beat Eton, Harrow and Charterhouse and reached the semi-final of the Public Schools Doubles Championship at Queen's Club. There they lost 4-3 to Marlborough in a thrilling game in which Jardine's play in the rallies attracted particular commendation from *The Times*. 'He returned the ball well and steadily, got up the service consistently and did something with it, and finished the easy ball with some certainty.'[12] To those of a cricketing bent, Winchester provided a perfect setting for playing the game in New Field with its picturesque water meadows down by the River Itchen. The school could boast a proud cricketing tradition. From 1825 there had been an inter-school week at Lord's in which Eton, Harrow and Winchester played each other, and although Winchester stopped playing there in 1854, to this day the first XI is still called Lord's. The war years produced five of the best cricketers the school had seen: J.C. Clay, a future captain of Glamorgan who played one Test for England, the three Ashton brothers and Jardine. The latter was later to write that Winchester was fortunate to have such an array of coaching talent at one time. The cricket master was the much-loved Rockley Wilson, a gifted all-rounder for Cambridge and Yorkshire. Years away during the war in no way diminished his class. After a rich haul of wickets in the summer of 1920, aged 41, he was given leave by Winchester to tour Australia with MCC. There he played in his sole Test and ruffled feathers for filing reports back to the *Daily Express*. A renowned wit, an astute judge of character and a supreme tactician, not least in placing the field, he hated slackness and conceit, but despite his Yorkshire will to win, he maintained a great reverence for the finer traditions of the game. Finding a ready disciple in Jardine, he exerted a substantial influence over him in his final year when his batting scaled new heights, not least the cultivation of his classic on-side play.

Wilson was assisted by Harry Altham, captain of the great Repton XI of 1908, a double Oxford Blue and a county cricketer during the school holidays. Joining Winchester in 1913 as a classicist, he fought with distinction on the Western Front during the war and returned to the school in 1919, inspiring generations of Wykehamists with his enthusiasm and kindness, as well as his cricketing expertise.

The coach was Schofield Haigh, a medium-paced bowler good enough to win 11 England caps and a highly valued member of the great Yorkshire sides at the turn of the century. Appointed to Winchester in 1913, his cheerfulness and geniality made him a universally popular figure, widely mourned on his premature death in 1921.

After a slow start to the 1916 season, which might have cost him a place in the XI, Jardine excelled in the Junior House competition and, along with W.M. Leggatt, he was Cook's inspiration in their innings victory against Kenny's in the Toye Cup Final. Not only did he captain the team and score a valuable 36 batting at No.6, he bowled unchanged in both innings to finish with match figures of 10-53. He also took plenty of wickets in the Turner Cup, the Senior House competition, that year and the two subsequent years, but he was never more than a useful change bowler in the XI with his round-arm leg breaks.

Jardine began 1917 with an impressive performance in the senior cricket trial, known as the Two Guinea Match. He was picked for the XI and cemented his position with 65 against the Royal Garrison Artillery. Being wartime, the fixture list against opposing schools was severely restricted and the traditional two-day games against Eton and Harrow were reduced to one-day. Opening the batting, Jardine made 27 against Charterhouse and 28 against Harrow, putting on 60 for the first wicket as Winchester strolled to an eight-wicket victory. According to *The Times*, he looked a player of promise.

He once again looked the part against Eton with some really fine strokes, but despite his 30 Winchester could only manage 90 all out, and Eton won by one wicket.

The following summer he continued to score freely for his house, but disappointed for the XI. In five school matches he made little impact aside from a sedate 33 against Harrow and 13 innings yielded only one fifty, against a local RAF side. 'Not so successful with the bat as was expected,' reported *The Wykehamist*, the school magazine. 'Has not yet developed enough driving power. Plays beautiful strokes on the on-side, and is a very sound back player. … Good fielder in any position.'[13]

In his last half (term), Jardine added to his scroll of honour, which included his position as a school prefect, with his appointment as captain of Lord's. On one level he seemed the obvious choice, but his dissenting views had upset the two previous captains and his predecessor John Firth, concerned about his ability to unify the team, advised against his appointment. The fact that he was made captain might have owed something to his housemaster, Charles Little, who had overseen the cricket in Rockley Wilson's absence, as well as the recommendation of Schofield Haigh, with whom he'd established an excellent rapport. Although Winchester's record over the previous several years had fluctuated somewhat, their prospects for 1919 seemed highly encouraging. Seven of the side – Jardine, Claude Ashton, William Baldock, Richard Hill, Jack Frazer, Tom Raikes and Mark Patten – went on to play first-class cricket, the first five playing in the County Championship.

Forming a productive opening partnership with his rackets partner Hill, Jardine struck form immediately, hitting 93 against New College, 63 and 140 against the Old Wykehamists and 77 against the Free Foresters. A rare failure came against Charterhouse – a school against which he never scored runs – when he was dismissed for the second year in succession by Raymond Robertson-Glasgow, later a team-mate at Oxford and a lifelong friend.

With wins against Cheltenham, Marlborough and Wellington, and having much the better of the draw against Charterhouse, Winchester travelled to Eton for the restored two-day match unbeaten, but Jardine wasn't taking anything for granted. Conscious of their defeats in the two previous years, he insisted that the whole team go and pray in the Eton chapel the evening before the match.

On an easy-paced wicket, Winchester batted first and made steady progress through Jardine and Claude Ashton before the former was out for 35, prompting a collapse. They were all out for 135 but with Eton making only 109 in reply, Jardine and Hill began their second innings at 3.50pm with a lead of 26. They batted carefully against steady bowling, most notably against rival captain Clem Gibson, later a double Cambridge Blue, putting on 72 for the first wicket; then, in the final hour, Jardine began to play shots of the highest calibre. He ended the day 89 not out and his side on 170/2. Although he failed to add to his score the next day, he always looked back on this innings as the one that gave him the most satisfaction. Winchester went on to make 295 and win by 69 runs, their first victory against Eton – excluding the war years – since 1907. Their triumph earned them a rapturous reception at Winchester station on their return home. Locals joined Wykehamists in the celebrations and Jardine was carried shoulder-high through the city streets to the College gates. 'Jardine captained the side excellently and placed the field well,' wrote *The Wykehamist*. 'Of his batting it would be difficult to speak too highly. He never looked like getting out, and always seemed to master the bowling. Owing to lack of driving power, he is not an attractive batsman on the eye, but his defence is very strong, and he seldom missed any chance of scoring on the on side.'[14]

He gave further notice of his potential with an undefeated 135 against Harrow, but while rain brought proceedings to a premature end, it enabled the XI to finish the season unbeaten, emulating his achievement when captain of Horris Hill. *The Wykehamist* congratulated Jardine 'on his extraordinary consistency with the bat this season, and in success in keeping his team together and in good heart, due to his patience, coolness and sound knowledge of the game'.[15] According to Harry Altham, he was the best schoolboy captain he ever knew – a master of field tactics and a fine psychologist – while in the opinion of Gerry Dicker, an opponent of Jardine's in house matches, he had a confidence and self-sufficiency beyond his years.

As a sporting colossus and leader of men, Jardine gained a cult following at Winchester. Douglas Jay, a future Labour cabinet minister, who arrived at Cook's a full year after Jardine left, recalled the adulation that he still commanded within the house. Yet such an autocratic and uncompromising personality wasn't without his critics. Determined to win the Inter-House competition, he took umbrage against anyone whose commitment didn't match his own by subjecting them to additional fielding practices, a sanction that prompted some bitter memories. E.T.R. Herdman, a contemporary of Jardine's in Cook's, alluded to his style of leadership in his memoir *Winchester 1916-1921*: 'But he really expected so much of the team and was so scathing if they made any mistakes that he had them all in a twitter of nerves. One poor man missed a catch early on in the final [sic] and the man he missed went on to score a century [C.T. Ashton, 107]. For the rest of his career, he never heard the end of it, how he lost us the cup.'[16] In posting the results of one house match, Jardine named only himself and another player, consigning the rest to oblivion on the grounds that they had barely featured. His action caused outrage and he later apologized.

'I have never known anyone who could put on such charm when he felt like it, or such withering sarcasm to anyone he disliked,' declared Winchester contemporary and friend Guy Turner.[17] A former team-mate, Cecil Verity, recollected that 'Jardine's captaincy soured us and I for one took up rowing at Cambridge as I no longer wanted to see cricket in any form.'[18] A.O. Elmhirst had been put down for school nets every week by Jardine when he was asked by the Officer Training Corps to go to Bisley to shoot for the Ashburton Shield, which they won. 'But Jardine rightly assumed that I had ignored his selection of me for school nets; consequently, on his end-of-term round when he awarded cricket distinctions, he said to me, "Elmhirst, if you hadn't gone bloody shooting, I'd have given you your 2XI cap, but as it is, you'll only get Senior Club.'" [the name given to 1st and 2nd XI middle practice games].[19]

In 1983 a profile of Jardine in *The Cricketers' Who's Who*, edited by Iain Sproat MP, an Old Wykehamist, claimed that the result of the final of the 1920 Turner Cup between Cook's, captained by Jardine, and College remained in dispute, with the College scorer declaring that College had won by one run and the Cook scorer maintaining it was a tie. Jardine, acting in his capacity as captain of Lord's, sent for both scorers, found a mistake, beat both scorers and announced that Cook's had won by one run. The allegation, based on information from fellow Wykehamist Jay, who admitted that he couldn't vouch for it, and made public in the national press in May 1983, prompted a fierce backlash from Wykehamists who resented a slur on Jardine and a calumny on the school. The truth was that Jardine had left the year before and during his whole time in the school his house neither reached the Turner Cup Final, nor did they play College in any round in his year as captain of Lord's. According to Tony Pawson of *The Observer*, himself a former captain of Winchester, Jardine could only beat his own man with the permission of his housemaster, and it would have been unthinkable for him to beat a member of another house. 'I can't of course say what his reputation was within his own House,' recollected Dicker. 'Outside he was highly respected. To me he was a man who was never "young". He was always mature beyond his years – a real leader in every sense. Jardine was also a very determined and fearless man; quite ready to back his own judgement and follow his own high principles. Cricket masters then at Winchester were of the calibre of Rockley Wilson – and Harry Altham – and Douglas was never afraid to argue the toss with them and to do what he felt to be right.'[20]

Mark Patten, who played for two years in the XI with Jardine, said, 'We had every possible respect for him at Winchester. He was very determined, obstinate at times, and somewhat reserved. But he was an extremely honest and upright man. And with his quiet sense of humour he was a charming companion for those of us who were his friends.'[21]

He was also fiercely loyal to those he respected. On Schofield Haigh's death in 1921, he organised a collection for his widow and on his first appearance for Surrey away to Yorkshire at Sheffield, he sought her out to offer a sympathetic word. It was a hard game and Jardine hadn't received the most enthusiastic of receptions from the crowd, but during the tea interval he made his way through the popular enclosure to where he thought Haigh's widow would be sitting. When they encountered each other, he was surprised to hear that she had been looking for him. He told her he was deeply touched by her determination to seek him out. 'Oh, Mr Jardine,' she replied. 'Schofield would never have forgiven me if I hadn't tried to have a word with you.'

Despite Jardine's astounding success at Winchester, he remained in the main an elusive figure, rarely able to relax in company. 'Poor old Douglas,' recalled Guy Turner. 'I have never known anyone so reserved as he was, and out of all his hundreds of friends I cannot think of one with whom he was really intimate.'[22] His daughter Fianach Lawry, reflecting on his life many years later, thought that he was to an abnormal degree the product of his boyhood. Already something of a loner, Winchester made him a complex, introvert character who concealed his hurt and vulnerability. 'I think a lot went on underneath the surface that didn't necessarily come out, for this is the way Winchester worked in those days. The silences and the things he didn't say perhaps made people think he was a hard man. The idea was not to let anyone see that you were hurt or upset. He was bad at communicating in today's terms, but there again we're back to Winchester.'[23]

**Endnotes:**

1  *The Guardian*, 29 May 2015
2  *The Fettesian* 1888, p147
3  H.F. MacDonald (ed), *One Hundred Years of Fettes*, p68
4  *The Times of India* , 5 December 1916
5  Philip Derriman, *Bodyline*, p18
6  *Summer Fields School Magazine* 1914
7  Quoted in Allen and Jardine. Summer Fields and Horris Hill 1914, pdf
8  Ben Travers, *94 Not Out*, p64
9  John Firth, *Winchester College*, p121
10  Quoted in Christopher Douglas, *Douglas Jardine: Spartan Cricketer*, p211
11  Richard Holt, *Sport and the British*, p81
12  *The Times*, 25 April 1919
13  *The Wykehamist*, 13 August 1918, p263
14  Ibid, 9 July 1919, p355
15  Ibid, 28 July 1919, p380
16  Quoted in Douglas, *Douglas Jardine: Spartan Cricketer*, p16
17  Ibid, Preface to the 2002 edition, xiii
18  Ibid, xiv
19  A.I. Elmhirst to James Sabben-Clare, 16 January 1987, Winchester College Archives
20  *The Cricketer*, July 1983, p19
21  Ibid
22  Douglas, *Douglas Jardine: Spartan Cricketer*, preface to the 2002 edition xiv
23  Derriman, *Bodyline*, p21

# CHAPTER 2

# AN OXFORD IDOL

JARDINE'S 997-RUN aggregate at an average of 66 for Winchester in 1919 – a school record till surpassed by the Nawab of Pataudi, later captain of India, in 1959 – gained him selection for the Rest against the Lord's Schools at Lord's in early August. Opening with Robertson-Glasgow, he played a leading part in his side's comprehensive victory with scores of 44 and 91 – out in both innings to Clem Gibson. From the two XIs a side was picked to play Plum Warner's XI and Jardine enhanced his reputation as the most promising schoolboy batsman in the country by scoring two more fifties. E.B. Noel wrote in *Wisden*, 'Jardine, of all the school cricketers had, perhaps, the soundest defence, the greatest patience and the best judgement, and he was the most difficult of any to dislodge. He had a wonderful record – an average of over 50 for Winchester, making big scores against Eton and Harrow, and four big innings without a failure in the matches at Lord's.

'It must not be imagined that Jardine is a player without strokes. He can and does hit the ball very hard on the on-side and indeed he lets off very few chances of scoring. He has, too, the off-side strokes, though he does not use them as often as he might. He is a cricketer with an old head on young shoulders, and I shall be very surprised if he doesn't follow his father's footsteps and get into the Oxford side as a freshman.'[1]

In October 1919, Jardine went up to New College, Oxford, which had a historic connection with Winchester, at a time when many ex-servicemen in their twenties helped swell numbers. Shunning the more decadent lifestyle associated with the 'Brideshead generation' that dazzled Oxford from the early 1920s, he led a more solitary, sober existence – in his first year, in particular, it is noticeable how many times he returned to Winchester to play in various fixtures – although he did belong to an arcane Oxford dining club called the Boojums. Any close friends he had emanated mainly from his circle of Old Wykehamists, most notably Jack Frazer, who died in a skiing accident in 1927, and Mark Patten, or from fellow cricket Blues such as Raymond Robertson-Glasgow, who wrote: 'We got on well from the start. Under a somewhat grave and even forbidding exterior he failed to conceal a golden heart and a mine of humour.'[2]

Building on his expertise at rackets, Jardine took up real tennis, the king of all racket sports, played in an indoor court with sloping surfaces, openings and a main wall with a kink in it. Representing the Combined Universities against Queen's Club, *The Times* correspondent singled him out as a player of great promise. While noting his weak service and his tendency to overdo the volley, he highlighted his attributes, notably his beautiful swing, his strong reach and tactical acumen, and predicted a great future for him in the game if he could spare it the time. 'The remark made in court that "Jardine has enough heart to drive a broken-down caterpillar" was deserved; it is thus that matches are won.'[3]

Although missing out on a half-Blue in 1920, he gained it the following year when he and Victor Cazalet, later a Conservative MP, beat Cambridge. Up against the brilliance of his former rackets partner Richard Hill, Oxford soon found themselves two sets down, but Jardine and Cazalet were nothing if not fighters and as Cambridge tired, they found a second wind to pull through 3-2.

Although a damaged knee sustained on the cricket field prevented him from representing Oxford against Cambridge the following year, he continued to play real tennis whenever he could, and in 1924 he, Hill and C.H. Bruce combined to win the Old Boys' Public Schools Tennis Tournament, beating Eton 3-0 in the final.

He played in goal for the Oxford Centaurs, the university football 2nd XI, and helped New College to win football 'cuppers', the university inter-collegiate competition, but any hope of them repeating their triumph the following year vanished when Jardine gifted the opposition a goal in the final.

He also represented the Old Wykehamists in the Arthur Dunn Cup, a football competition featuring the alumni sides from England's public schools. First played in 1903, the Old Wykehamists, one final aside, hadn't made a great impact in the competition, but this all changed in 1919/20 with a vintage team that comprised three Ashtons in the forward line – Claude, the youngest was still at school – and Max Woosnam, a brilliant all-round sportsman who captained Manchester City and England, at centre-half.

After beating Old Albanians in the second round and Old Reptonians in the third round, Jardine excelling himself with several outstanding saves, Old Wykehamists went on to beat Old Salopians 2-0 in the semi-final. He also distinguished himself in the final at the Queen's Club when the Ashtons ran Old Malvernians ragged to win 4-0.

He was in goal again the following year when Old Wykehamists were surprisingly beaten 3-2 in the third round by Old Aldenhamians on heavy ground which stymied their quick style of play.

In common with the post-war popularity of sport and entertainment, cricket at Oxford in the 1920s was all the rage. One of three freshmen of outstanding ability – the other two being Greville Stevens, who'd represented the Gentlemen against the Players while still at school, and Lionel Hedges, the prolific Tonbridge batsman – Jardine was part of a golden generation which adorned university cricket in the 1920s. *The Times'* cricket correspondent wrote: 'Mr Jardine, the son of the old Oxford Blue, whose glorious fielding and great innings of 140 in the Oxford and Cambridge match of 1892 are remembered to this day, is a sound, steady batsman – a born No 1 – with a fine defence. He does not drive much at present, that will come, but he is extremely good on the leg side, and as a first batsman is needed his prospects of a Blue are good.'[4]

Having carried his bat for 60 in the Freshmen's Match, Jardine was picked to open the batting by the Oxford captain Frank Gilligan, whose two younger brothers, Arthur and Harold, both went on to captain England. Dismissed without scoring in his first game against Warwickshire – bowled by Freddie Calthorpe, a future England captain – Jardine made a well-played 29 in the second innings before falling to the same bowler.

Narrowly defeated by Warwickshire, Oxford then beat that year's county champions, Middlesex, with Jardine winning

48

plaudits for his stylish 60, his effortless timing breaking the opposing captain Plum Warner's stranglehold in the field. He then caused something of a sensation in the win against Essex with his occasional leg-breaks. The omens didn't look at all promising as the visitors, in reply to the university's first innings of 331, made hay on the second morning, reaching 201/1. Having bowled five innocuous overs before lunch, Jardine returned for a second spell and caused immediate mayhem. He dismissed Jack Russell for a fine 117, his partner John Freeman for 40 and then bowled Essex's leading batsman, Percy Perrin, for a duck. The county lost nine wickets for 19 runs as they succumbed to Jardine, who took 6-6 in seven overs and three balls after lunch. 'He made the ball break both ways and had a deceptive flight which seemed to puzzle all the later Essex batsmen,' reported *The Times*.[5] It really was something of an aberration; the odd useful wicket aside, Jardine never came close to emulating such success again.

After missing several games because of exams, he returned in time for the Varsity Match at Lord's. In an era suffused with outstanding amateur players, Oxford could draw on the talent of Jardine, Hedges, Stevens, Robertson-Glasgow and Reg Bettington, a highly accomplished leg-spinner from Australia, while Cambridge, led by Gilbert Ashton, had Hubert Ashton, two future England captains in Arthur Gilligan and Percy Chapman, the former Eton captain Clem Gibson and 'Father' Marriott, a leg-spinner whose one game for England yielded him 11 wickets. In a game blighted by bad weather, Oxford made 193 – Jardine 13 before becoming one of Marriott's seven victims – and Cambridge replied with 161/9.

Jardine spent the rest of the summer playing wandering club cricket, most notably for the Harlequins and the Incogniti.

The Harlequins, founded in 1852, was an Oxford club open to Blues and a few others who just missed a Blue, elected on the recommendation of the current university captain. Jardine's father continued to play for the club till well into his late fifties and Jardine himself, like Warner before him, took advantage of amateur protocol which permitted a Harlequin to bat in its quartered cap of dark blue, maroon and buff when playing for any other team. Under the astute captaincy of Harry Altham, the Harlequins toured Sussex and Kent every August, playing a high standard of cricket on picturesque grounds such as the Saffrons at Eastbourne and Mote Park at Maidstone. In this congenial atmosphere and amid select company, many of whom he knew well, Jardine felt very much at home, which helps to explain his lifelong commitment to wandering-club cricket.

That August he was invited to tour the United States and Canada with the Incogniti, the third oldest of English wandering clubs. Organised by Major E.G. Wynyard, one of the great all-rounders of the Victorian era, and captained by Evelyn Metcalfe, an Etonian who later played for Queensland, it also included Tom Lowry, later captain of New Zealand, and the actor Desmond Roberts. After a nine-day Atlantic crossing on board the RMS *Mauretania*, the side based themselves in Philadelphia, where they played the majority of their games. With American cricket in decline, the side went through their nine-match tour, winning seven and having the better of two draws. After a lean start, Jardine found his form against the two New York sides, scoring 157 and 133 respectively, and scored a half-century in their final match against Toronto.

Bolstered by his success in club cricket, Jardine returned for his second year at Oxford a more complete player. In a disappointing season for the university, he emerged as their leading batsman. Robertson-Glasgow recalled bowling to him in the nets in the Parks on a summer's evening. Here, in this enchanting setting, a carefree Jardine would display every stroke in the book, all played with grace and power, and with an abandon which he rarely allowed himself in a match.

As an undergraduate, he was the most complete batsman that Robertson-Glasgow ever saw, the supreme example of orthodoxy. Tall, lean, ruddy-faced, cold-eyed and long-nosed, his patrician pose, complete with baggy cream flannels, Harlequin cap and silk scarf, exuded authority. He resembled his hero C.B. Fry with his upright stance, intense concentration and powerful will to improve. Central to his batting was his impregnable defence. Blessed with quick eyesight and rapid reflexes, his still head and balanced body meant that he was in the perfect position to judge the line of the ball. His ability to play it late made him an expert against swing bowling, not least the art of determining when to play and when to leave the ball. Selling his wicket as dearly as any professional, he took his time playing himself in and proceeded sedately, his patience and mental strength proving particular attributes in a crisis. It is no coincidence that many of his finest innings were played against top sides such as Nottinghamshire and Yorkshire when others had fallen by the wayside. Hostile fast bowling posed few terrors. With his tall frame, high left elbow and soft hands, he had few equals playing the short ball; similarly, his quick reflexes and long reach made him well-equipped to deal with the turning ball. In the third Test at Melbourne in 1928/29, when England were subjected to a vicious Australian 'sticky', Jardine was promoted to No.3 because of his immaculate technique. 'I don't think I ever met such a studious batsman,' recollected his county captain Percy Fender. 'He had a wonderful instinct for "reading" the bowling. He might be out, having made a mistake, but he would know what the bowler had done, and where he, the batsman, had gone wrong.'[6]

Like Fry, Jardine was the master of the back stroke – the right leg well over the ball, the left leg away from the stumps. With his high backlift and the great power of his wrist and forearm, he was a forceful driver – he rarely lofted the ball – especially on the leg side, and he deflected with ease and grace. According to Fender, he was the most perfect strokeplayer in the post-war era, and if quick runs were needed, he could accelerate with the best of them.

If he had a weakness it was his indeterminate footwork, particularly early in his innings. Alec Kennedy, a Hampshire medium-pacer, dismissed him 11 times over the years – mainly bowled or lbw – with his inswingers, and Bert Ironmonger, the Australian left-arm spinner, then aged 50, established something of a hold over him in the 1932/33 series, taking his wicket four times.

Jardine began 1921 with 8 and 60 against Hampshire and 53 and an unbeaten 54 against Middlesex, a useful warm-up for the visit of Warwick Armstrong's Australians to Oxford. They were a great side who followed up their 5-0 thrashing of England in Australia the previous winter with a 3-0 win that summer on a tour where they remained unbeaten till their final match, against A.C. MacLaren's XI at Eastbourne. In order to permit the tourists a rest day before the first Test at Trent Bridge, Oxford agreed to restrict the fixture to two days. Before a fashionably dressed crowd at the Christ Church ground, the university batted first on an easy-paced wicket and Jardine looked very much at home against Jack Gregory, Australia's intimidating fast bowler, and Armstrong before he was caught and bowled by leg-spinner Arthur Mailey for 35. Later Mailey was to recount his first impressions of Jardine: 'He never spoke to any of the Australians, and as far as I know he seldom mixed with any of his own team. He was so withdrawn it seemed an effort for him to whisper, "Two legs, please", to the umpire when he came in to bat. He drew my attention more than any other [Oxford] player mainly because his features were so like a caricature. He had a hawk-like face with very high cheekbones, slanting eyes and the immobility of an Aztec.'[7]

In reply to Oxford's disappointing total of 180, the Australians made 294 all out, but their progress was hampered by bad weather. After an early lunch on the second day, Oxford began their second innings and reached 35/0 before rain forced another 90-minute delay. On the resumption at 4pm, Eric Bickmore was out immediately for 19, but Jardine and Romilly Holdsworth proved secure in defence, and once they'd seen off the threat of defeat, they began to play with real fluency, the former especially strong off his legs. Had they run with a greater sense of urgency, Jardine would almost certainly have reached his century. As it was, he ended not out on 96 – the highest score against the tourists to date – when stumps were drawn with Oxford 174/1. Given his failure to reach his hundred, it has subsequently been suggested that his long-standing grudge against the Australians stemmed from their refusal to give him an additional over to complete his century. This view was given substance by Jardine's cousin, Peter Wilson, the renowned *Daily Mirror* sportswriter. In his autobiography, published in 1977, he claimed that Jardine had told him that he'd taken umbrage at the Australian decision to leave the field earlier than previously agreed, but there is absolutely no evidence of an altercation in any of the contemporary match reports. The fact that the rickety Christ Church scoreboard failed to display the batsman's tally suggests that the question of a century for Jardine wouldn't have preoccupied him or the opposition.

Resentment or not, Jardine's chanceless 96 further enhanced his reputation and prompted calls from Plum Warner that he be included in the England side that summer. The fact that it took him another seven years to win his first Test cap is surprising given his commendable consistency throughout the 1920s, although various injuries and unavailability because of business commitments didn't help.

Jardine didn't have long to wait for his maiden first-class century when he scored 145 for Oxford against the Army, followed by another one against Sussex. Unfortunately, he failed to do himself justice in the Varsity Match as Oxford, following an encouraging season, fell at the final fence. Despite fielding nine Blues, they were outsmarted by a vintage Cambridge side captained by Gilbert Ashton and containing his two brothers Hubert, who'd scored the first century against Armstrong's Australians, and Claude. Other members included Chapman, Marriott, J.L. Bryan, later a consistent batsman for Kent, and Gibson, who, along with the Ashtons, helped A.C. MacLaren's XI to their famous victory over the Australians. Batting first, Cambridge amassed a formidable total of 415 against a ragged Oxford attack, Jardine proving their most successful bowler with 2-27 off 10 overs, but he scored only 5 and 18 as Oxford lost by an innings. According to *The Cricketer* magazine, his performance wasn't helped by the fact that he had to play Cambridge at real tennis, and against 'Shrimp' Leveson Gower's XI at Eastbourne before the Varsity Match. The truth was that the real tennis match against Cambridge usually coincided with the cricket and Jardine had managed to rearrange the date so that he could play in both.

By virtue of his family home being at Walton-on-Thames, Jardine was invited to play for Surrey at the end of the university season. Led by their inspirational captain Percy Fender and boasting a formidable batting line-up, they were in with a chance of winning the Championship. With their revered opener Jack Hobbs absent because of illness, Jardine took his place. On his debut against Lancashire at the Oval, he hit 27 and, following several moderate scores, displayed his promise against Yorkshire. Having been caught and bowled by his old schoolmaster, Rockley Wilson, for 25 in the first innings, he scored a fighting 60 in the second. No other batsman shaped up and Surrey only avoided a heavy defeat because of bad weather.

His other notable performance came in the Championship decider against Middlesex at Lord's. In order to be crowned champions, Surrey needed to win the match outright, but, in front of a 20,000 crowd, Middlesex drew first blood by reducing them to 56/3. Tom Shepherd and Jardine, now batting at No.5, made amends with a fourth-wicket partnership of 144 before Jardine was bowled by fast bowler Jack Durston for 55. With no one else contributing anything of note, Shepherd was 128 not out in Surrey's total of 269.

Excellent bowling by Surrey on the second morning dismissed Middlesex for 132, but they batted carelessly in their second innings and were all out for 184. Needing 322 to win, the home side were 19/0 at the close and, in front of a large final-day crowd, a magnificent second-wicket partnership of 229 by Richard Twining and J.W. Hearne was chiefly responsible for their memorable six-wicket victory. For the second year running,

Middlesex won the Championship in dramatic style by beating their old rivals at Lord's.

Despite his disappointment in the Varsity Match and the Championship decider, Jardine had enjoyed an auspicious season, topping the Oxford batting averages on 46.62 and making a solid start with Surrey. One disappointment concerned his failure to win the captaincy of Oxford for the following year. The choice lay between Greville Stevens and himself and while there was no disgrace losing out to an outstanding cricketer, who later captained England in one Test against South Africa, it was Jardine's sardonic reserve that appeared to be his undoing. In the event it proved something of a blessing, given his subsequent knee injury.

During Oxford's first match against Hampshire, he displaced his right kneecap while bowling and had to be carried to the pavilion. The injury was severe enough to incapacitate him for six weeks. He returned against Leicestershire as captain in place of Stevens, who had flu, but he had to retire because of his damaged knee. He missed the next game against Surrey and although he marked his return against MCC at Lord's with an impressive unbeaten 30, *The Times'* correspondent remarked that he shouldn't have played because of his lack of mobility. He played against Leveson Gower's XI, but, once again, his knee gave up on him and on specialist advice he not only missed the Varsity Match – easily won by Cambridge – but also the rest of the first-class season. Despite his injury, his sporting exploits won him nomination by *Isis*, the Oxford University publication, as one of its Men of the Year.

After aggravating his knee injury playing real tennis, Jardine, a fourth-year student, now reading Law having gained a fourth in Modern History, missed Oxford's first four matches in 1923.

He returned a more circumspect player, partly the result of his injury and partly the responsibility he carried as Oxford's leading batsman in a side deemed weak in batting. Following a careful 38 against Gloucestershire, he failed against the Army, bowled in both innings by Captain James Hyndson. Before he was out in the second innings, he stopped one of Hyndson's inswingers with his pads, a tactical ploy that was strongly advocated by the Oxford coach Tom Hayward, the former Surrey and England batsman, and one which Jardine increasingly used. His action won the approval of *The Times'* writer covering the game, but not the sports journalist and editor of *Wisden*, Sydney Pardon. Without singling him out, Pardon decried the growing tendency of batsmen to use their pads as a defensive weapon, a tactic first employed by the former England captain Arthur Shrewsbury some 40 years earlier. He described it as a detestable practice, a rank injustice to the bowler, and called for an amendment to the lbw law so that a batsman could be given out to a ball that pitched outside the off stump and hit him in line. His salvo prompted a series of letters to *The Times*, specifically from R.H. Lyttelton, an enthusiastic club cricketer and a long-time opponent of pad play, who later wrote a book on the subject. Although the row failed to deter Jardine from continuing to use his pads – he remained a staunch defender of the existing lbw law – it only served to deepen his mistrust of the press.

After missing out in Oxford's match against the touring West Indians, he found some form with a chanceless 63 against the Free Foresters, dispatching Chapman for four fours in one over; then, after a half-century against Sussex, he scored 95 against Surrey at the Oval, his fourth-wicket stand of 161 with fellow Wykehamist John Guise largely instrumental in Oxford's three-wicket victory.

For the Varsity Match, Oxford, under Reg Bettington, started favourites against Cambridge, captained by Claude Ashton, and by exploiting good fortune, they chalked up what is still the most overwhelming victory in the history of the contest. Batting first on a beautiful wicket, Oxford made solid progress with a second-wicket stand of 101 between freshman Claude Taylor and Jardine, their cause helped by a serious side strain to Gubby Allen, Cambridge's leading bowler. Batting at No.3, Jardine looked in no trouble, scoring 39 before lunch, but was out immediately afterwards, expertly caught at slip by Claude Ashton as he sparred outside the off stump.

Led by Taylor's century, Oxford amassed 422 and, following heavy overnight rain, Cambridge were caught on a drying wicket. Bundled out for 59 in their first innings, with Stevens taking 6-20, they could only manage 136 in their second attempt, with Bettington the destroyer this time with 8-66.

On returning to Surrey, Jardine happily settled into the batting order at No.5, a position which he occupied, the odd game aside, for the rest of his career. By scoring 127 to help his side avoid defeat against Hampshire at Bournemouth, he won high praise from *The Times*, who described it as an innings quite out of the common. 'Mr Jardine is admittedly deficient in off-side hitting – he has been from his schooldays – but there can be no doubt about his class. Very few amateur batsmen today have anything like his strength in defence.'[8]

Another century followed against the touring West Indians as Surrey went down to a ten-wicket defeat. He then showed his more adventurous side against Yorkshire with some splendid hitting in the latter stages of his 74 not out, which won him his county cap. Finishing second in the county averages with

49.14, *Wisden* called his batting exceptional and with his future now committed to Surrey he was appointed vice-captain for the following season.

**Endnotes:**

1   *Wisden 1919*, p260
2   Douglas, *Douglas Jardine: Spartan Cricketer*, p210
3   *The Times*, 14 January 1921
4   Ibid, 6 May 1920
5   Ibid, 21 May 1920
6   Richard Streeton, *P.G.H. Fender: A biography*, p152
7   Derriman, *Bodyline*, p21
8   *The Times*, 30 July 1923

# CHAPTER 3

# 'THE BEST AMATEUR BATSMAN IN ENGLAND'

THE 1920S were in many ways the heyday of the County Championship. In an era when cricket was the undisputed national summer game and followed by all classes, it received unprecedented coverage through the introduction of the newsreel and the wireless and the expansion of the popular press. Crowds flocked to the larger grounds, especially for derbies such as the Roses Match or for Surrey's fixtures against its northern rivals, Lancashire, Yorkshire and Nottinghamshire. With a more hard-nosed post-war ethos and the growth in popularity of the leagues, the balance of power shifted northwards. Middlesex's Championship triumphs in 1920 and 1921 were the south's only success in the inter-war years, when Yorkshire claimed the title 12 times, Lancashire five, and Nottinghamshire and Derbyshire once each.

Although the First World War brought about rapid social change with the expansion of the franchise and the growth of trade union power, the old order remained entrenched in cricket. Power remained very much the preserve of the privileged MCC and the amateur captains with their blazers of many colours. Aside from being addressed by the professionals as 'Mr' or 'Sir', they stayed in superior accommodation, changed in separate dressing-rooms and entered the field by separate gates. While some of these captains sank without trace because of their limitations as either leaders or cricketers, others won undying allegiance from their players for their adventurous approach or their concern for others. No one better exemplified the latter type than Percy Fender, captain of Surrey between 1921 and 1931.

An outspoken maverick, much favoured by cartoonists for his crinkly black hair, horn-rimmed spectacles, toothbrush moustache and grotesquely long jersey, Fender always marched to his own drumbeat. A popular entertainer, he played a pivotal role in Surrey's Championship success in 1914 and was one of the leading cricketers of the inter-war period: a wily leg-spinner, an outstanding slip fielder and an inspirational captain, noted for his tactical ingenuity. At a time when Surrey's limited attack laboured long and hard on the Oval's placid surfaces, his success in keeping his side in the upper echelons of the county table was judged to be a near miracle.

With Fender away playing for England against South Africa during the summer of 1924, it fell to Jardine to step into his shoes now that he was Surrey's vice-captain. Although he had missed out on the captaincy of Oxford, his potential for leadership was unquestioned, especially with Fender as his mentor. For the Surrey v Cambridge University match of 1925, Fender left himself out of the side so that Jardine could be captain. For three days he sat in the Oval pavilion and at each interval told Jardine what errors he'd made in a game in which Cambridge, set 426, won with half an hour to spare. Their hero was Ranjitsinhji's nephew, the brilliant Kumar Shri Duleepsinhji, who beat the packed off-side field by steering everything round to leg. When Jardine placed seven on the leg side, he started guiding the ball to third man. *The Times* called it the finest batting seen in London that season.

Besides a mutual respect for their playing and leadership ability, Fender and Jardine were close friends, the ebullience of the former helping the latter to relax. On one occasion after they returned to the dressing-room following a long day in the field when the Surrey attack had been hammered, Fender asked the Oval dressing-room attendant if he could get them some provisions. 'Just slip out and get me 20 Players,' he said. 'Make that 20 bowlers,' added Jardine.

With a long-established batting order of Hobbs, Sandham, Andy Ducat and Tom Shepherd, who had 400 first-class centuries between them, Jardine happily took his place at No.5, proving himself a great retriever of lost causes. Although missing out against the touring South Africans, Jardine began 1924 with consecutive half-centuries against Glamorgan and Somerset in the Championship; he then marked his first two games in charge with a convincing win against Glamorgan and enjoying much the better of a draw against Gloucestershire, scoring two more fifties in the process. He again led from the front with a masterly 91 to help Surrey earn a draw against Lancashire at Old Trafford.

His good form continued with 105 not out and 63 against Oxford University, but his captaincy attracted some flak for an over-generous declaration. Setting the university 316 to win in four hours, the Surrey attack were undone by the brilliance of John Guise, who scored an unbeaten 154 to steer Oxford to a notable four-wicket victory.

Jardine's innings of the season came in the return match against Lancashire at the Oval when he made 122. Opening the innings in place of Hobbs and Sandham, who were away on Test duty, he impressed with the quality of his driving. The *Morning Post's* Plum Warner wrote: 'Jardine was a little lucky at the start of his innings in snicking two or three balls, but he possesses great defence and sound judgement. He late cuts well, and is very strong on the leg side. He completed his 1,000 runs for the season, and at the moment stands at the top of the amateurs in the batting averages. He seems destined to play a big part in the cricket of the near future.'[1]

His form tailed off in August save for one typical effort against Middlesex when his stoical 87 rescued Surrey from a terrible start. With wins against Sussex, Yorkshire and Leicestershire, Surrey finished the season on a high by coming third in the Championship – up one place on the previous year. Describing Jardine as the county's most consistent batsman after Hobbs and Sandham, *Wisden* wrote: 'Stronger, perhaps, in defence than any other amateur now playing first-class cricket in England, he again and again showed his best skill when nerve and steadiness were most needed.'[2]

The 1925 season will always be recalled for the stupendous batting of Hobbs and Sandham, who scored 16 Championship centuries between them. Their runs, and the bowling of Fender, who took 124 wickets, primarily accounted for Surrey's rise to second place.

Jardine, while living in Hobbs's shadow, batted consistently in a season in which he scored 40 or more on ten occasions. His only real failures came in the side's two defeats: against Lancashire at Old Trafford, where they were routed by the Australian fast bowler Ted McDonald, and against the champions Yorkshire at Bradford, where England's George Macaulay took 11 wickets.

Following the Lancashire defeat, Jardine made a flawless 79 against Essex, but then, shortly afterwards, he was forced to miss three weeks of cricket because of an injury sustained when playing for the Essex batsman Colin McIver's XI against the Surrey club Ashtead. Facing up to the local postman, he was struck a nasty blow on his collarbone which left him writhing on the ground. After he was bandaged and retired to bed, the novelist Joan Grant, his companion for the day, went to comfort him. She found him upset at the thought that he would miss playing for the Gentlemen against the Players and wouldn't get another chance. She took him to her home on Hayling Island, near Portsmouth, where he stayed until he recovered. The following year he paid her the great compliment of taking her with him to inspect the wicket at Lord's, but, according to Grant: 'I was secretly so tired of watching even Douglas play cricket that my cup was filled to overflowing when he decided the wicket was not fit for play and so was free to take me to the cinema.'[3]

Jardine returned against Gloucestershire at Gloucester and made useful runs before Surrey's Bank Holiday fixture against Nottinghamshire at the Oval. In front of a crowd so vast that they blocked the sightscreens and reduced the size of the boundaries, Jardine came face to face with Nottinghamshire paceman Harold Larwood for the first time. From humble mining stock, the 5ft 8in Larwood appeared to lack the physique to bowl fast. But determined to succeed at cricket to escape life down the pit, he perfected his craft through superb coaching and dedicated practice. Possessed of great upper-body strength and stamina, he generated exceptional pace and accuracy through his wonderfully smooth run-up and classical side-on action. After making his debut at the end of 1924, he soon became the talk of the counties in 1925 with 40 wickets in 12 matches, although Jardine remained sceptical; he'd heard such talk before about fast bowlers who failed to live up to expectation. 'He doesn't look fast to me,' he remarked to Fender as he watched Hobbs and Sandham comfortably negotiate his opening overs. Jardine played admirably for 53 but was given a rough baptism against Larwood when the latter returned for a second spell in which he cleaned up the Surrey innings. 'Larwood's first ball was being returned by the wicketkeeper Lilley as Douglas completed his stroke,' Fender later wrote. 'The second ball was on its way through to Lilley when the stroke was completed. The third ball Douglas finally made contact. He immediately turned round to the pavilion and raised his cap to me.'[4]

Bowled neck and crop by Larwood, Jardine recalled the paceman's fixity of purpose and his ability to block out anything extraneous, while Jardine had impressed Larwood with his willingness to get into line against the short ball and take a blow on the body. It was the beginning of one of the most significant relationships of Jardine's career.

Hobbs's prodigious form yielded him 12 centuries by mid-July, an astonishing achievement for a 42-year-old. One more would place him on a par with W.G. Grace's record aggregate of 126 first-class centuries, a landmark that captivated the nation. Carrying their hopes on his shoulders proved a heavy burden for Hobbs, and for the next month his batting lacked its customary authority. Even cameo fifties were treated as failures, and by the time Surrey travelled to Taunton to play Somerset on 15 August the strain was beginning to show. In front of a large crowd and in perfect conditions, Somerset batted poorly and were dismissed for 167 by tea on the opening day. Once again, a nervous-looking Hobbs batted tentatively but with lady luck on his side he survived to the close undefeated on 91, with Jardine, yet to score, at the other end.

Following a day of mounting excitement on the Sabbath, Monday dawned bright and fair. All routes led to Taunton as spectators, many travelling down from London, along with journalists and photographers, poured into the small ground. So great was the crush that the scheduled start had to be delayed by nearly half an hour. A tumultuous ovation greeted Hobbs and Jardine on their appearance before the crowd settled down in silence as the Somerset seamers Robertson-Glasgow and Jim Bridges gave nothing away. A pull for four off the former which took Hobbs to 98 lifted the tension before a hush descended once again. A quick single to point followed and then, after what seemed an eternity, a leg-side push off Bridges gave Hobbs his coveted century. Well before the single was completed, the crowd let out an ecstatic roar as they rose to their feet, waving their hats and cheering their idol wildly. As a beaming Hobbs accepted the congratulations of all the Somerset side, Fender appeared from the pavilion bearing a celebratory glass of Hobbs's favourite ginger beer. Hobbs raised his glass high and took a swig, bringing the crowd to its feet once again.

When play resumed, he was soon out for 101, but Jardine continued to play sensibly before he was run out for 47. Surrey made 359 and although Somerset rallied second time round, their target of 183 proved a mere formality as Hobbs and Sandham knocked off the runs without being separated, the former finishing with 101 to surpass Grace. No wonder Jardine christened him 'The Master'.

Although Jardine failed to reach three figures in 1925, *Wisden* was appreciative of his efforts. 'D.R. Jardine, sound as ever in defence, put together a number of excellent scores and altogether rendered the side very fine service.'[5] He'd also established himself as a reliable gully, missing very few chances that came his way, and a courageous if rather impetuous short leg.

Disappointed by his form, Jardine worked hard at tightening up his game and restricting his range of strokes. 'I am not a natural batsman like Sutcliffe, Hammond, Leyland, Paynter and these fellows,' he later told Bill Bowes, the Yorkshire fast bowler. 'I am a made cricketer, dull and without sparkle, but I can get runs if I play within my limitations.'[6] He began 1926 with a spirited 79 against Hampshire, scoring all 34 runs in a last-wicket partnership with Stanley Fenley before national politics briefly intervened.

A long, drawn-out struggle between the miners and the mine-owners over pay and conditions in the pits escalated into a full-blown crisis in May 1926, whereby the former, supported by the trade union movement, challenged Stanley Baldwin's Conservative government by calling a General Strike. Although the trade union leaders were by and large loyal, patriotic types who felt deeply uneasy about resorting to such drastic action, the radical slogans of a firebrand such as A.J. Cook, the General Secretary of the Miners' Federation of Great Britain, sent shudders through the Establishment. As public transport ground to a halt, City bankers, undergraduates and First World War veterans rallied to the cause by volunteering as special constables and tram drivers. MCC appealed to cricketers' sense of duty and Jardine, a committed Conservative, along with his amateur team-mates, Alfred Jeacocke, Errol Holmes and Donald Knight, was among those who signed up, Jardine as a special constable, leaving Surrey rather depleted for their match against the Australians. Despite the scarcity of transport, a large crowd gathered at the Oval to watch the tourists compile a big score before rain disrupted the game, an all-too-familiar occurrence throughout most of that season.

After nine days during which the government remained rock-solid in its refusal to make concessions to the strikers, the dispute petered out, leaving the miners to fight on alone, and Jardine and Co. could go back to playing cricket. He did get the chance to play against the Australians when picked for the South of England but failed to do himself justice. Having looked uncomfortable against opening bowler Jack Gregory, he lashed out at leg-spinner Arthur Mailey and was stumped for seven. He then led Surrey in their first-ever defeat by Glamorgan, bagging a pair in the process, the only one of his career.

After missing two matches to take his final law exams which enabled him to qualify as a solicitor, he returned to his best against Yorkshire at Bramall Lane. Finding himself at the wicket at 7/3 in reply to the home side's 398, Jardine temporarily halted the surge with a chanceless 82, sharing a fourth-wicket partnership of 150 with Shepherd. Thereafter, Surrey collapsed again and were all out for 228. Following on 170 behind, Jardine again batted admirably for 63, but his was a lone hand as his side slid to an innings defeat.

He continued to impress with a classic 85 for the Gentlemen against the Players at Lord's. His team-mate Bob Wyatt, the Warwickshire all-rounder and later his vice-captain in Australia, recalled: 'I thought he was a great player, though concentrating mainly on the on-side. His defence seemed impenetrable, and he had endless guts. Fast bowling never worried him. When I got to know him better, I found that in spite of his aloof manner he could be surprisingly thoughtful and kind, and had considerable personal charm.'[7]

Jardine made the same score for Surrey against Kent at the Oval, but only after being the recipient of good fortune. Given out lbw for 2, he remained at the crease, at which point the umpire reversed his decision, and after being dropped on 38, he then added 98 with Bob Gregory at more than a run a minute.

Bad weather again ruined Surrey's return match against the Australians, with the county in real trouble at 82/6 in reply to the tourists' 432. On a spiteful wicket, ideal for the spinners, Jardine was the only man who played leg-spinner Clarrie Grimmett with any conviction and he remained undefeated on 20 when rain washed out the final day. The county's form had fluctuated all summer, but, inspired by Hobbs and Jardine, they began to raise their game, remaining unbeaten for the rest of the season. Against Warwickshire at Edgbaston, Surrey collapsed to 67/6 before Jardine led a spectacular recovery. Shunning his normal caution, he took the attack to the opposition, putting on 110 in 70 minutes with all-rounder Alan Peach and 107 in under an hour with wicketkeeper Ted Brooks. He finished with 167, paving the way to a high-scoring draw.

He finished in style with a quick-fire 69 not out against Leicestershire, prior to playing Brutus to Hobbs's Caesar against Middlesex at Lord's. Up against a powerful attack of Jack Durston, Gubby Allen, Nigel Haig and Greville Stevens – all of whom played for England at one time or another – Hobbs dispatched them to all parts of the ground with shots of effortless timing, one powerful drive killing a sparrow. Jardine gave him solid support and was undefeated on 72 when Surrey closed at stumps on 460/3, Hobbs 256 not out. 'Mr Jardine's innings would have looked to be a very good one in ordinary circumstances,' wrote *The Times* reporter. 'On Saturday it appeared laboured in comparison with Hobbs's artistry.'[8]

They extended their partnership to 270 on Monday before Jardine was out for 103, but Hobbs went remorselessly on to make an undefeated 316, a career best and the highest score made at Lord's, a record he held until Graham Gooch's 333 for England against India in 1990.

Jardine wasn't finished yet. Given a rare bowl, he picked up three cheap wickets, his victims including F.T. Mann, a former England captain, in Middlesex's first innings, and Patsy Hendren, one of England's finest batsmen, in the second, as Surrey won comfortably to finish fifth in the Championship.

Invited to play for an England XI against the Australians at Folkestone, Jardine deputised as wicketkeeper for Warwickshire's Tiger Smith on the opening day when a severe thunderstorm disrupted the latter's journey to the game. It proved no easy assignment as he was keeping to Larwood at his fastest, the paceman finishing with 7-95. Opening the innings, Jardine looked more assured against Gregory than he did earlier in the summer and his 38, spread over three days because of poor weather, convinced Australia's Bill Woodfull that he was one of England's best young batsmen.

Like many amateurs, Jardine enjoyed an affluent lifestyle totally beyond the means of his professional team-mates. Living in some style in London's fashionable West End, he dressed smartly, ate out, frequented exclusive clubs and pursued expensive hobbies such as fishing and shooting. Although comfortably off, his financial resources weren't so limitless that he could afford not to work. Having completed his legal training with Crawley, Arnold, Ellis & Ellis, he worked at Barings Bank and as a legal adviser to several commercial firms, primarily on lucrative matters such as conveyancing and probate. Later, he worked at the merchant bankers Helbert, Wagg & Co.

Because of his business commitments he played relatively little cricket between 1926 and 1931, notwithstanding the tour to Australia in 1928/29, which helps explain why he won a mere 22 Test caps. In 1927 he played in only three Championship games for Surrey, but what cricket he did play that year cemented his reputation as a batsman of the highest class.

Having warmed up with a century in his opening match, for the Harlequins against Oxford University, he then scored 147 for Surrey against Leicestershire and 143 against Lancashire, a side greatly strengthened by the inclusion of Ted McDonald. Having settled in England to play in the Lancashire League, McDonald, now in his fourth year in county cricket and still a fearsome bowler, had Surrey on the defensive at 94/4, but Jardine stood firm against the rising ball. Unperturbed by the numerous blows he took on the body, he gradually got the measure of McDonald, driving him mercilessly as he began to tire. It took a fine delivery to bowl him in the final over of the day, by which time he'd made 143, his third century in consecutive matches.

His rich vein of form continued with 118 against Cambridge University. According to Warner, Jardine looked a much-improved player, a view shared by the former England all-rounder Gilbert Jessop. He wrote: 'The Surrey player, though somewhat overshadowed by the compelling personalities of Hobbs and Sandham, has for some seasons past been recognised as a batsman of more than ordinary promise, and this latest effort should suffice to convince our authorities that in him we possess a cricketer blessed with a temperament fitted for great occasions.'[9]

His words were given substance by Jardine's fifth century of the season in the Gentlemen–Players fixture at Lord's, a game disrupted by the weather. In saturnine conditions and on a sodden pitch, he rescued his side from an uncertain start with imperious shots on both sides of the wicket. The *Times* correspondent, commending him for his improvement as an off-side player, called his 123 the one outstanding achievement of the day, and *The Cricketer* rated him the leading amateur batsman in England. His performance gained him the captaincy of the England XI in the second Test trial following the late withdrawal of the incumbent Percy Chapman, despite his unavailability for the forthcoming tour to South Africa. With more bad weather robbing his side of a probable victory in the final trial at Lord's, he finished his abbreviated season top of the national averages with 91.09, a feat that gained him recognition as one of *Wisden*'s Five Cricketers of the Year. Having acknowledged his many attributes as a batsman, *Wisden* opined that, provided he could spare the time, he would be on the boat to Australia the following autumn, expectations that were to be fully realised as his batting continued to flourish.

**Endnotes:**

1  *Morning Post*, 12 August 1924
2  *Wisden* 1925, p130
3  Joan Grant, *Time out of Mind*, p87
4  Quoted in Hamilton, *Harold Larwood*, p49
5  *Wisden* 1926, p70
6  John Arlott (ed), *The Great Captains*, p55
7  Gerald Pawle, *R.E.S. Wyatt: Fighting Cricketer*, p92
8  *The Times*, 30 August 1926
9  *The Scotsman*, 1 July 1927

## CHAPTER 4

# THE MULTI-COLOURED CAP

AFTER HIS prodigious run-scoring in 1927, Jardine began 1928 in the unusual position of being a prime contender to lead MCC in Australia that winter without having yet played Test cricket. 'Last summer D.R. Jardine exhibited such form as to ensure inclusion in the best side we could then produce,' wrote Jessop. 'It will need a repetition of such brilliance before I, for one, would be convinced that he should receive preference over such consistent batsmen, so temperamentally fitted for great occasions, as Holmes, Ernest Tyldesley and Sandham.'[1]

Aside from an assured 58 against the touring West Indians, Jardine only managed two other first-class innings in May because of work and bad weather prior to Surrey's traditional Bank Holiday fixture against Nottinghamshire. On a flat Trent Bridge pitch Surrey toiled in the field for 159 overs while the home side piled on the runs with the genial George Gunn, a year off his 50th birthday, scoring a century. When he'd reached 97, Jardine sidled up to him and said, 'I say, Gunn, do you smoke a pipe?' Gunn's eyes glistened, 'Yes, Mr Jardine, I do.' 'Well,' continued Jardine, 'I wish you would get back to the pavilion and light up.'

'As a rule, you know, I'm satisfied to get a century and then throw my wicket away,' Gunn later recounted, 'but after Mr Jardine had spoken to me I determined that I would delay that pipe-lighting until I had scored 200 runs.' As it was, Gunn was irritated with himself for getting out for 122.

In reply to Nottinghamshire's 457, Surrey could only manage 288, but spared the follow-on, they struck back with a vengeance. Taking advantage of some rank bad batting, Fender and Peach took all ten wickets between them to bowl their opponents out for 50 and Surrey, led by Sandham, chased down the 220 required to win by seven wickets, with Jardine administering the *coup de grâce*.

Following a masterly unbeaten 73 against Leicestershire, he hit an admirable century for the Gentlemen against the Players at the Oval. Entering at 7/2, he began uncertainly and was badly missed by Ewart Astill at third slip when on 23. Ignoring some mild barracking during a passive afternoon, Jardine changed tack after tea. Laying into some weary bowling, he duly completed his century before racing to his third fifty in 45 minutes with some scintillating strokes, and he continued to sparkle till he was out in the final over of the day for 193. According to *The Times,* he showed himself as good an attacking batsman as he was a defensive one.

His performance helped ensure his appointment as captain of the Rest against England, captained by Chapman, in the Test trial at Lord's. Once again, he proved himself the complete batsman with scores of 48 and 74 not out. Coming in at No.7 in the second innings to give others a chance, he batted faultlessly to earn his side a hard-earned draw. 'He played great cricket on a wicket which afforded help to spin bowlers like Freeman and

Jupp,' wrote Warner. 'A most polished player, Jardine's defence is, probably, as good as that of any other player in the country, and he is in particularly fine form just now. He gets the ball very consistently in the middle of the bat.'[2]

After his sterling performance, Jardine well merited his England debut against the West Indies at Lord's, helped by the fact that Hobbs was injured. It was at pre-match practice that he first came across Bill Bowes, who was then on the MCC ground-staff and who had been deputed to bowl at England's captain Chapman. On returning to the pavilion, Jardine asked Chapman whether he had any money on him and when Chapman replied that he hadn't, Jardine said, 'Oh, never mind. It's usual to give the two bowlers a drink and I've left my change in the pavilion.' With the help of the pavilion attendant, Jardine sent his two bowlers half a crown, but Chapman said to his two: 'Jolly good thing Douglas reminded me, I should have forgotten. But I'll make a deal with you. If I get 50 tomorrow, I'll give you ten bob each; if I don't get 50, we're all square because your bowling didn't do me any good.' 'This was the difference between the two great England amateurs at the time,' wrote Bowes. 'Douglas Jardine was coldly efficient and did the right things. Percy had a way of saying the right things and getting you to like him straight away. He brought a touch of adventure into the game and he got you "with him".'[3]

West Indies, under Karl Nunes, were playing their first Test series, but despite possessing three genuinely quick bowlers in George Francis, Herman Griffith and Learie Constantine and several attacking batsmen, they flattered to deceive, losing all three matches by substantial margins. On a glorious day and in front of a large crowd, England batted first and although Jardine, batting at No.5, made only 22, he looked very much the part, one straight-driven boundary off the back foot as memorable a stroke as anything seen all day. England made 401 and won by an innings.

Returning to county duty, Jardine remained in the runs with 91 against Somerset at the Oval and a chanceless 157 against Yorkshire – aside from one piece of luck. He'd only scored one when he stepped back to a ball from spinner Wilfred Rhodes and appeared to play on. He was leaving the wicket before he was called back by wicketkeeper Arthur Wood, who explained that he'd accidentally dislodged the ball with his pads. In reply to Yorkshire's 406, Surrey were struggling at 96/5, at which point Jardine found a reliable partner in Fender and together they took the score to 264/5 at stumps. They continued their epic stand the next day, adding 294 in little over four hours, beating the previous highest sixth-wicket stand against Yorkshire by K.J. Key and W.H. Lockwood at the Oval in 1890, which enabled Surrey to gain a first-innings lead.

Jardine again showed his pedigree in the Gentlemen–Players fixture at Lord's. Replying to their opponents' first innings of 423, he scored 86 in less than two hours with majestic shots all around the wicket. Particularly impressive was the way he used his feet to leg-spinner 'Tich' Freeman, who finished with 6-93. Following on, Jardine again looked in sparkling form before he was brilliantly run out by Yorkshire's Maurice Leyland for 40. Despite half-centuries from Bob Wyatt, Aidan Crawley and Chapman, the Gentlemen lost by nine wickets.

England welcomed back Hobbs for the second Test at Old Trafford and drew first blood by dismissing West Indies for 206. Although unsettled by some hostile short-pitched bowling, Hobbs and Sutcliffe opened up with a century partnership and, after the fall of three quick wickets, Hammond and Jardine consolidated. Having progressed to 26, the latter incensed the West Indians when he hit his wicket but refused to walk, claiming that he'd completed his shot and therefore the ball was dead. According to Constantine, Jardine was within his rights but the haughty way he had behaved rankled.

Technically correct at all times, not least against the rising ball, Jardine helped Hammond add 120 for the fourth wicket and, according to *Wisden*, played masterly cricket, before he was run out for 83 when Maurice Tate failed to respond to his call. He gave Tate an icy stare as he left, leaving some to conclude that their relationship never quite recovered from this misunderstanding.

West Indies, 145 in arrears, once again batted poorly and lost by an innings. Although unavailable for the third Test, Jardine was guaranteed a place in the MCC side to tour Australia. The question was: would he be captain? He'd led the Rest in the Test trial with flair, but while a superior batsman to Chapman, the latter's halo still shone bright. Not only had he won back the Ashes in 1926, he'd captained capably against West Indies and fielded brilliantly. In addition, he was idolised in Australia in 1924/25 and his cheerful, outgoing personality was more suited to the captain's ambassadorial role on tour than Jardine's aloof demeanour. More surprising was the appointment of Somerset's J.C. White as vice-captain, the assumption being that his affable personality would get more out of the team than Jardine, the third amateur in the party, who was co-opted to the selection committee, as was Hobbs, making his fifth tour to Australia.

On 15 September Jardine was part of the advance party that left England on board the SS *Otranto*, seen off by a buoyant crowd of 2,000 at Victoria station. The rest of the players, detained by a match between Lancashire, the champion county, and the Rest, travelled across France by rail and joined the *Otranto* at Toulon.

Protocol dictated that the three amateurs kept their distance from the rest of the team, eating at separate tables, much to the amazement of the other passengers, and Jardine caused some consternation by refusing his autograph to a pretty Australian girl. An early riser, he trained every morning and kept himself trim by playing quoits and deck tennis.

After an agreeable voyage the players were in high spirits when they disembarked at Fremantle, Western Australia. They were given a warm reception by the large crowds that had gathered and under Chapman's genial leadership they proved popular wherever they went. With Hobbs, Sutcliffe, Hammond, Hendren and Jardine constituting a formidable batting line-up and Tate and Larwood leading the attack, it was a powerful side which prepared for the challenges of an Australian tour. Apart from seven months away from loved ones and the arduous inter-state rail travel, the playing conditions were very different from those back home: the intense heat, the glare of the light, the timeless Tests, the bland wickets, the vast grounds and the huge crowds. Unlike the demure nature of English crowds, Australian ones tended to be much more vociferous and while they could turn on their own players if they weren't performing, most of their criticism was directed at the auld enemy. Although previous MCC sides had taken exception to their behaviour, much of it was harmless banter and those like Hendren who responded to it with witty repartee made friends for life.

From the first game, Jardine lived up to his reputation as the best amateur batsman in England by scoring centuries in three consecutive innings, a record for a touring team in Australia. Beginning with 109 against Western Australia, he followed this with 104 against Victoria, and, best of all, a peerless 140 against New South Wales. Dominating an opening stand of 148 with Sutcliffe, he played opening bowler Jack Gregory with consummate ease, driving him imperiously through mid-on. Completing a chanceless century in 153 minutes, he gave a vintage exhibition of strokeplay until he played on. According to *The Times*, he batted in magnificent style, while the distinguished Australian cricket journalist Johnnie Moyes wrote in the Sydney *Daily Telegraph*: 'Jardine gave a charming display. His on-side play was as usual absolutely faultless and the ease and precision with which he deflected the ball into the vacant spaces won universal admiration.

'It was altogether one of the finest exhibitions of batsmanship seen for a very long time, and Jardine has firmly established his reputation as one of the finest English amateur batsmen seen on the famous Sydney Ground.'[4]

On a day when the crowd remained good-tempered, the *Toowoomba Chronicle* noted there was hearty applause from all quarters when Jardine posted his century, and *The Times* reported that he returned to the pavilion to a standing ovation, both accounts at variance with the playwright Ben Travers, who was following the side around Australia. In his memoir *94 Declared*, he wrote that the incoming batsman Hendren, sensing the crowd's hostility towards Jardine on his dismissal, said, 'They don't seem to like you very much here, Mr Jardine,' to which the latter is alleged to have replied, 'It's mutual.'

Even an authority such as Jack Fingleton isn't entirely correct when attributing Jardine's unpopularity in Australia to his habit of wearing the Harlequin cap, because it failed to impress egalitarian Australians. Aside from the fact that the wearing of such a cap was no bar to the immense popularity enjoyed by other amateurs such as Arthur Gilligan and Chapman, Jardine's headwear was more an object of fascination than derision. 'Take your hat off,' called one barracker in the opening match and Jardine doffed his cap in reply. 'The crowd took to him right away,' noted Velox in the *Queensland Figaro* after the first Test. 'They liked his batting and they liked his cap – a real harlequin – breathing a real breath of England's high-class collegian world. Hence his sobriquet of "Rainbow", a harmless little threat, which I am sure, even Mr Jardine himself quietly appreciates, and which no doubt will surely find mention when his cricketing memories are being written.'5

Not everyone liked his cap, it is true, but this was down to form and taste rather than class, as evident in an editorial in the weekly periodical *The Australasian*. 'Jardine, with his ugly Harlequins cap, was next man, and why the members of the English team are not compelled to wear their proper colours is a sign that superstition overrides nationalism. It gives the team a ragged appearance, and it may be mentioned that Jardine is not the only delinquent.'6

It is certainly the case that Jardine often irked the crowd, but this was overwhelmingly the result of his slow scoring, exacerbated by his growing disdain for their hostility. During his century against Victoria, when the Australian batsman 'Stork' Hendry, fielding at slip, apologised to Jardine for the crowd's hostility, Jardine launched into such a bitter tirade against Australians that Hendry berated him in turn, the only occasion he ever swore at a fellow cricketer. It was the last time that they spoke to each other on the tour. Weeks later, when Hendry was on 96 in the second Test, Jardine told Chapman to call for drinks. Hendry later recalled the incident:

'That mongrel Jardine must have given instruction that one of the glasses was to have whisky in it. Jardine didn't like Australians. He told me during a game against New South Wales [sic] that all Australians were uneducated and an unruly mob. I wasn't going to take that from anybody, an insult to my countrymen, so I said, "you bugger off".

'When the drinks came out, I stood at the batting crease and they said, "aren't you going to have a drink with us, Stork?"

Before I could get it to my lips, Patsy Hendren said: "Stork, that is loaded with whisky," so I said to him: "Get a glass, Pat, I am going to drink to a magnificent sportsman."'[7] Having downed their drinks, the quick hit of alcohol made Hendry's head spin, but he still retained enough composure to complete his only Test century.

According to Fingleton, Jardine wasn't a good mixer and he didn't respond to the friendly informality of the Australian character. 'He did not proffer his hand more than necessary. He was aloof and discerning with a cold, judicial mind in gauging people and events before committing himself. He did not want to be rushed with friendship and gusto – he preferred to do his own picking and choosing. He was of that proverbial English type which shares a railway compartment on a journey and never enters into a conversation.'[8] At a train halt on their way north to the first Test the three amateurs, Chapman, White and Jardine, strolled along the platform to stretch their legs. When a stranger accosted them with a cheery greeting, Jardine, in contrast to Chapman and White who warmly shook hands, replied with a supercilious stare and complete ignorance of the proffered hand.

Possibly because of its youth or remoteness from older centres of civilisation, Fingleton continued, the Australian felt the need to publicise his country and its many achievements. 'But Jardine was not amused by such understandable insularity. He was bored immeasurably, and that, in turn, nettled Australians, who abhor bored and critical visitors. The Australian wants to like his visitor; just as important, he wants his visitor to like him.'[9]

In a country intolerant of class distinctions in sport, Jardine's first public action was to gather exclusively the Varsity men of the South Australian team and wine and dine them. He made ideal barracking material – one spectator shouted, 'Eh, eh, Mr Jardine, where's the butler to carry your bat for you?' – but according to Fingleton, he could have won them over, as Gilligan had done, or Chapman was to do, with a wave or a cheery comment. 'No crowd is quicker to condemn, no crowd quicker to applaud, than the Australian, and none is more easily won over.'[10]

After drawing their first four matches, MCC beat an Australian XI, despite Jardine's double failure, twice dismissed cheaply by his former Oxford team-mate Reg Bettington, and Queensland to enter the first Test as favourites. Jack Ryder's Australia had lost Herbie Collins, Charlie Macartney and Warren Bardsley to retirement, and although the side contained some fine batsmen, such as Bill Woodfull, Bill Ponsford and debutant Don Bradman, their ageing attack lacked penetration.

In the first Test held in Brisbane, staged at the city's Exhibition Ground, England appeared to have wasted first use of a perfect wicket when Jardine was out for 35 at 217/5, but Hendren came to the rescue with a magnificent 169, aided by 50 from Chapman and 70 from Larwood.

Replying to a total of 521, Australia ran into Larwood at his most hostile and were dismissed for 122, but, despite a lead of 399, Chapman, conscious of having only three frontline bowlers, chose to bat again. Phil Mead made 73 and Jardine showed his class with an undefeated 65 although his cautious approach taxed the patience of the crowd. When appraised by Ben Travers of his suspicion that debutant spinner Bert Ironmonger, aged 46, possessed a suspect action, Jardine replied, 'Of course, he throws. But don't for God's sake tell anybody.' His confidence was well founded on that tour but, four years later, it was a different story when Ironmonger dismissed him four times in the Tests. No wicket gave him greater pleasure, since he didn't care for Jardine and his fellow amateurs, believing them to be snooty. 'A friend of mine told me that Jardine, who hardly scored a run off me, dismissed me with the words: "Ironmonger's easy enough to play but hard to score off." That's the sort of blokes they were.'[11]

Set 742 to win, Australia found themselves batting on a drying wicket and with slow left-armer White in his element they could only muster 66, their defeat by 675 runs remaining the biggest defeat by runs in Ashes history.

The first Test marked the end of two great Australians – Gregory whose injured knee finally gave way, and Charles Kelleway who succumbed to illness – and the arrival of Bradman, who was dropped after scoring 18 and 1. Appointed 12th man for the second Test at Sydney, he fielded as a substitute for 11 hours following Ponsford's broken hand on the opening day, an injury which ruled him out of the series. Dismissed for 253 in their first innings, Australia made England struggle for runs on a drab second day. At stumps, they were 113/2 with Hammond on 33 and Jardine 23. The following morning Jardine proceeded carefully in comparison to Hammond, his caution once again provoking the crowd. On 28, he responded slowly to Hammond's call for a brisk single and was run out by the bowler Don Blackie, who raced to the ball, retrieved it and threw down the stumps. His dismissal proved a fleeting success for the home side as England, led by Hammond's 251, scored 636, paving the way to an eight-wicket win.

The third Test at Melbourne was altogether a closer affair with Bradman scoring 79 and 112 on his recall, his performance inviting comparisons with the youthful exploits of previous Australian greats such as Clem Hill and Victor Trumper. Thanks to another double century from Hammond and 62 from Jardine, England gained a first-innings lead of 20, but centuries from Woodfull and Bradman took the home team to 347/8 at the end of the fifth day.

A torrential storm that night turned the wicket into a lottery when play resumed at 12.30pm the following afternoon. The appearance of a hot sun soon afterwards only added to their woes as Hobbs and Sutcliffe began the gargantuan task of scoring 332 for victory. Walking in to lunch, Jardine met Hugh Trumble, the former Australian off-spinner and secretary of the Melbourne Cricket Club, who reckoned England would be lucky to make 70 on such a surface, let alone 100. Immediately on resumption, Hobbs survived a simple slip chance, but despite the ball turning and lifting venomously, he and Sutcliffe proved equal to everything the Australian bowlers threw at them, employing the dead bat to great effect. According to Bradman, it was the worst sticky wicket he ever saw, along with the finest batting in such conditions, their cause aided by the failure of the Australian bowlers to locate the right length.

After tea Hobbs, on the pretext of changing his bat, signalled to the dressing-room and Jardine, fathoming that he had something of importance to impart, made it his business to take a replacement out to the middle. There Hobbs told him that he should come in next because he had the best technique to handle the conditions. Jardine conveyed Hobbs's advice to Chapman who readily accepted it, so that when Hobbs was out for 49, it was Jardine who replaced him. Hit in the solar plexus by his first two balls, he was fortunate to survive a confident lbw appeal from Blackie before he'd scored; thereafter, he looked distinctly uncomfortable against him and Grimmett, but his defensive technique against the latter, with his bottom hand removed from the bat, certainly helped. At one point he withdrew from the wicket as Hendry was about to bowl because of a late change in the field, a gesture which, quite unjustifiably, earned him a wigging from the crowd, but Jardine ignored them and survived with Sutcliffe to the close.

Needing another 172 to win on the final day, they proceeded cautiously on an improving wicket, taking the score to 199 whereupon Jardine was bowled off his pads by Grimmett for 33, one of the innings that, in retrospect, gave him the greatest satisfaction. Sutcliffe's 135, the innings of his life, was primarily responsible for England's miraculous three-wicket victory and their retention of the Ashes.

From Melbourne MCC travelled to Tasmania for two fixtures against the island. Jardine batted superbly in the first one to score a career-best 214 and missed the second one to go fishing, catching a 6lb sea trout, which he called one of the highlights of his life.

He continued his run spree with a century in the return fixture against South Australia, despite being subjected to a slew of bouncers from their fast bowler Jack Scott, later a leading Test umpire.

Now that the Ashes had been lost, the Australian selectors bowed to popular demand and gave a first cap to their 19-year-old prodigy Archie Jackson, who was later to die tragically young of tuberculosis. Although Hobbs and Sutcliffe gave England the perfect start at Adelaide with an opening partnership of 143, only Hammond prospered thereafter with 119 not out.

Replying to England's 334, Australia lost early wickets, but Jackson proved peerless from the outset, hitting a brilliant 164. Facing a deficit of 35 on first innings and losing Hobbs and Sutcliffe for 21, the tourists were in some trouble when Jardine joined Hammond. In scorching heat, they concentrated on occupying the crease, avoiding anything hazardous against the spinners and enjoying their share of good fortune. Once, when Grimmett moved to the leg side to take a caught and bowled from Hammond, Jardine at the non-striker's end blocked his path. At the time Grimmett made light of the incident, but in discussions afterwards with umpire George Hele, the latter told him that had there been an appeal he would have given Hammond out because of obstruction by Jardine.

Jardine's competitiveness was obvious to Hammond. Refraining from any banter between overs to ease the tension, the batsmen dispensed nothing more than a mutual nod of approval. By continuing to bat carefully, interspersed with the occasional sweep to leg off the over-pitched ball, they took the score to 206/2 at the close.

The next morning Jardine, missed twice by Hendry at slip in Grimmett's opening over, remained in defensive mode, until, on 98, he drove medium-pacer Ron Oxenham hard to

Woodfull at silly point. He'd batted for 347 minutes and added 262 with Hammond. The *Sydney Morning Herald* called it the dreariest partnership of the series and the crowd taunted Jardine throughout, although he scored at a faster rate than Hammond, who hit his second century of the game. Requiring 349 to win, Australia seemed destined for glory with 29 needed and three wickets left, at which point Bradman was run out for 58, prior to White dismissing Grimmett and Blackie to give him match figures of 13-256 and England victory by 12 runs.

The longer the tour went on, the more Jardine's relationship with the spectators deteriorated, a situation exacerbated by the amount of time he spent patrolling the boundary, a position he took up to preserve the energy of his more elderly team-mates. Subjected to lengthy spells of heckling when batting, he was forced to listen to many a jarring comment when fielding, not least for his stiff-legged running. During the Sydney Test, Ben Travers observed that when Jardine was fielding in front of the Hill he received constant abuse. He ignored his detractors till he was moved elsewhere, whereupon he turned his head, spat on the ground and strode off. C.R. Ashford, a cricketer from the Upper Hunter Valley who played against MCC in 1932/33, later wrote: 'In the 1928-29 season, one of, if not the, most objectionable remarks I ever heard on a cricket ground was made to Jardine in Sydney. I had been seated in the Sheridan Stand and in a few minutes before stumps I moved down to the fence where Jardine was fielding at fine leg. A very dirty, smelly newspaper seller had just sold his last paper. He moved to the fence, leant over it and touched Jardine on the shoulder and said, "Hey, Jardine, I'd like your nose full of rum."'[12]

Confronted with comments like this, Jardine found it hard to hide his disdain for the average Australian spectator. 'His face set more sternly, his walk became stiffer, he froze more Antarctically beneath his cap of many colours – and the barrackers became more voluble, and less respectful,' wrote Fingleton.[13] Their mutual animosity came to a head in MCC's return game against Victoria during the home team's first innings of 572. After one spectator had baited him incessantly when he was fielding on the fence, Jardine walked up to him and said politely, 'My man, does your wife not allow you to speak at home? You seem to have so much to say here.' So did many others when Chapman brought back Larwood to bowl at last man Ironmonger. As the crowd vented its disapproval, Jardine accompanied his captain to the boundary to try to restore order, but unable to hear themselves speak amid the din, Chapman halted play and the team sat down on the field before Ryder declared. Alluding to the unrest later, Jardine called it 'unbelievably childish'.

'It might have been expected that the spectators, in view of the size of their side's total, would be in good humour, or at least would not object to a side which had fielded out for 600 runs taking the advantage which a new ball, every 200 runs, confers on the fielding side.

'But no. It was considered unsporting of the English team to take a new ball, and to put on a bowler who ordinarily used the new ball against a tail-end batsman such as Ironmonger.

'The whole occurrence was, however, attributed to the lack of humour on the part of the English team.'[14]

After MCC were forced to follow on against Victoria, Jardine rescued his side with a chanceless 115 to secure a draw, but his sixth century of the tour wasn't devoid of controversy. Objecting to the young fast bowler Harry 'Bull' Alexander running on the wicket, Jardine appealed to the umpire. His appeal was upheld, much to the irritation of the crowd, who began to heckle him when he turned around to survey the field before Alexander bowled, at which point Jardine stepped back and wouldn't face the next ball till the noise abated.

Throughout the tour Jardine remained detached from the rest of the party, spending much time with his own circle of friends off the field, and, unlike his fellow amateurs, rarely ate with the professionals. 'Jardine was not an easy man to get on with,' recalled wicketkeeper Les Ames. 'I suppose he was a bit of a loner, for socially he didn't mix, at least not with the professionals. In fact, I didn't see much of him, except on the field, and he was perfectly all right then. But I don't think he was a particularly friendly man.'[15] His singular approach manifested itself in his early departure from the final Test and the subsequent match against Western Australia, so that he could catch a boat to visit friends in India. This unusual state of affairs required Ryder's reluctant consent for a substitute fielder in Australia's second innings, who, ironically, happened to be Chapman.

Still recovering from illness and loss of form, Chapman opted to leave himself out of the final Test at Melbourne, handing over the baton to White. With Sutcliffe also incapacitated because of an arm injury, Jardine stepped up to open with Hobbs. As was the case in every Test, he once again incurred the crowd's displeasure with his slow scoring, his 19 taking the best part of two hours. Led by Hobbs's 12th and final Test century against Australia, England made 519 before bowling out Australia for 491. Jardine, wearing his MCC cap for the first time in the series, was then out first ball, caught down the leg side, and looking something of a spent force, England went down to a five-wicket defeat, their first of the tour, on the eighth day of the match.

Jardine's early dismissal saved him the expense of chartering a plane to Adelaide to catch the Great Western Express to Perth in order to join the mailboat *Maloja* at Fremantle. Asked what he thought of the tour, Jardine laughed and said there were several appreciative things that he wished to say but it was against the rules of the team. On board ship, he was confronted with a newspaper story that he'd spat at the Melbourne crowd when they'd barracked Larwood in the Victoria game, an allegation he firmly denied, but he left Australia an unpopular figure in the eyes of most Australians. Contrasting his lack of popularity with the likes of Chapman, Hendren and Tate, the *Adelaide Mail* wrote that 'an impression has got abroad that Jardine has exclusive social tastes – and that added to his painfully slow scoring methods – deprives him of popular sympathy'.[16]

*The Referee* thought along similar lines. The crowd hadn't taken to him, it opined, partly because of his amateur status and partly because of his turgid batting and exaggerated stylishness.

It wasn't just the crowd. Ben Travers recalled dining one evening with an Australian girlfriend when Jardine came over and joined them uninvited, much to his girlfriend's horror, fearing that she would be cold-shouldered by her Australian friends because of her association with Jardine.

Not surprisingly, *Wisden's* assessment was more flattering. 'As everyone expected, Jardine was also a success. He began with three successive hundreds and, if he had his days of failure, he played many delightful innings. He impressed everybody with his great strength in defensive strokes no less than by his power in forcing the ball away when going back on to his right leg. One of his best innings was his 98 at Adelaide when all except Hammond and Tate failed. The manner in which he dealt with Grimmett on that occasion was masterly. Time after time he would step right out with his left foot and sweep the ball round to leg. He has also imprinted his mark on international cricket in Australia.'[17]

Jardine's time in Australia came at the expense of his work and there was a reckoning to be had on his return. Throughout the summer of 1929 he didn't play at all and, early in 1930, he resigned the Surrey vice-captaincy on the assumption that he would only be available intermittently. In those circumstances, therefore, it seems puzzling that he should play in the Test trial match at the end of May. With some pundits such as Frank Mitchell, the former England and South African cricketer, touting him as captain for that summer's Ashes series, it may well be that he would have reconsidered his availability had he landed the great prize.

Entering to warm applause from the crowd at Lord's to mark his first match back, Jardine, appearing for Surrey against MCC, batted competently in both innings. He then made a polished 47 against Glamorgan and a solid 25 for MCC against the Australians before he was lbw to a half-volley from opening bowler Tim Wall.

The following week he played for Surrey against the Australians, a match which was given added piquancy by Fender's criticism of Bradman when reporting on the 1928/29 series. He wrote that Australia's new idol was unwilling to learn and predicted that his technique would be exposed in English conditions. Having already scored 236 against Worcestershire and 185 against Leicestershire, Bradman now turned his attention to the Surrey attack, scoring an unbeaten 252 out of 379/5, a sublime innings even by his standards. 'I wonder what Percy will say in his newspaper tomorrow?' he commented as he returned to the dressing-room.

Rain washed out the rest of the match and interrupted the Test trial match at Lord's. Opening for the Rest, Jardine made only 15 before he was caught off the leg-spinner Walter Robins in a match ruined by the weather. With Chapman reconfirmed as captain, Jardine opted out of the series and, apart from making a century for the Free Foresters against Oxford University, he didn't play again until August when he appeared in three games for Surrey with little success. England, nevertheless, missed him in their 2-1 defeat by Australia and their 1-0 defeat in South Africa that winter. It thus came as a considerable relief to the selectors when he declared himself available for the coming season.

**Endnotes:**

1  *The Scotsman*, 8 June 1928
2  *Morning* Post, 20 June 1928
3  Arlott (ed), *The Great Captains,* p48
4  *Daily Telegraph* (Sydney), 10 November 1928
5  *Queensland Figaro*, 8 December 1928
6  *The Australasian*, 5 January 1929
7  *Sydney Morning Herald*, 17 December 1988
8  Fingleton, *Cricket Crisis*, p75
9  Ibid
10 Ibid, p78
11 Max Bonnell, *Dainty: The Bert Ironmonger Story*, p115
12 Derriman, *Bodyline*, p24
13 Fingleton, *Cricket Crisis,* p78
14 Douglas Jardine, *In Quest of the Ashes*, p294
15 *Wisden Cricket Monthly*, December 1982, p9
16 *Adelaide Mail*, 9 February 1929
17 *Wisden* 1930, p658

## CHAPTER 5

# THE GREATEST PRIZE IN SPORT

JARDINE'S AVAILABILITY for the whole of the 1931 season was good news for Surrey and England. He began with 80 not out against Somerset, putting on 181 with Fender in 80 minutes, as Surrey amassed 579/4, and he then showed his class in totally different conditions when playing for MCC under Chapman against the touring New Zealanders.

Bowled out twice in one day for 132 and 48 to lose by an innings, his contributions of 62 not out and 19 were the only signs of resistance in the rout – made all the worse by Chapman's pair.

Jardine's limited availability in 1929 and 1930 had only temporarily stymied his claims to the England captaincy, since Chapman's star had lost some of its lustre against Australia in 1930. After England won the first Test, Bradman's superlative 254 at Lord's helped his side to a mammoth 729/6 in their first innings and although Chapman hit a gallant second-innings century, there were those who thought he should have shunned attack for defence. England lost by seven wickets and were saved by the weather at Headingley after Bradman had pummelled them for 334. In another rain-ruined draw at Old Trafford, Chapman was reckoned to have been tactically flawed and, amid growing concern about his predilection for drink, he was dropped for the final Test at the Oval. Such a change during a series wasn't without precedent – Johnny Douglas had given way to Lionel Tennyson against Australia in 1921 and Chapman himself had replaced Arthur Carr for the final Ashes Test in 1926 – but his demotion caused a storm of protest from press and public alike. Their consternation was barely mollified when England, under their new captain Bob Wyatt, went down to an innings defeat as Bradman helped himself to yet another double century.

With Chapman already chosen as captain for the winter tour to South Africa, he had the chance to restore his flagging reputation, but it wasn't to be. In a series which England lost 1-0, he averaged only 10 with the bat and his miserable start to the 1931 season further undermined his position. He wasn't helped by the reappointment of Plum Warner as chairman of selectors, with the remit to win back the Ashes in 1932/33. Fully alive to the threat posed by Bradman on his home wickets, Warner greatly appreciated the need for England to develop new ideas and tactics under a leader with the necessary discipline, the vital missing ingredient in South Africa under Chapman. Background aside, Jardine seemed the obvious candidate, his credentials greater than the brave but uncharismatic Wyatt. Not only was he England's finest defensive batsman, his tactical nous and his assessment of a player's strengths and weaknesses was unrivalled. Warner was later to write: 'When in 1931 I came into closer contact with Jardine I realised – it was easy to do – that there was a man who was a thorough student of the game of cricket, keen and competent, one who had thought much and pondered deeply over the tactics and strategy of the game and, incidentally, a stern critic of his own cricketing abilities.'[1]

While Fender wrote approvingly of Jardine's appointment in *The Star*, others were more guarded. 'As a Test Match batsman, his ability is indisputable,' wrote *The Times*, 'but for the moment, with so many others claiming the honour of captaining England, his claim has yet to be proved.'[2]

'One cannot imagine the recently-selected England captain, D.R. Jardine, indulging in anything but orthodox tactics, for his cricket is strictly in accordance with the text-books,' commented Gilbert Jessop in *The Scotsman*. 'It seems unfortunate that we should be unable to find at the moment, from amongst those who have regularly devoted to the game, someone with a greater experience of captaincy than Jardine ...

'If it can be assured that Jardine will be available for the next tour to Australia, then the choice of this year's captain is a happy one, for there is no denying his great merits as a batsman. Whether his capacity for leadership is as sound as his batsmanship remains to be discovered.'[3] Loudly cheered by his home crowd when he went out to bat for the Gentlemen against the Players at the Oval, Jardine made a polished 56. He followed up with an undefeated 46 in the second innings, 56 not out against Sussex and a faultless unbeaten 106 for MCC against Cambridge University, playing their aggressive fast bowler Ken Farnes with ease.

The New Zealanders under Tom Lowry may have been on their first official tour of England, but after their comprehensive victory over MCC, they weren't to be underestimated. In perfect weather, and in front of a near capacity crowd at Lord's, the first Test had a dramatic start with 17 wickets falling on the opening day. Batting first on a flawless wicket, the tourists began promisingly, lunching at 132/2, before collapsing in the afternoon and fighting back with the ball in the final session. Captaining

England for the first time, Jardine remained something of an enigma even to his closest acquaintances. Reserved, sardonic and lacking the common touch, he was very much the opposite of Chapman, whose laid-back style he didn't approve of, and, according to Ian Peebles, he was rather too anxious to assert his authority. Instead of placing the 44-year-old Frank Woolley at slip, his usual position, Jardine sent him down to fine leg in front of B Stand, but Woolley, unaware of the lettering of the Lord's stands, used his own judgement to station himself in front of C Stand. As Hammond was running in to bowl, Jardine stopped the game and called out in his stentorian voice from mid-off, 'I said B, Woolley, not C,' a rebuke which affronted the veteran who felt he had been humiliated in front of a large crowd.

Relations between the two men deteriorated further when, at the end of the New Zealand innings, Jardine went to the Professionals' Room to discuss the batting order. 'Woolley, will you bat at number five and I shall bat at number six,' he said, 'but if there is a crisis, I shall bat at number five and you will go number six?' His words were soon given added meaning when England, in reply to New Zealand's 224, slumped to 31/3, at which point Jardine preceded a disgruntled Woolley to the wicket. Woolley was further aggrieved when, coming in at 62/4, Jardine advanced up the wicket, indicating that he had something to say, but he stood his ground impassively, forcing Jardine to come to him. 'Woolley, we have a very nice wicket for you today,' he commented. Staring at him in amazement, Woolley replied, 'What about you?' but Jardine, without answering him, turned about and returned to the non-striker's end.

While Jardine played second fiddle, Woolley went for his shots and after the former was out for 38, he continued to flay the bowling. On his dismissal for 80, Peebles was sent in as nightwatchman, but the ploy failed, since he took a liberty against Bill Merritt's leg-spin and was stumped without scoring, an act of impetuosity which earned him a dressing-down from his captain.

When England resumed their innings after the weekend, Ames asked his partner Gubby Allen what he knew about Merritt. Allen replied that he didn't like stick, a comment much to Ames's approval as he relished the prospect of going after him. Under assault from both batsmen, Merritt soon lost his length and suffered some fearful punishment as both Ames and Allen hit centuries in the course of a record eighth-wicket partnership for England of 246. During the stand, leg-spinner Walter Robins amused himself by making cutting remarks about the identity of the last man out, Peebles, and the 0 against his name, a form of humour which tested his captain's patience. Eventually he told Robins he wanted a word with him on the balcony, whereupon they went outside and Jardine berated him for undermining a young cricketer's confidence.

Declaring 230 ahead, England took the field again in a commanding position, but New Zealand, helped by some wayward bowling, especially from Voce, played with wonderful resolution. Centuries from Stewie Dempster and Curly Page permitted Lowry to declare, setting England 240 to win in 140 minutes, a challenge they declined.

While New Zealand's spirited performance earned them two additional Tests, Jardine's captaincy attracted mixed reviews. 'Douglas Jardine is on trial at the moment and with all respect to the Surrey amateur, it must be confessed that as a leader he is out of his element,' opined the *Daily Herald*. 'This was strikingly demonstrated in the Test match against New Zealand.'[4]

'D.R. Jardine is a thoughtful and painstaking captain, and a good fighter,' wrote Frank Mitchell in *The Cricketer*. 'He tried every sort of experiment with his bowling in order to get the New Zealanders out, but it was not the field for I.A.R. Peebles, twice placed wrongly in the second innings. He should always keep an orthodox field. To bowl without a slip, and with four or five men on the on-side – without a long-on – is a tactical mistake.'[5]

For the second Test at the Oval, England, strengthened by the return of Sutcliffe from injury, took first use of an easy-paced wicket to score 416/4 declared with Sutcliffe, Duleepsinhji and Hammond all hitting centuries.

New Zealand, without Dempster with an injured leg, fell prey to Allen who took the first four wickets to finish with 5-14 and although Lowry hit a gallant 62, they were all out for 193. Following on, they struggled on a lively wicket and lost by an innings. 'D.R. Jardine led England well,' reported *The Cricketer*. 'He kept Allen off for an hour and twenty-five minutes after that bowler had taken four wickets for 4 runs, but, apart from this, he managed his bowling with judgement and discretion, and his tactics were justified by events.'[6]

The third Test at Old Trafford was a depressing affair, with persistent rain limiting the game to three hours on the final afternoon, when England scored 224/3 of which Sutcliffe made 109 not out and Jardine an unbeaten 28. According to Peebles, the New Zealanders, thinking there would be no play, had begun celebrating and were in no fit state to bat. When elements of the crowd began calling for a declaration, Lowry sent Jardine a message begging him not to declare, but the protesters continued until Jardine opened the dressing-room window and gave them one of his looks, which reduced them to silence.

Jardine played spasmodically for Surrey during the closing stages of an extremely wet summer and finished with a sterling century for the Rest of England against Yorkshire, the champion county, at the Oval. Bowled out cheaply in their first innings, the Rest were only 28 ahead with four wickets left in their second innings, but Jardine found a stalwart ally in Wyatt, who'd retired hurt the previous evening with a bruised hand. Forced to play practically one-handed, Wyatt nevertheless helped Jardine add 126 for the seventh wicket and by displaying such raw courage he raised his stock in his captain's estimation.

Despite being hit on the wrist by Bowes, Jardine dealt with his rising deliveries effortlessly. (After the game he was going to Scotland to fish and when he was out, the first thing he did was to get out his fishing rod to see if the wrist injury prevented him from casting.) He did enjoy a couple of pieces of good luck. Veteran Emmott Robinson was in the middle of his delivery action when he noticed the non-striker Jardine advancing several yards down the pitch. He stopped and stood with the ball over the bails and warned an astonished-looking England captain that if he continued to pinch a yard or two every time he bowled, he would run him out. Jardine said nothing, walked majestically back to his crease but didn't offend again.

He was also fortunate to avoid being run out by wicketkeeper Arthur Wood when he slipped and strayed from his crease, but otherwise he gave a faultless display, mixing solid defence with a glorious array of shots. Eventually out for 104, and with the match safe, he declared to give Sutcliffe the opportunity to score his 3,000th run of the season. 'If ever a hundred was deserved it was the one Jardine got yesterday,' wrote Leveson Gower in the *Morning Post*. 'It is nice to think the last century of the First-Class

Season has been got by this year's England captain – at a time when it was so badly needed and against a county that possesses the strongest attack.'[7] *The Times* expressed similar sentiments, noting that some of the crowd called it the best innings they'd ever seen at the Oval.

Yet despite his success in his first year as England captain and a season's average of 64.94, Jardine had yet to win over all of his critics. Looking ahead to Australia, the editor of *Wisden* wrote: 'There remains the big question who shall captain the side. A year ago, everything pointed to the probability of the post being offered to Jardine. The old Oxonian not only possesses the experience born of a tour in Australia but can look back upon a series of fine performances accomplished out there and, if he was out of first-class cricket in 1930, he showed last year that he has lost nothing of his qualities as an exceptionally sound watchful batsman. On the other hand, he does not seem to have impressed people with his ability as a leader on the field. Whether Jardine lacks some of the essentials for a successful captain or not, the impression appears to be widely entertained that Chapman, were he in form, would again be given charge of the team.'[8]

That winter Surrey decided on a change of leadership, a change rather shrouded in mystery and one which reflected badly on the club. Having captained them with rare brilliance since 1920, Fender offered to resign before the 1931 season in favour of Jardine, to help his friend gain the England captaincy. He admired him greatly as a cricketer, especially his ability to read a game, his calibre as a batsman and his iron will. 'He loved a challenge,' Fender later recalled, 'and was one of the few amateurs to play irregularly for Surrey who would deliberately choose the tougher matches to play in; he never avoided Yorkshire or our other hard games, like some of the part-timers.'[9] Standing together in the slip-gully cordon, they would exchange ideas, but while Jardine deferred to no one in his admiration for Fender – he thought he should have captained England in the mid-1920s – he was ultimately his own man.

The committee, with whom Fender had always had a tense relationship, declined his offer, but they began to have second thoughts throughout 1931 when his combative leadership landed him in several on-the-field scrapes. There is the suggestion that Lord's encouraged Surrey to make Jardine captain, since he was the prime candidate to lead MCC in Australia in 1932/33, but even if this was the case Surrey appeared reluctant to do Lord's bidding. For, having dismissed Fender at the end of January 1932, it took them another six weeks to appoint his successor. Their dithering was made public when, in response to rumours about Fender's deposition, they released a statement on 20 February declaring that nothing had been decided except that a change of leadership was desirable, provided a suitable successor could be found. Their reluctance to automatically appoint Jardine probably stemmed from his lack of availability over the previous five years during which he'd played in only 22 Championship matches. That said, he was captain of England and once he'd indicated his willingness to play all summer it would have been hard to ignore him. On 17 March they finally announced that Jardine had been appointed captain for 1932 with Maurice Allom as his deputy.

Despite his shabby treatment, Fender continued to play under Jardine, offering advice when it was sought and captaining the side in his absence. (The players continued to call him 'skipper' and Jardine, 'Mr Jardine'.) Rather like his contrasting leadership style to Chapman, Jardine's approach differed markedly from

Fender's. According to Surrey's Monty Garland-Wells, Jardine was a very good captain, but Fender was a genius – a glorious original. Opening bowler Alf Gover thought Fender's thinking far deeper than Jardine's and all-rounder Freddie Brown didn't know of another captain who schemed almost every ball like Fender did. He also made more allowances for the spinner compared to his successor. 'As a spin bowler himself I felt he understood me better than Jardine. Fender did not mind if I got hit for four. It's an exaggeration, of course, but one boundary hit and Jardine might take me off.'[10]

In addition to being more cautious and detached than Fender, Jardine was more of a disciplinarian. He used to speak to Hobbs tersely for getting out after scoring a hundred rather than going on to greater things, he moved fielders without consulting his bowlers and came down hard on any player who lacked ambition or team spirit. Gover recalled the experience of Gerald Mobey, Surrey's reserve wicketkeeper, who joined Jardine in the middle at the non-striker's end when his captain was in full flow. Jardine immediately played a ball to leg and Mobey, thinking that the ball had gone past the fielder, called him for a run, only then to realise that leg slip had retrieved the ball, and sent him back. Jardine was run out by two yards.

In the second innings Mobey found himself batting with Jardine again. Jardine played the ball in front of the wicket, called for a run and when Mobey was halfway up the wicket, he sent him back to be run out. As Mobey passed Jardine, his captain said, 'That will teach you to say yes or ruddy no, young man.'

Jardine marked his ascent to the captaincy in appropriate style with a magnificent 164 against Worcestershire, described by their veteran bowler Fred Root as one of the best centuries he'd ever seen. Before Jardine faced him, he warned the three short legs that they would be in danger within a few minutes. 'When I hit hard, I hit hard,' he told them, and sure enough, they were soon ducking and weaving in full retreat. 'He has a most peculiar and effective stroke for a ball just short of a good length, sending it between short leg and mid-on,' recalled Root. 'He doesn't pull you, but makes a sort of drive.

'Jardine's wonderful innings was notable because he came in at a critical juncture, with three wickets down for nine, and himself captain of Surrey for the first time. I liked the way he spoke to some of the youngsters about running between the wickets and so on. There was a fatherly way about it that marks the true skipper.'[11]

He also acted in a paternal manner towards Sandham following the latter's loss of form in 1932, suggesting that he play for the 2nd XI. The team thought his demotion to be harsh but the decision was fully vindicated. After several fifties in the 2nd XI, Sandham marked his return to the first team with a double century against Somerset, much to Jardine's pleasure. 'Andrew, I'm delighted,' he told him, 'we missed your presence in the side.'

For all their respect for Jardine, the senior professionals weren't devoid of a touch of mischief-making. On one occasion Hobbs rang Jardine on the old-fashioned intercom in the captain's room at the top of the pavilion to inform him that an argument was raging among his team-mates about the full extent of the follow-through for the off-drive. Would he come and settle it for them? At which point Jardine and Fender descended to the rabbit hutch that purported to be the professionals' room.

'Now then, skipper,' Hobbs said, handing Jardine a bat, 'you've got that model off-drive they taught you at Winchester, would you mind showing us your follow-through?' Jardine duly obliged but not to Hobbs's satisfaction. 'Oh no skipper, that's nothing like your follow-through,' and this time Jardine swung more extravagantly, only to knock out the overhead light. Both he and Fender beat a hasty defeat.

Following New Zealand's first official tour of England the previous year, India, admitted to the Imperial Cricket Conference (ICC) in 1926 after three previous tours of England, were the visitors in 1932. At a time when princely patronage governed Indian cricket, the captaincy was entrusted to the Maharaja of Porbandar, a man of minimal cricketing ability, following the withdrawal of the Maharaja of Patiala owing to ill health. Acknowledging his limitations, Porbandar stood down for the sole Test in favour of C.K. Nayudu, a free-hitting batsman, a useful change bowler and an austere warrior leader who gave no quarter. By no means popular with all of his team, his appointment provoked a rebellion on the eve of the match, forcing Patiala to intervene from back home to quash it.

Boasting a formidable opening attack of Amar Singh and Mohammad Nissar, India shocked the capacity Lord's crowd on the opening morning by taking the first three England wickets for 19. The situation called for a captain's innings and Jardine responded. Batting at his very best, he added 82 with Hammond and after the latter was bowled for 35, he continued to play effortlessly before falling to Nayudu's quicker ball, caught behind for 79. With Ames contributing an attractive 65, England recovered to 259 all out and India ended an absorbing first day 30/0.

They continued to bat steadily on the second morning in front of King George V and another large crowd, Nayudu making a determined 40 despite nursing a badly bruised hand. They were 153/4 at lunch, but then lost their last six wickets to Bowes and leg-spinner Robins for 29, giving England a first-innings lead of 70.

Once again, the home side started uncertainly and at 67/4 the game remained very much in the balance, but Jardine again showed his mettle, adding 89 with Eddie Paynter before the close. The next morning, he took the game to India, driving and cutting with great power. Foregoing the opportunity of scoring a maiden Test century, he declared when on 85, setting India 346 to win in five hours. They began solidly but up against a probing attack, well marshalled by Jardine, and excellent fielding, they lost by 170 runs. 'England, for their part, had a hard part to fulfil,' wrote *The Times* correspondent, 'and that they came so well out of the test is due primarily to D.R. Jardine, who twice prevented an imminent collapse, and in all other respects captained his side admirably. He achieved, in fact, a personal triumph, which was none the less remarkable because he is the last of men to admit it.'[12]

Bowes recalled that before England took the field at the start of India's first innings, Jardine sent for Voce and him. 'Did you notice that Holmes, Hammond and Ames got out to full tosses?' he said. 'It was very difficult to see the ball against the blackness of the pavilion or against the glare of those white seats above the sightscreen. I want you to bowl at least one full toss each over.'

Neither said anything. At the end of the game Jardine sent for them and asked why they hadn't obeyed instructions. Instructions, they enquired innocently, what instructions? But such evasions didn't wash with Jardine. Voce said he could do better by avoiding full tosses and as for Bowes, he thought an

England bowler wouldn't be picked if that was the best he could do. Jardine told them that if they played under him, they would do as he said and not what they thought, but being in good humour in the hour of victory, he let them off lightly.

Jardine's supreme performance at Lord's made him the clear favourite to lead England in Australia, especially given the high esteem in which Warner held him. The appointment of Chapman as captain of MCC against the Indians in preference to him earlier that season suggested that the former still had his supporters, primarily on diplomatic grounds. Yet aside from Jardine's greater prowess as a batsman and tactician, the selectors appreciated the need for a firmer hand at the tiller than had been the case in 1928/29.

The only real doubt concerned Jardine's inclination to tour. Aside from the financial cost, which the £150 expense allowance didn't cover, and the time away from his work, there were his unhappy memories of Australia. It has been suggested that his reluctance was such that Warner appealed to his old friend Malcolm Jardine to get Douglas to reconsider, which his father did by stressing honour and duty. I suspect that this account has been exaggerated. Whatever reservations Jardine might have had about touring, they paled in comparison to the opportunity to lead MCC in Australia.

The choice was broadly welcomed, not least by Wyatt, the last man to have captained England against Australia. *The Times* wrote: 'The MCC in their selection of D.R. Jardine to captain their team in Australia, have paid a well-deserved compliment to a cricketer who has earned the respect of all with whom he has played, and who will carry with him the fullest measure of confidence. His experience of captaining a side is not long established, but he is an astute student of the game, knows his own mind, and can be relied upon to face any difficulty with composure.'[13]

'D.R. Jardine has gradually forced his personality upon the country,' wrote Neville Cardus, the *Manchester Guardian*'s cricket correspondent. 'He is not exactly a man for the crowd; there is something aloof and angular in his aspect ... Jardine does not suffer fools or folly gladly; he is a plain speaker and so keen on the game that he is not prepared to indulge in those nuances of terminology which usually win for a man the name of an artist intact. If a cricketer serving under Jardine commits a fault of carelessness, he will hear about it from his captain in direct and unmistakable accents.

'He ought to prove the ideal captain against the Australians ... They will get "no change" out of him, or if they do, it will only be just right – for D.R. Jardine is a true son of his own country.'[14]

The day after the announcement of his appointment, Jardine was cheered all the way to the wicket by a 15,000 crowd at Bramall Lane. With Bowes in his element, Surrey were in deep strife as they responded to Yorkshire's total of 241. Not for the first time Jardine rose to the challenge but with little support from his team-mates, he was forced to farm the strike by taking a single off the last ball of each over. When he called the last man Jack Parker for an impossible single which led to Parker being run out, Jardine let loose a string of expletives at his partner which earned him a gentle rebuke of 'Nay, nay, Mr Jardine', from Yorkshire's Maurice Leyland.

All out for 126, Surrey performed even worse in their second innings and lost by 178 runs, their first defeat of the season.

As ever, Jardine flourished for the Gentlemen against the Players, hitting a chanceless 123 not out in a high-scoring draw at the Oval, followed by a sedate 64 at Lord's. He declared at the beginning of the third day with a lead of 129 and it needed a monumental unbeaten 161 from the 49-year-old Hobbs to save the game for the Players.

Jardine continued in prime form for England against the Rest in an unbroken century partnership with Duleepsinhji in a severely truncated match at Cardiff. Afterwards Wyatt, the Rest captain, was appointed vice-captain in Australia, much to Jardine's pleasure – as expressed in this missive to Wyatt.

> Dear Bob
>
> A private line of private congratulations from one who, if I may say so, has always been a peculiarly interested admirer of yours.
>
> I am so very glad that you have been asked to go to Australia. You have deserved the honour so very thoroughly. May you have a great and happy and most successful tour. I know you will be a tower of strength to me both on and off the field.
>
> Good fortune, and very sincere congratulations,
> Yours ever,
> DOUGLAS[15]

Jardine once again saved Surrey when they played Kent at the end of July. Coming in at 39/3, he rarely looked troubled, playing Freeman off the back foot with ease, before he was brilliantly run out by Chapman for 74.

His most stylish innings came in a memorable match against Middlesex at the Oval. Having dismissed their opponents for 141, Surrey took the opportunity to compile a huge lead and in a classic innings of 126 Jardine batted beautifully. Even with five men on the leg side, his on-drives repeatedly pierced the field during an entertaining stand of 247 in 85 minutes with Freddie Brown, who made 212.

Middlesex were 265 behind on the final morning with nine wickets in hand, but, with centuries from Hendren and Jim Sims, they kept Surrey in the field for most of the day. When they were finally out, the home side needed 57 in 20 minutes, which equated to seven overs, four from Jack Durston and three from Nigel Haig. Amid mounting excitement and with batsmen running to the wicket to save time, it was down to Jardine to score 10 off the final three balls of the last over bowled by Durston. Missed off the first ball at mid-off which yielded two runs, Jardine then delicately late cut the next for four, before driving the final ball to the pavilion railings to win a thrilling game by six wickets.

It was a different story when Surrey played Yorkshire in front of a large Bank Holiday crowd at the Oval, the men shrouding their heads with handkerchiefs to protect themselves from the heat. On a perfect wicket, Hobbs and Jardine stood alone against the short-pitched assault from Bowes and Macaulay, who also bowled two beamers at Jardine, which he coolly avoided. With the crowd's patience sorely tested by his 35 in the best part of three hours, Jardine couldn't contain his glee when Yorkshire's captain Brian Sellers turned to the occasional leg-spin of Leyland, but it was the Yorkshireman who had the last laugh. Attempting an ugly swipe at his second ball, Jardine was clean bowled and although he dropped anchor again in the second innings for 29, Yorkshire won a low-scoring match by three wickets to give them the double over Surrey, their only defeats of a season in which they finished fifth in the Championship, their best position for six years. 'As captain he [Jardine] led his side admirably,' reported *The Cricketer*, 'never overworking any bowler, and he was vigilant in the field besides bringing off some catches quite in the style of Chapman himself.'[16] At a club dinner to bid him and Brown farewell for Australia, Jardine declared that he wanted more of the northern spirit to epitomise their cricket. 'We, in Surrey, are just a little lacking in determination that has carried Yorkshire to the top of the table.'

Although the MCC side to Australia took nearly two months to be fully chosen, it contained few surprises. Sutcliffe, Hammond, Wyatt, Duleepsinhji, Leyland and the Nawab of Pataudi, along with Jardine, constituted a strong batting line-up; the wicketkeepers, Ames and Duckworth, selected themselves, as did the fast bowlers, Larwood, Voce and Allen. Another seamer, Tate, a success in Australia on his two previous visits, suffered something of a nervous breakdown prior to departure, and with his fitness in jeopardy – he subsequently joined the boat at Toulon – the selectors now added Bowes, twice a match-winner against Surrey that summer, as a last-minute replacement.

Hedley Verity was the main spinner, supported by Freddie Brown, who'd just completed the double of 1,000 runs and 100 wickets, and when Robins was forced to withdraw because of business commitments, his place was taken by Derbyshire leg-spinner Tommy Mitchell. A more serious casualty was Duleepsinhji who had to cry off because of a serious attack of tuberculosis, an ailment which cut short a glorious career. He wrote to Jardine informing him of his fate and Jardine replied in suitably affectionate tones.

How very nice of you to write to me, though I wish you had not exerted yourself to do so. Thank you for your charming letter. I haven't written since I went up to Scotland for fear of worrying you, but now I can only say that with the exception of yourself, there is none more sadly disappointed at your tragic bad luck than myself.

I know I could count on you and looked forward so much to your help and advice in our difficult task – believe me I do not forget how you have gone out of your way to be helpful to my face and behind my back [sic]. I am very grateful – but apart from all that, Duleep, I like you so much and value your friendship so much that I can only hold out my hand to you in silent sympathy, while also sympathising with myself on losing the right-hand man of the team. Take care of yourself – think of us often and let me know how you get on.[17]

Duleepsinhji was replaced by Paynter, who'd impressed Jardine with his half-century against India at Lord's and who brought more variety to the party with his left-hand batting.

A surprise decision was the appointment of Warner as co-manager – Richard Palairet, his Oxford contemporary and, until recently, the secretary of Surrey, was responsible for the financial side – because of his other responsibilities as chairman of selectors and cricket correspondent of the *Morning Post*. On the eve of departure, he used his column to write in glowing terms about Jardine. 'We are taking out a team of magnificent triers, with a skipper who will get the last ounce out of them. The English public, perhaps, have not yet appreciated Jardine's qualities to the full. Only those who know him best realise what a magnificent fighter his somewhat shy exterior hides. In the long-drawn-out and strenuous struggles of the Tests, he will give 100 per cent. He is a thinker, a classic batsman and a great gentleman.'[18]

Within weeks he would be regretting such sentiments as he repeatedly clashed with his captain in Australia. A more perceptive analysis of Jardine's character came from Fender when paying tribute to him at the Surrey dinner.

'Douglas is difficult and never so difficult when you are trying to get him out. I am sure the Australians will find him equally difficult and they will be sick of the sight of his cap, his bat, his front and his side; and that before he has finished with them the bleachers on the Hill at Sydney will have faces as white as their shirts. Douglas is difficult and many people have found him difficult to understand. But those who have the brains to understand him will quickly learn what a great captain and cricketer he is.

'If the team will only follow him as they should, and endeavour to understand him, he will get away with the Ashes triumphantly.'

It proved to be a typically acute assessment from a highly shrewd cricketer who knew Jardine as well as anyone.

## Endnotes:

1   Howat, *Plum Warner*, p107
2   *The Times*, 11 June 1931
3   *The Scotsman*, 12 June 1931
4   *Daily Herald*, 16 July 1931
5   *The Cricketer*, 9 July 1931, p299
6   Ibid, 8 August 1931, p458
7   *Morning Post*, 17 September 1931
8   *Wisden* 1932, p306

9  Streeton, *P.G.H. Fender: A Biography,* p152

10  Ibid, p153

11  *The Referee,* 6 July 1932

12  *The Times,* 29 June 1932

13  Ibid, 5 July 1932

14  Neville Cardus, *Cardus on the Ashes,* p104

15  Gerald Pawle, *R.E.S. Wyatt: Fighting Cricketer,* p88

16  *The Cricketer Winter Annual 1932-33,* p23

17  Barry Rickson, *Duleepsinhji: Prince of Cricketers,* p71

18  *Morning Post,* 16 September 1932

# CHAPTER 6

# TAMING BRADMAN

THE MCC tour to Australia in 1932/33 was the most contentious in the history of the game because of Jardine's deployment of Bodyline bowling. According to Fingleton, 'Bodyline was not a cricket revolution which grew overnight. Unrest among bowlers, because of the difficulties and injustices of their job, had been simmering for years. It was purely a coincidence that Bradman, bringing to the game a particular outlook, should have synchronised with a period when the art of doped wickets was at its height. All it required to touch off the fire of bowling revolution was somebody like Bradman, somebody who could throw into bold relief just how one-sided this game of cricket had become in its lauding of, and consideration for, the batsman, always at the expense of the bowler.'[1]

Cricket in the 19th century was an off-side game, but as hitting to leg became more fashionable, so did bowling on or outside the leg stump to a strong leg-side field in order to curtail scoring. The England bowlers George Hirst and Frank Foster employed it to good effect in Australia in 1903/04 and 1911/12, and Fred Root, the Worcestershire medium-pacer, was a past master of it either side of the First World War. Australia, too, had their exponents, most notably Hugh Trumble, their revered off-spinner, Warwick Armstrong, the captain of the victorious side of the early 1920s, and Jack Scott, South Australia's fast bowler. By then, in a more professional age, the growing dominance of the bat, brought about by timeless Tests and featherbed wickets, was compounded by incessant pad play. Batsmen, especially in Australia, knowing that they could not be given out if the ball pitched outside the off stump, were tending to move across their stumps and use their pads as a second line of defence. Feeling that the dice was loaded against them, frustrated bowlers increasingly abandoned off theory for leg theory and bowled short with greater frequency.

Larwood resorted to leg theory in the Adelaide Test of 1928/29 to break a partnership between Bradman and Jackson. He failed to take Bradman's wicket in that series and only dismissed him once in 1930, a series in which Australia's new idol plundered the England attack for 974 runs. Although Jardine had been unavailable for Test duty that summer, he'd played for Surrey when Bradman scored 252 not out and had seen enough of him to know that on Australia's unblemished surfaces he needed to be tamed if England stood any chance of winning. Having absorbed charts of his innings and sought advice from bowlers who'd claimed his wicket, as well as taking soundings from Fender with his many Australian contacts, he watched footage of Bradman's 232 in the Oval Test. There, batting on a damp wicket, he appeared to flinch against Larwood. Spotting his discomfort against the short ball, Jardine shouted, 'I've got it. He's yellow.'

Jardine's theory about Bradman's weakness was given added weight by the reflections of the veteran South African batsman

Herbie Taylor, who visited England in the summer of 1932. Taylor had played against Bradman in Australia in 1930/31 and although the latter had flayed the South African bowlers to all parts, he was deemed vulnerable to the short ball. In particular he'd struggled against the left-arm medium-quick Neville Quinn, who'd attacked him on leg stump and, briefly, against opening bowler Sandy Bell when he bowled at his ribs in the Adelaide Test.

With Jardine determined to cut Bradman down to size, he looked to his opening bowlers, Larwood and Voce, to put his daring new plan into effect. Ever since his first confrontation with Jardine in 1925, Larwood had consolidated his reputation as England's most lethal fast bowler. Making his Test debut against Australia in 1926, he helped win back the Ashes at the Oval and, responding positively to Arthur Carr's leadership at Nottinghamshire, he'd proved the killer element in their attack, laying out a number of batsmen in the process. In 1928/29 he played his part in retaining the Ashes in Australia, but after taking 6-32 in the first Test, he'd faded as over after over on bone-hard wickets yielding minimum movement took their toll. Now with Australia beckoning again and Bradman in his pomp, he acknowledged that something different was needed this time.

While Larwood had the pace, lift and accuracy crucial to Jardine's plan, his Nottinghamshire team-mate, close friend and fellow ex-miner Voce would prove to be the perfect foil. Tall, strong and barrel-chested, he was less hostile than Larwood, but his left-arm in-swingers, delivered from a great height, and the bounce he extracted made him no soft touch. Not only had he been crucial to Nottinghamshire's Championship success in 1929, he was England's leading wicket-taker in the West Indies in 1929/30 and in South Africa the following winter.

When Surrey played Nottinghamshire at the Oval in late July and early August 1932, Jardine arranged with his rival captain Carr to entertain Larwood and Voce at the Grill Room of the Piccadilly Hotel. In these ornate surroundings, the evening began awkwardly before Jardine raised the topic of Bradman, a man he considered to be a brash upstart. It wasn't only the England captain who felt like this. Even many Australian cricketers resented his cockiness at the wicket, his undiluted pleasure in demolishing attacks and his tendency – deliberate or otherwise – to hog the limelight to the exclusion of his team-mates.

With the Oval Test of 1930 in mind, Jardine alluded to Bradman's weakness on leg stump and quizzed Larwood as to whether he could bowl persistently short at his body on leg stump. Larwood assured him that he could and the more they discussed the plan the more he warmed to it, his enthusiasm driven by his disdain for Bradman, whom he thought aloof, conceited and driven by money. He also resented his failure to walk for a caught behind off his bowling before he'd scored at Headingley in 1930, a particular grievance given that he went on to make 334.

During the final matches of the season, Larwood and Voce began to experiment with this new form of attack, and teams wilted before their bombardment. Even the aged Woolley wasn't spared the treatment in a festival match at Folkestone, and, in Surrey's game against Yorkshire at the Oval, Bowes caused uproar with the large crowd by bowling bouncers at their idol, Hobbs. Amid the chorus of press criticism, by far the most trenchant came from Warner. 'I am a great admirer of Yorkshire Cricket,' he wrote in the *Morning Post*. 'I love their keenness and the zest with which they play, but they will find themselves a very unpopular side if there is a repetition of Saturday's play. Moreover, these things lead to reprisals, and when they begin goodness knows where they will end.'[2]

Later Warner was to pen an even more damning critique in *The Cricketer*. 'Bowes should alter his tactics. He bowled with five men on the on-side and sent down several very short-pitched balls which frequently bounced head high and more. That is not bowling. Indeed, it is not cricket, and if all fast bowlers were to adopt his methods, there would be trouble and plenty of it.'[3] His words would be recalled by Australian cricket writers months later, since Bowes's late-season form was rewarded with his last-minute call-up for Australia – approved by Warner – taking the number of fast bowlers to four, a rarity for those days.

On 17 September 1932 a vast crowd thronged St Pancras station to bid farewell to Jardine's men as they boarded the boat train to Tilbury. At every station along the route, they were cheered by well-wishers and on their arrival, they faced a battery of cameras on the bottom deck of the oriental liner, the SS *Orontes*, where they were greeted by the captain. Jardine, immaculately attired in homburg hat, suit and I Zingari tie, thanked everyone for coming and expressed the hope that he would return with the Ashes.

Throughout the month-long voyage he lived up to his reputation as a martinet, quizzing his team daily about their sleep and health and supervising a rigorous programme of physical exercise. He permitted them minimum time for sunbathing, he reprimanded Brown for drinking too much, he forbade them to go ashore at Aden on the grounds of security, and warned them not to mix with the press. Although preferring his own company, smoking his pipe and reading Chaucer, he did have a long chat with Verity, which helped clear the air between them following their disagreements over field placings when Verity had previously played for England. As a result of this conversation the Yorkshireman found Jardine to be a kindred spirit who took the game seriously and, once taken into his captain's confidence about his intended role in the forthcoming series, not least in containing Bradman, he was completely won over.

Jardine also conveyed to Larwood the result of his discussion with the former England all-rounder Frank Foster, who bowled leg theory with great success on the 1911/12 MCC tour to Australia. Larwood's biographer Duncan Hamilton relates how during the early days at sea, as the rest of the team were running around the deck, Jardine found Larwood and Voce lounging in chairs, staring out to sea, cigarettes in hand. Why weren't they exercising with the others, he asked. 'We're relaxing after a hard season to get ready for the tour, Mr Jardine. We need our rest,' replied Larwood. Jardine nodded, moved on and made no further demands on them.

Jardine tried to impress upon his players that the only way to beat the Australians was to adopt a policy of hate, an attitude opposed by Allen, who subsequently refused to bowl Bodyline. Quite early during the voyage, Jardine fell out with Warner, one disagreement ending in a major row in which the former tore into the latter. 'Plum was warned about Jardine by any number of people on the boat, but he wouldn't listen,' recalled Allen. 'Once or twice, Douglas was ruder to him than I would have thought possible and the whole way through the tour they were utterly hopeless.'[4] Several days before their arrival in Australia, Allen wrote to Warner's wife Agnes in rather ominous terms. 'There have been no rows and everyone seems very happy but I am terrified of Douglas [Jardine]. For a well-read and well-educated man, he is easily the stupidest I know and conceited as well. I am not saying I don't like him, as I do, but one can't help noticing his shortcomings.'[5]

On 19 October at 8am the *Orontes* arrived at Fremantle to a regal reception from a large and enthusiastic crowd. The crew of HMAS *Canberra* lined the deck to welcome the tourists while the band played 'See the Conquering Hero Comes' and Jardine was met with prolonged cheers as he disembarked. The welcome was just as cordial along the route to the Palace Hotel and on their arrival there. 'Jardine would have been chosen on his merits as a batsman, in any case,' reported the *Sydney Morning Herald*, 'but he had been marked for promotion because of his undoubted ability for leadership. That the game and its credit will lose nothing in his hands is beyond question.

'In D.R. Jardine the Australian cricket-loving public will find a strong, purposeful leader, a man thorough to a degree, a sportsman who would scorn to take an unfair advantage of an opponent. He will not ask a favour nor will grant one, and in this he is to be compared with the Australian captain W.M. Woodfull.'[6]

The Australia that Jardine was returning to was a country in the grip of depression, its plight exacerbated by the Wall Street Crash of October 1929. The withdrawal of British capital, the fall in export prices and the beginnings of a severe financial crisis brought about a cut in wages and mass unemployment. The Bank of England's Sir Otto Niemeyer visited Australia in 1930 to propose further austerity measures. His remedy was fiercely opposed by the populist Labor premier of New South Wales Jack Lang, who'd introduced widespread social reforms for the working class. Objecting to paying interest to British creditors, his refusal to be bound by financial stringency ultimately saw him defy federal statute, leading to his dismissal by the governor of New South Wales, Air Vice-Marshal Sir Philip Game. The domination of British bankers over the Australian economy fuelled nationalist resentment towards the mother country, especially among the working class and those of Irish descent. Yet despite this rift, Anglo-Australian ties remained strong, symbolised by the biannual tussle for the Ashes. With the country desperate to find a distraction from their economic travails, this tour was eagerly anticipated more than most.

For the first few days all was sweetness and light as MCC were fêted in Perth. Jardine charmed a group of press photographers by padding up and giving them 20 minutes of him playing all the shots, but his mask slipped once he came face to face with the Australian press corps. When Claude Corbett of the Sydney *Sun* suggested to him that if the team was released each morning, his journal, an afternoon paper, would be able to get a scoop, Jardine looked at him with disdain and said, 'What damned rot. We didn't come here to provide scoops for yours or any other bally paper.' When another journalist told him that Sydney and Melbourne were waiting, Jardine retorted that 'Sydney and Melbourne could bloody well wait.' He also upset his hosts by turning up late for a pitch inspection on the second day of the opening match against Western Australia after heavy overnight rain. Corbett wrote: 'Douglas Jardine, England's cricket captain, doesn't consider the feelings of anybody but himself. He showed that today when he kept the whole of the Western Australian cricketers and officials waiting on the ground till 12.35pm before he arrived, formally to declare the match off for the day.

'Certainly, it was obvious that play was impossible because of heavy rain and the deplorable state of the wicket, but there were formalities, which should have been complied with.'[7]

Unhappy with Corbett's depiction of him, Jardine tried to build bridges with the journalist in Adelaide, but his peace initiative backfired when he riled Corbett with his stated intention of ignoring letters from Australians.

MCC had much the better of the draw against Western Australia, as they did in their next game against a Combined XI, a side strengthened by the inclusion of Stan McCabe, Fingleton and Bradman, whose presence brought Perth to the edge of hysteria. 'No prince could have had a more regal entry into Perth,' wrote Fingleton. 'As the long and dusty eastern train jolted to a stop, thousands crammed the station, the adjoining roofs and buildings, the exits and the streets outside. Police had to force a passage for Bradman, and the Palace Hotel, where we stayed, was in a constant simmer by day and night.'[8] After Jardine frustrated the locals by batting on late into the second day – they cheered heartily when he was out for 98 – a capacity final-day crowd saw a nervous-looking Bradman dismissed cheaply twice as the Combined XI, following on, struggled to stave off defeat.

When Jardine came in to bat in the next game against South Australia, the warm reception he was given by the majority was offset by a few jeers from the terraces. Their hostility caused something of a stir with *The Australasian* which, like the English media, was unsparing in its criticism of his treatment, and Warner appealed for the end to such antics. Undeterred, Jardine batted fluently, becoming the third centurion in MCC's score of 634/9 declared, which set up a comfortable innings victory.

It was at Adelaide that Jardine crossed swords with Bowes after Vic Richardson hit him to the square-leg boundary. Twice Bowes asked for another man on the leg side and twice Jardine refused, whereupon the Yorkshireman started bowling long hops till he was taken off. That evening Jardine asked to have a word with him and Bowes told him that if it occurred again, he would act in a similar manner. 'Anyone who plays for me does as I say, or he goes home,' declared Jardine. 'Right,' snapped Bowes. 'I go home,' his defiance catching his captain off guard. Having established that Bowes was indeed prepared to take the next boat home, he told him to forget their scrap and shook hands on it. 'From that moment,' Bowes wrote, 'Jardine ceased to be the big bad wolf I had imagined him to be. Until there is an exchange of confidences friendship is impossible, and that evening I had the first of many an exchange of confidences with D.R. Jardine, who can be a powerful friend but a relentless enemy.'[9] He explained to Bowes that in Australia bowlers should concentrate on either leg theory or off theory and that was what he had meant when he said that he couldn't have one more fielder but he could have five.

Following their win against South Australia, MCC were equally dominant against Victoria in a game in which Hammond emulated the form of his previous tour to Australia with a vintage 203. Before he went in to bat Jardine warned him about the danger posed by 'Chuck' Fleetwood-Smith, Victoria's back-of-the-hand spin bowler. 'I want you to murder him. We don't want him to ever play for Australia. Now's the time to destroy him. It's up to you, Wally.' Hammond did precisely that, hitting Fleetwood-Smith out of the attack and out of contention for the Tests.

Days later, while Jardine was 200 miles away fishing in the Kiewa River, near Albury, MCC, with Larwood, Voce and

Bowes all playing, employed Bodyline for the first time against an Australian XI at Melbourne. Bill Woodfull, the captain, received a fearsome blow over the heart from Larwood and Bradman looked decidedly uncomfortable against this form of attack. Dismissing him twice for 36 and 13, Larwood drew satisfaction from the fact that it had worked better than expected. 'The bowling looked very dangerous stuff,' reported Hobbs, who was covering the tour for the *News Chronicle* and *The Star*. These were real shock tactics. Bradman, wonderful player though he is, ducked away like anyone else. Most of all, I was impressed with the form of Larwood. I don't think he has ever bowled faster.'[10] Fitter and stronger than on his previous tour to Australia, Larwood noted a surprising change in the pitches; they were now much faster and more variable of bounce, causing the ball to rear alarmingly. These were conditions he was able to exploit much more effectively than the Australians because of their lack of genuine pace.

Jardine's absence from the match has puzzled many historians, lending credence to those who have questioned the premeditated origins of Bodyline, despite Larwood's confirmation of their strategic discussions at the Piccadilly Hotel in his memoirs. (Others, like Stork Hendry, then a columnist for *The Age*, claimed that Jardine had deliberately absented himself to spare himself the popular backlash to Bodyline.) They point to Bob Wyatt's memoirs where he makes great play of the fact that he, Allen and Ames knew nothing about the Bodyline plan prior to the match against the Australian XI.

It is quite possible that having discussed the plan with Larwood and Voce, Jardine didn't mention it to those such as Wyatt and Allen, who were thought likely to oppose it. It is also worth noting that Bodyline formed only part of Jardine's strategy

– hence his explanation to Bowes against South Australia that whether bowling off-theory or leg-theory, the key was accuracy. Apart from Jardine's uncertainty that the plan would work given the strength of the Australian batsmen on leg stump, there was little need to implement it during the early matches, especially when Larwood wasn't playing and Bradman was out of kilter.

What Wyatt instigated at Melbourne wasn't so much Bodyline as old-fashioned leg theory. Knowing that the ball in Australia lost its shine after a few overs and that the Australians, predominantly bottom-handed batsmen, were inclined to play on the leg side, he moved a number of fielders across there to curtail their scoring. Although the bowlers didn't overdo the short ball in this game, the success of the plan, especially against Bradman, encouraged them to expand it in future. Hence its use in the New South Wales game in which their batsmen showed discomfort against Voce – Larwood wasn't playing. And so, the plan hatched primarily for Bradman was now employed in the first Test, even though he wasn't playing.

Whatever the reservations expressed about Bodyline at Melbourne, most notably by Bradman to delegates of the Australian Board, MCC were given a heartfelt welcome on their arrival at Sydney. In a witty speech at a reception hosted by the New South Wales Cricket Association, Jardine hoped that the great struggles on the cricket field would always take place in a manner worthy of both countries.

His words seemed hollow in the build-up to the match against New South Wales. While the team practised at the SCG, he refused to sign autographs or talk to the locals, even those who had helped out as net bowlers, and when he encountered several of the New South Wales team, he gave them stony looks.

Larwood was rested for the match, but his absence provided scant relief for the home side as, batting first, they were battered by Voce, many batsmen taking painful blows to the body. No one suffered more than Fingleton, their 24-year-old opener. He recalled several of MCC's close-in fielders offering condolences to his team-mates, 'but a continuation of such courtesies would, in the circumstances, have been hypocritical and embarrassing to the giver and receiver alike'.[11] He battled through his ordeal to make a courageous undefeated hundred, but his achievement was overshadowed by a feeling of hurt at the methods employed by his opponents. 'It was the consciousness of a crashed ideal,' he wrote.[12] 'I was revolted by that particular day's play,' recalled Herbert Evatt, the renowned Australian High Court judge and politician. 'It made me feel that I never afterwards wanted to see a single day's play of that series.'[13] It was a feeling shared by Fingleton's mother. A dedicated follower of the game, she refused to watch another day that summer, including her son's Test debut against England.

After bowling out the home side for 273, MCC, led by 182 from Sutcliffe, replied with 530. Batting at No.7, Jardine clashed with Australia's fiery leg-spinner Bill O'Reilly, telling him that he shouldn't be following through on the pitch, thereby damaging the surface. 'If that's a complaint I advise you to address it to the umpire,' O'Reilly retorted.

Dismissing New South Wales for 213 in their second innings, MCC clocked up yet another innings victory. Once again Bradman, physically run-down and locked in a contractual dispute with the Australian Board over his right to report on the forthcoming series, appeared all at sea against the quick bowlers, scoring 18 and 23, giving him a paltry aggregate of 103 runs in six innings against the tourists. Of equal concern was the manner of his dismissals. At Melbourne he was lbw in the first innings attempting to hook Larwood, and in the second he was bowled by him swinging wildly; while in his second innings at Sydney, he was bowled by Voce retreating to outside his off stump. According to Fingleton, 'A hush fell on the ground, an unbelievable hush of calamity, for men refused to believe what their eyes had seen. Bradman left the wickets in silence.'[14]

Amazed by the tendency of the Australian batsmen to move across their stumps and play everything to leg, thereby increasing the chances of being hit, Jardine wrote to Fender after the match to inform him that the plan was working and that more fielders were needed on the leg side.

With MCC unbeaten so far and victorious by an innings over South Australia, Victoria and New South Wales, they entered the first Test as favourites, especially with Bradman absent because of illness, but which Jardine attributed to him suffering a nervous breakdown.

Although the Australians under the chivalrous Woodfull boasted a notable batting line-up, their bowling, for all the efforts of paceman Wall and leg-spinner O'Reilly, the finest bowler Bradman ever witnessed, couldn't compete with their opponents.

Like a medieval knight, Jardine treated the series as a kind of crusade rather than a game of cricket. He refused to name his team in advance to keep the opposition guessing, he sent his 12th man into the Australian dressing-room clutching autograph books to divine the latest intelligence and was quick to remonstrate against any perceived impropriety, such as opposition fielders moving behind the batsman once the bowler had begun his run-up or bowlers running on the wicket. (During the Melbourne Test he is said to have employed a spy in the Australian dressing-room to ensure there was no tampering with the wicket on the rest day.) Shunning any pleasantries with the Australians, he spoke about them in derogatory terms and he displayed no emotion when any opponent was injured, figuring that any show of sympathy would be construed as weakness. When the popular Vic Richardson was struck painfully by Larwood on the hand, Jardine walked up to the latter and said, 'Well bowled! You made that rise nicely on to his thumb!' 'Off the field he could be quite amiable, but changed immediately he stepped into the cricket arena,' recalled wicketkeeper Bertie Oldfield. 'He would order his men about with the firmness of a general marshalling his troops.'[15] Umpire George Hele, who recalled Jardine as communicative and personable during the previous MCC tour, now found him much more abrupt in his quest for victory.

After losing the toss, Jardine led his players out of the historic Sydney pavilion, with its mint-green tiled roof, on to the ground in stony silence. A capacity crowd watched transfixed as Larwood and Voce worked up a ferocious pace, supported by fielders who adhered to Jardine's command to always return the ball to the wicketkeeper, a practice the home side found to be unduly intimidating.

With Larwood at full throttle post-lunch, Australia were teetering at 87/4 before McCabe counter-attacked in thrilling fashion. Taking on the short ball with abandon and riding his luck with several mishits, he forced Jardine to dispense with his short legs. According to Fingleton, McCabe that day wore the mantle of the legendary Victor Trumper, playing the most brilliant innings he ever saw. Never before or thereafter did he see respectable gentlemen give vent to such exuberant feelings as when McCabe returned to the pavilion. His 187 not out was primarily responsible for Australia's total of 360, but with their attack posing few terrors in contrast to Larwood, Voce and Allen, chosen in preference to Tate despite his refusal to bowl Bodyline, the England openers Sutcliffe and Wyatt began in confident fashion. They did little, however, to quell Jardine's renowned pessimism. For much of his side's innings he sat behind a pillar watching the occasional ball. Hoping to raise his spirits, Wyatt, after he was out, went to sit with him and assured him that they would score 500 on that wicket. Jardine told him he was crazy but with centuries from Sutcliffe, Hammond and Pataudi, England duly reached 524, and with Larwood taking 5-28 in the second innings, giving him match figures of 10-124, they won by ten wickets. Featuring in a British Pathé newsreel afterwards, a smiling Jardine spoke in clipped tones of his pride in victory, but cautioned against complacency given the renowned fighting spirit of the Australian team.

Although Bodyline was only used spasmodically at Sydney, it stirred passions and divided opinions. While the English papers accused the Australians of squealing, the Australians attacked a form of bowling they considered unsportsmanlike and likely to foment bitterness between the two countries. 'It would be silly to disregard the hostile feeling which has been created by this type of bowling,' Warner wrote to William Findlay, the secretary of MCC, after the Test. 'One of these days there will be a terrible accident.'[16]

The next day Jardine wrote to Findlay in entirely different vein. 'So far our bowling has in general been a shock and an unpleasant surprise to the old hands of Australia. The papers have put up a squeal rising to a whine about bowling at the man.

Nothing of the sort, but we have by dint of hard work, and, I hope, clear thinking got a field suitable for attacking the leg stump.'[17] Later, alluding to the controversy when visiting Tasmania, he claimed that Bodyline was merely a term that had originated in the Australian press. Calling it leg theory, he declared that it was exactly the same type of attack on the leg stump that had been tried many times from village cricket to Tests. The only difference was the field they adopted.

Jardine missed the first match against Tasmania at Launceston to go fishing, but on returning for the second at Hobart, he walked straight into a major storm. After heavy rain had all but washed out play on the opening day, he strongly objected to the prompt resumption the next morning given the sodden state of the wicket and he appealed to the chairman of the Tasmania Cricket Association, Colonel L.M. Mullen, to overrule the umpires. (This was out of character since Jardine was a great stickler for the laws of the game and hence the authority of the umpire.) With the umpires' view prevailing, Jardine, unwilling to risk his frontline attack in the atrocious conditions, upset the sizeable crowd by bowling Paynter, Ames and himself for most of the home side's innings. Mullen called his tactics an insult to Tasmanian cricket, the *Hobart Mercury* branded him a sulky schoolboy and Joe Darling, the former Australian captain, declared that he'd never witnessed a bigger farce in first-class cricket. That and the team's turbulent crossing of the Bass Strait back to the mainland by steamer provided an unfortunate backdrop to the Melbourne Test.

Prior to the match, Jardine pressed Allen once again to bowl Bodyline. Although Allen was happy enough to field in the leg trap and serve up a mean bouncer, he wouldn't resort to Bodyline, a show of defiance which irked his captain. 'Douglas is difficult and whines away if he doesn't have everything he wants,' Allen wrote home after the first Test. 'We all try very hard with him, but I know as time draws on that someone will have the very hell of a row with him. It won't be me, so don't worry, but sometimes I feel I should like to kill him and today is one of those days.'[18] Larwood and Voce attributed Allen's refusal to bowl Bodyline to his desire to keep in with his relatives in Australia and when Jardine passed on their theory, which contained an element of truth, Allen seethed with indignation. 'Well, I burst and said a good deal about swollen-headed, gutless, uneducated miners, and that if it had been a question only of popularity, I could have bowled "bouncers" years ago,' he informed his father. 'I concluded by saying that if he [Jardine] didn't like the way I bowled he still had time to leave me out not only of this match but until he came to his senses ... He said "Well, I am afraid you will have to or Larwood won't try." I told him I had no intention of doing it but he walked away by then and the matter was left.'[19]

Having consulted Warner about their exchange, Allen agreed to let sleeping dogs lie, but warned that if the matter resurfaced in future, he would adopt a similar line and inform the MCC committee about it on his return.

Anticipating a fast wicket at Melbourne, England erred badly by leaving out Verity, their sole spinner, for Bowes; Australia, in contrast, were buoyed by the return of Bradman, now fully recovered from illness. Entering at 67/2 on the opening day after Woodfull had won the toss, he received a rapturous reception from the 63,000 crowd, the like of which Fingleton hadn't known the equal. Facing up to Bowes's first ball, Bradman swivelled outside his off stump to dispatch a long hop to leg, only to drag the ball on to his stumps. While the normally taciturn Jardine celebrated with a war dance, a stunned silence descended across the ground as Bradman began his long walk back to the pavilion.

Led by a battling 83 from Fingleton, Australia made 228; they then turned the tables on England by dismissing them for 169.

Batting continued to be a taxing business in the home side's second innings, but Bradman, after a run of failures against Jardine's men, finally came good. Playing at his very best, he delighted a world-record cricket crowd of 68,000 with his audacious strokeplay against Larwood and Voce on this most docile of wickets. Long before he reached his century, Jardine had moved all the leg-side fielders to the deep, but remained in close himself. It was a challenge Bradman couldn't resist. He crashed ball after ball at him, causing considerable bruising to his hands, but Jardine didn't flinch once. He did, however, take out his frustration on Allen who, at the end of a tiring spell, bowled a slow long hop which whistled past his nose. 'Well bowled, thanks so much,' he barked sarcastically, a comment which Hammond judged the worst he'd ever heard on a cricket field. 'But this is a Test, so you must forget it,' he said to Allen as they passed at the end of the over.

Bradman's 103 not out was largely responsible for Australia's total of 191 and their win by 111 runs as England, with another abject display, succumbed to the spinners, O'Reilly and Ironmonger on a wearing wicket. Jardine, who endured a miserable game scoring 0 and 1, told umpire Hele that the three balls he faced from Ironmonger in the second innings were the finest he'd ever faced in a row, but he was distinctly unimpressed when his nemesis caused Pataudi to self-destruct. 'That man won't play for England again under my captaincy,' he fulminated, and he didn't. He calmed down enough to earn applause from the ecstatic thousands assembled in front of the members' reserve with his concession speech congratulating his opponents on a 'jolly good show'. Whatever else, Bradman was back in business and the Ashes remained in play. All roads now led to Adelaide.

**Endnotes:**

1  Fingleton, *Cricket Crisis*, p132
2  Howat, *Plum Warner*, p107
3  Ibid
4  *The Bulletin*, 14 December 1982, p70
5  Howat, *Plum Warner*, p107
6  *Sydney Morning Herald*, 19 October 1932
7  *The Sun*, 23 October 1932
8  Fingleton, *Cricket Crisis*, p40
9  Bill Bowes, *Express Deliveries*, p100
10  Quoted in Fingleton, *Cricket Crisis*, p49
11  Ibid, p50
12  Ibid
13  Ibid, p51
14  Ibid, p52
15  Bert Oldfield, *Behind the Wicket*, p204
16  Howat, *Plum Warner*, p115
17  Quoted in Ric Simmons and Brian Stoddart, *Cricket and the Empire*, p72
18  Brian Rendell, *Gubby Allen: Bad Boy of Bodyline?* p21
19  Quoted in David Frith, *Bodyline Autopsy*, p146

CHAPTER 7

# 'WELL BOWLED, HAROLD!'

IT IS often said that there was little love lost between Jardine and Australians, and while there is much truth in this statement, it doesn't convey the whole truth. 'Many people have claimed over the years that Douglas Jardine didn't have a friend in Australia,' wrote Larwood. 'It was not so. He was very much in demand, especially by socially prominent families and spent a great deal of his leisure time in their company.'[1] Not only was he the recipient of many an enthusiastic reception when coming out to toss/bat, he was cheered to the echo when he visited Melbourne High School, where Woodfull taught, and when he gave away the prizes at Launceston Grammar School.

For the most part he took his off-the-field duties seriously and his speeches were invariably gracious, even if some of his sentiments about playing the game in the right spirit smacked of platitudes. In Perth, he was presented with the Western Australian Incogniti cap at a ceremony and wore it the next day in the field; he also visited York Jockey Club, near Perth, where two boys donned boxing gloves to fight for the honour of selling a programme to him. As the fight became increasingly ferocious, he stopped it, declaring the result a draw and, amid much cheering, bought a programme from both. In Sydney, he asked that the New South Wales team should also attend an official reception by their cricket association at the Hotel Australia, and he received rich plaudits for allowing their reserve wicketkeeper Hammy Love to play against MCC when Oldfield contracted influenza. In December, he made an appeal for funds on behalf of the Australian Legion in their quest to provide Christmas dinners for unemployed soldiers and their families, describing the Anzacs at Gallipoli as the bravest thing God ever made; then at practice before the second Test, he rendered first aid to a youth who had his eye cut by a ball from Bowes which bounced out of the net.

Although he rarely curried favour with his opponents, Jardine wasn't averse to making the occasional goodwill gesture. Noticing that South Australia's Richard Whitington, later an eminent cricket writer, was wearing an Adelaide University cricket cap when MCC played the state, he walked off the field with him and spent some time talking to him about the latter's Surrey ancestry at lunch. Away from cricket, Whitington found him delightful company. He recalled how Jardine sought permission from the headmistress of St Peter's Girls' School, Adelaide, as to whether he and Pataudi could escort five of her pupils to Glenelg and spend the day at Luna Park funfair. 'Those five girls, all married women now, swear that the very sun shone out of Jardine,' Whitington later wrote.[2]

One of Jardine's favourite Australians was Oldfield and when he had flu, he not only phoned him to wish him a speedy recovery but sent his family a bouquet of flowers; later, following his nasty accident in the Adelaide Test, he sent a telegram to his wife and two Shirley Temple dolls to his young daughters.

He extended the hand of friendship to O'Reilly by inviting him to his team's Saturday night dinner at their hotel during the Brisbane Test, a dinner at which Jardine sat next to the proprietor's fourteen-year-old daughter, Peggy Maguire, later a Hollywood actress, and gave her a gold watch. He also took a shine to Fingleton by twice rendering first aid to him when the latter was afflicted by cramp in the New South Wales game; later, after Fingleton made a pair in the Adelaide Test, he sought him out to commiserate, assuring him that some very good players had suffered the same fate. 'I got on well with Jardine in the little I had to do with him,' Fingleton wrote in *Cricket Crisis*. 'I did not admire the tactics of his team, but I had a liking for the man, and few Australians will be found to say that.'[3]

According to Arthur Mailey, another admirer of Jardine, there was something in his make-up which prevented him from seeing the human side of Australians. When waiting at Ballarat station for the train to Melbourne, a friendly engine driver scooped some hot cinders into his shovel and shouted across, 'Hey, Mr Jardine, here are the Ashes. Would you like to take them back to England with you?' Jardine tossed his head back and ignored him.

His failure to respond to other friendly gestures didn't endear him to Australians. Early in the tour he instructed the baggage master Bill Ferguson to refuse an offer by a whisky agent to supply his product free; in Melbourne, prior to the second Test, he upset the locals by cancelling the players' appearance at a dance in their honour, and when a young autograph hunter approached him after practice in Sydney, he brushed him aside with arrogant disdain that disgusted Alan McGilvray, later the voice of Australian cricket. 'I saw more of Jardine than most people did,' declared Canon E.S. Hughes, the president of the Victoria

Cricket Association who conducted Bradman's marriage, 'and I did not like the gentleman.'[4] This followed an apparent insult during the final Test at Sydney when Jardine greeted him with, 'Well, did you come to see leg theory bowled?' before marching off briskly without waiting for an answer. 'Had Jardine come to Australia in the 18th century and been clothed in authority, he would have strutted the stage with the early Governors,' wrote Fingleton. 'Coming when he did, an Englishman needed a new approach, and many Australians considered that Jardine did not have that approach.'[5] On one occasion when taking a single after a long period of inactivity, a young local player said to him, 'Well hit, Jardine,' to which the batsman replied, 'Mister Jardine, to you.'

Incapable of unbending, his attitude to Australian journalists travelling with the MCC team was invariably one of icy aloofness and frequently of downright rudeness. For most of the time he was inaccessible to them, while still ready to discuss team news with their English counterparts. When Gilbert Mant, an Australian journalist covering the tour for Reuters, introduced himself to Jardine on the voyage out to Australia, Jardine merely looked up from his book and said, 'I see' before he carried on reading. 'The silence between us was becoming unbearable,' recalled Mant, 'so I muttered something or other and moved away, somewhat flabbergasted by his churlish attitude. It was not what I expected from a captain of England.[6]

'He really was a paranoiac Australian-hater. We had hardly any communication throughout the tour, though I was the best of friends with everyone else in the team.'[7] At the end of the trip, Jardine was the only person not to offer Mant best wishes for his marriage.

Jardine's dislike of Australian journalists was heightened by his belief that they were out to cause trouble. On one occasion the *Sydney Morning Herald*'s Tom Goodman, a highly respected cricket writer, approached Jardine after a practice session at Sydney to ask him about a cablegram stating that his fiancée had broken off their engagement. 'The Australian press has had its last jibe at Jardine,' he snapped as he stalked off. Goodman went after him, trying to convince him that the message was from England, but Jardine wouldn't listen.

There were other grievances. Aside from rebuking a group of journalists in the bar of the team hotel for apparently plying Larwood with drink during the Brisbane Test, he objected to their invention of the term Bodyline and to allegations about divisions in the MCC party. 'The newspapers and general public in this country … are simply dreadful,' Allen wrote home prior to the Adelaide Test. 'They never leave Douglas alone for a minute and they publish the most unfounded statements which are certainly libellous but, of course, we can do nothing about it. DRJ asks for it with his [offensive] manner and is then hurt when they say nasty things about him.'[8] The following editorial in the *Port Lincoln Times* in mid-tour was by no means the most damning verdict: 'It is doubtful if England has been led by a captain more unpopular with Australians. Starting off with the handicap of having that superior manner which makes some types of Englishmen obnoxious to every nation on the face of the earth, he has made himself offensive – though in all probability unwittingly – by foolish speeches.

'It is a great pity, as the great mass of the Australian people do not want to disturb in the slightest their friendly feeling towards the English. Jardine should remember that cricket is only a game after all, and does not call for the military efficiency of the German military machine.'[9]

Critical press coverage about Bodyline, in addition to events on the field, exacerbated the rift between Jardine and the crowd. Dismissing the notion that Australian crowds were fair-minded, he took exception to their hostile partisanship and lack of taste, and found it hard to understand why the authorities made no effort to suppress their boorishness. 'Unlike most Englishmen the Australian, while impatient of criticism from without, is not given to criticizing with himself or his country,' he wrote in *In Quest for the Ashes*, his account of the tour. 'Ask any cricketer who has played cricket for England in Australia during the last twenty years and he will tell you that boasts about the impartiality of an Australian crowd are so vain as to be almost pathetic.'[10] Exposed to greater abuse than on the previous tour, primarily because of Bodyline, Jardine continued to treat the crowd with contempt. Wyatt recalled him being hit on the shin by a full-blooded hook by McCabe while fielding in Larwood's leg trap. As blood began seeping over his boots, Wyatt suggested Jardine should go off for treatment, to which he replied, 'What? And let 50,000 convicts know I'm hurt?'

With the series all square, thousands headed for Adelaide, the most decorous of all Australian cities, although even this haven of tranquillity hadn't escaped the ravages of the depression. Mass unemployment had precipitated an ugly clash with the police two years earlier, and tensions remained high after welfare cuts to help meet the punitive interest repayments to British creditors and also Bodyline. Given her position as one of Britain's largest customers and her large-scale sacrifices in the First World War, Australia prided herself on being the most loyal of dominions. She had fully embraced the traditions of Empire, not least the code of British fair play which Warner had promulgated so religiously, only to see the England team ride roughshod over that code in pursuit of victory. 'Australian cricket had a strong tradition of following spirit and convention,' wrote Ric Sissons and Brian Stoddart in their book *Cricket and the Empire*, 'so to have the very envoy of cricket's ultimate authority destroy them was a shattering blow.'[11]

Jardine's mood had soured by recent events. Recriminations in Tasmania and defeat in Melbourne was followed by a provincial match at Bendigo in which he displayed little interest, especially following another failure with the bat. He also managed to fall out with Larwood owing to an insensitive piece of captaincy. Instead of allowing his strike bowler to put his feet up and relax for the Adelaide Test, he made him 12th man in Bendigo. When the team was posted up in the hotel, Larwood immediately informed the press that not only would he refuse to perform his duties, he would be absent from the ground. In the end he complied and bowled a few overs off his short run in a match that became 12-a-side – a breach of protocol that upset the Australian Board – but his resentment with Jardine remained all too obvious, a state of affairs which continued on arrival in Adelaide.

At an England pre-match practice, a section of the 4,000-crowd goaded Jardine, cheering wildly when Bowes spreadeagled his stumps, 'a display of hooliganism' which prompted him to have the ground closed to the public the following day, the only time such a precaution had ever occurred at Adelaide. The decision did little to boost his popularity with the locals. Only an Englishman of his aloof temperament and upbringing could have lodged a protest because a few louts yelled at the spectacle of seeing him clean bowled at practice by Bowes, declared *Truth*, a Melbourne tabloid. The paper didn't excuse the outburst, but it was 'spontaneous and good-natured and could occur in any country, England not excluded.

'His appeal to have the practice conducted in private not only deprived Adelaide of six constables, it also made him look ridiculous. Everywhere this unhappy Englishman seems to be exercising a gift for "creating situations". His refusal to employ his shock bowlers in Hobart when the little Tasmanian capital had gone to considerable expense to give the tourists a good time; his plain unwillingness to exercise the diplomacy which his predecessor excelled; his and Warner's tautness to the press in Adelaide in refusing to allow the cameraman to photograph his team at practice are surely "over the odds."'[12]

Concerned about his poor form, Jardine insisted on leaving the rest of the selection committee while they considered his offer to stand down for the Test. They flatly dismissed it, but they did encourage him to open the innings with Sutcliffe as a way of soothing his nerves, advice that he accepted.

The next morning Jardine was given a polite reception when he went out to toss with Woodfull. Calling correctly for the only time in the series, he chose to bat first, only to fail once again, bowled by Wall for 3, his dismissal greeted with the loudest cheer of the match. Sutcliffe, Hammond and Ames soon followed as England slumped to 30/4 and during the lunch interval Jardine told Wyatt to drop anchor, but Wyatt, with the wicket becoming ever more benign, had other ideas. Twice smiting Grimmett for six, he saw his captain get up from his seat on the balcony and retire to the dressing-room, clearly unnerved by such recklessness. He need not have worried. Wyatt, playing better than Jardine had ever seen him, and Leyland added 156 for the fifth wicket and after they were dismissed in quick succession it fell to the left-handed Paynter, chosen instead of Pataudi, to rally the tail. Before a record ground attendance of 50,962 on the second day, he and Verity, recalled in place of Bowes, frustrated Australia with an eighth-wicket partnership of 96, enabling England to reach 341.

Australia began their reply in mid-afternoon and promptly lost Fingleton to Allen without scoring. Helped by the breeze at his back, Larwood pounded in from the Torrens End to near silence as if the crowd sensed something portentous. With the final ball of his second over, he struck Woodfull a vicious blow over the heart with a short delivery which deviated sharply. The bat fell from his hands and, clutching his chest, he doubled up in pain. As the England fielders went to his assistance, the ground erupted in unrestrained fury – not only on the terraces but also in the stands, where even the most venerable members of Adelaide society spat vitriol at Jardine and Larwood. The uproar lasted for several minutes during which Jardine strolled past the stricken Woodfull and, slapping Larwood on the back, bellowed, 'Well bowled, Harold!' in full earshot of Bradman in order to try and unsettle him. Before Larwood could bowl the first ball of his next over, Jardine stopped him in mid run with an imperious clap of the hand and gestured to his slip fielders to move across to the leg side. His provocative move roused the crowd to further outrage, especially when the next ball, a bouncer, knocked the bat from Woodfull's hands. According to the future Australian prime minister Robert Menzies, a staunch Anglophile and keen spectator at Adelaide, Jardine's action was a blunder of the first magnitude. He had in effect announced that Bodyline was designed as a physical attack; no more and no less. 'Jardine's action at the best was a terrible error of judgement,' concurred Fingleton. 'I thought that the crowd would split the skies. If it had not been that the match was in Adelaide, the "City of Churches", many of us felt that the crowd would have come over the fence and the match would have broken up in disorder.'[13]

Defying the crowd's antagonism, Larwood continued to pepper the Australian batsmen with bouncers. He dismissed Bradman, caught in the leg trap, and McCabe cheaply and when Allen bowled the obdurate Woodfull for 22 after he'd taken several more blows to the body, the home side were teetering at 51/4. As Jardine took up his position on the boundary, he was subjected to repeated taunts from spectators, the politest being, 'Do you call this sport?' and 'Why don't you play cricket, Jardine?' Later, at the close of play, the England captain, accompanied by Allen, chose to walk across the ground through a hostile mob instead of leaving by a side entrance. 'The crowd called for three cheers for me and jeers for Jardine,' recalled Allen. 'Oh, he had moral guts, too, to fight for what he believed in.'[14]

While Ponsford and Richardson saw out the final hour to take Australia to 109/4 at stumps, Woodfull had been receiving treatment for his bruises when informed that the England management would like to see him.

Given his previous experience of captaining two MCC tours to Australia, his standing in the game and his flair for diplomacy, Warner seemed the ideal man to manage the current tour. On the surface he had much in common with Jardine – Oxford, the Harlequins, the England cricket team, the Empire and Kipling – but in reality, they were very different. Whereas Warner was a softly spoken diplomat who sought popularity over confrontation, which made him evasive in the eyes of his critics –

Duncan Hamilton called him 'pious, unctuous and duplicitous' – Jardine was a blunt, uncompromising warrior who despised weakness. From the opening days of the voyage, they appeared at loggerheads over their different attitude towards Australians. Having taken against his manager, deeming him to be weak and insincere, Jardine treated him with cold disdain thereafter, his antipathy greatly upsetting Warner, who didn't believe a man of Jardine's standing could stoop to anything so demeaning. On 29 November, a week or so before the first Test, he wrote to his wife:

> D.R. Jardine is a very difficult fellow – such a queer nature – rather 'cruel' in some ways, and generally got his knife into some one for no reason at all. He is not easy or pleasant, really on the contrary but is *very* keen. Hates Australians and his special hate is now Bradman! Not an easy task to keep things nice and even, but so far, alright, but he is not the right fellow to be captain. Long ago, but for me, there would have been a row with the Press. He was entirely in the wrong as he was *very rude* to the Press for no reason at all. One *simply cannot* like him and I have tried very hard. He says cruel things of people and his language is poor at times. Not often but he uses awful words on occasions in talking, eg. of Bradman. He is very conceited, only He knows, and arrogant.[15]

Not only was there a clash of personalities, there also appeared to be a clash of cricketing philosophy, given Warner's ringing denunciation of Bodyline before the tour's departure and his repeated homilies in Australia about British fair play. Yet this ignores the fact that Warner was the chairman of selectors who appointed Jardine as captain for Australia, knowing full well the kind of person he was. 'There is a certain irony, in the light of later events, in Warner's own approach to the matter of winning, for he – just as much Jardine – sought success,' wrote his biographer Gerald Howat. 'His sense of history led him to hope that a side he had selected to go to Australia would be as successful as the two he had led there. So, with victory in mind Warner gave Jardine the bowlers he wanted – Larwood, W. Voce, Allen and, at the last minute, Bowes. What a fast bowler with a packed leg-side field could achieve, he well knew.'[16]

Opinion is divided as to whether Warner knew of Jardine's premeditated plan to use Bodyline. There is no evidence that they ever discussed it before their arrival in Australia, but from the make-up of the side – Bowes was selected after Warner had berated him for his intimidatory bowling against Surrey – he must have known what was cooking. Although his letters home expressed a growing disillusionment with Jardine as a person, he didn't take him to task over Bodyline. Even after the first Test when various Australian journalists castigated Warner for his apparent indifference to such tactics, he appeared more concerned about the diplomatic fall-out than the ethics of this form of attack. According to William Findlay, the secretary of MCC, 'Plum apparently has not told Jardine that he does not approve of this kind of bowling', and when Allen informed Warner of his row with Jardine over his refusal to bowl Bodyline prior to the second Test, Warner besought him to do nothing.[17] Even if we accept that Warner's reservations about Bodyline were entirely genuine, his failure to speak out against it, either because he felt unable to stand up to his captain or because he placed loyalty to MCC above anything else, exposed him to Australian charges of hypocrisy and led to the most painful encounter of his life. Having entered the Australian dressing-room with Palairet to express sympathy with an ashen-looking Woodfull, he was met with his stinging retort: 'I don't want to see you, Mr Warner. There are two teams out there; one is playing cricket, the other is not. The game is too good to be spoilt. The matter is in your hands.' 'They were simple words, simply expressed, with no flavour of heat and anger,' wrote Fingleton. 'The sting was in their meaning, and Warner, for once, could not produce the soft, sweet words which fell so readily from his lips.'[18]

Humiliated by this crushing rebuff, Warner retreated to the England dressing-room deeply upset. 'Warner – the epitome of all the game stood for,' wrote Howat, 'the quintessence of sportsmanship and high ideals; the chevalier of cricket – had been identified with a rejection of the very standards he had devoted his life to upholding.'[19] His distress, however, won him little sympathy from Jardine, who merely called his team together to inform them of what had transpired and insist that the altercation remained confidential.

Woodfull's words were witnessed by a number of the Australian team and one of them – Warner wrongly pinpointed Fingleton because he was a journalist – divulged the exchange to Claude Corbett the next day. Corbett shared his scoop with his fellow cricket journalists, and before play resumed after the weekend the contretemps was front-page news across Australia, fuelling the antipathy of the crowd towards England.

On Monday morning, in front of a tense crowd of 32,000 overseen by policemen stationed around the boundary, Ponsford, absorbing many a blow to the body, continued to hold the innings together, taking Australia to 185/5 at lunch. After he was out for 85, his partner, Oldfield, rallied the tail with a plucky 41 before tragedy struck. Attempting to pull Larwood, then bowling to an orthodox field, he played a tad too soon and the ball struck him on the temple with a crack that could be heard all around the ground. He dropped his bat, clutched his head in both hands, staggered away from the wicket and fell to his knees. As Larwood dashed up the pitch, terrified that Oldfield's condition might be fatal, the ground descended into uproar with some spectators shaking the picket fences. The bowler instantly apologised to Oldfield who reassured him that it wasn't his fault, while a grim-looking Woodfull in mufti strode to the middle proclaiming, 'This isn't cricket, this is war.' He eventually helped the dazed batsman to walk shakily from the field to the dressing-room where he was attended by a doctor before being taken away in an ambulance suffering from severe concussion. Fortunately, he recovered quickly enough to be able to play in the final Test.

Maintaining his poise throughout, Jardine, with a nod of his head, checked with Larwood whether he was ready to bowl. The latter took the ball again to a storm of abuse every time he ran up to bowl. Hoots from one section of the ground, counting out from another and cries of dismay from the women's stand made a bedlam of noise. Amid such fury, Tate, sitting in the enclosure, began to feel genuinely alarmed that the hotheads would take over and retreated to the dressing-room. So serious was the threat of crowd disorder that police reinforcements were rushed to the ground, some arriving on motorcycles. Halfway through his next over, Larwood bowled O'Reilly and when Hammond bowled Wall to end Australia's innings for 222, the England team left the field in frigid silence.

Back in the dressing-room, Sutcliffe and Wyatt looked quizzically at each other when they saw Jardine buckle on his pads, but despite the fears for his safety, the latter wouldn't be dissuaded by the crowd's clearly audible vitriol. Not only that. Knowing that Australians resented his millinery, he chose to wear his longest-peaked and most garish Harlequin cap and emerged with Sutcliffe to raucous abuse from his antagonists who encouraged opening bowler Wall to hit him on the head. Hoots and jeers rang out every time he faced a ball and when Bradman mimicked him by returning each ball he fielded to the wicketkeeper, the crowd roared their approval.

Oblivious to all the abuse, Jardine batted in his most obdurate style, making 24 in over two hours by stumps, at one stage going over an hour without scoring. On one occasion as he swatted off the flies settling on him, a barracker cried out, 'Don't swat those flies, Jardine – they're the only friends you've got in Australia.' (Jardine, himself, thought this less humorous than a remark from a Sydney barracker as he was being handed a drink on the field: 'Don't give the bastard a drink! Let him die of thirst!')

After stumps, Jardine rang Allen's good friend Ian Hayward and asked if he could take up his father's long-standing invitation to dine with them that evening. Knowing his father's reaction to events at the cricket that day, Hayward was horrified but reluctantly agreed. On his arrival at their home, Jardine asked Dudley Hayward if he'd been to the cricket, to which an embittered Hayward replied, 'Yes, and if that sort of thing happens again, I'm never going to another one.'

Jardine continued his vigil in front of a much smaller, subdued crowd the following morning, taking over four hours to score 56, his first and only half-century of the series. With

Hammond making 85, Ames 69 and Wyatt 49, England crawled to 412 all out, setting Australia an improbable 532 to win. A dazzling 66 from Bradman lifted spirits before he fell to Verity, leaving Woodfull to fight a lone battle. In the face of another onslaught from Larwood and Allen, he carried his bat for 73 as his team subsided to a 338-run defeat. Accepting that Australia had been beaten by a better side, Arthur Mailey wrote: 'Jardine, too, must be congratulated on the way he handled his team on the field. He played the game right up to the hilt and showed no quarter. This is the spirit that has earned the Australians the reputation of being the hardest fighters on the cricket field. Jardine relentlessly strove to drive home every advantage, and in doing this, he was a foeman worthy of our own steel.'[20]

Mailey was a minority voice among his press colleagues. 'Today the man who plays cricket in a fine sportsmanlike way that nobody in the world can excel is W.M. WOODFULL, captain of the Australian Eleven,' reported the tabloid *Smith's Weekly*. 'All the honours are with him and none are with Warner or Jardine.'[21]

In a letter to the Australian Board, Woodfull declared that the solution lay on the field, but as long as Jardine had the support of the powerbrokers at Lord's little could be achieved. He thought it most unfortunate that a feeling of enmity had intensified just at a time when England and Australia needed to be pulling together. Consequently, he felt everything should be done to find a way out.

In response to this pressure, the Australian Board, unwilling to meet Warner and Jardine, released the contents of a cable they had sent to MCC deploring the tactics of its team.

Body-line bowling has assumed such proportions as to menace the best interests of the game, making protection

149

of the body by the batsman the main consideration. This is causing intensely bitter feeling between the players as well as injury. In our opinion it is unsportsmanlike. Unless stopped at once, it is likely to upset the friendly relations existing between Australia and England.[22]

In Fingleton's opinion, even many Australians recoiled at the clumsy, blustering manner in which the Board cast aspersions on MCC's sportsmanship, since the charge of Bodyline was a vague one, and MCC, true to form, bristled at such allegations. According to the historian Patrick McDevitt, questioning a team's sportsmanship was the gravest charge one could level in the world of imperial sport in which cricket was a code of conduct and the expression of a British sense of right and wrong. 'Jardine's world view was that of the high Victorian period, when the British ruled the waves and waived the rules. Jardine's expectations of behaviour fit squarely in a world in which colonial subjects of the Crown deferred to Englishmen in matters of taste and culture, including in cricket.'[23]

In an age of sparse communication – letters took the best part of a month to arrive, there were no radio or television broadcasts, and no English national daily sent their own correspondent to Australia because of economic austerity – it was difficult for people back home to ascertain the true nature of Bodyline and the furore it generated. Jack Hobbs, working for the *News Chronicle* and *The Star*, was one witness who could have enlightened the nation of Bodyline's perils – but reluctant to criticise Jardine, his county captain, and his fellow professionals, he chose to overlook such matters. Bruce Harris, the correspondent of the London *Evening Standard*, knew little about cricket, and, as an apologist for Jardine, he tended to follow the party line. *Reuters* correspondent Gilbert Mant was privately critical but kept his reports strictly factual in his agency's tradition, and although Warwick Armstrong expressed reservations about Bodyline in the London *Evening News*, chiefly on aesthetic grounds, his main gripe concerned the failure of the Australian batsmen to combat Larwood.

On top of this, the *Daily Mail* complained about the barracking, the *Daily Herald* accused Australia of being bad losers, and Percy Fender, writing in the *Daily Telegraph*, dismissed the charge that Bodyline was dangerous; it was just that the Australians couldn't play it.

*The Times* pronounced rather pompously: 'It is inconceivable that a cricketer of Jardine's standing, chosen by the MCC to captain an English side, would ever dream of allowing or ordering bowlers under his command to practise any system of attack that, in the time-honoured English phrase, is not cricket.'[24]

Only Neville Cardus of the *Manchester Guardian* challenged the prevailing consensus by describing Bodyline as violent and intimidatory, a view held by several former England cricketers such as Sir Stanley Jackson, Frank Foster and Arthur Gilligan. 'This bodyline is disgusting,' the latter wrote in a letter which came to light many years later, 'and it is a miracle that Jardine has completely got away with it ... I admire Woodfull for the way he behaved in such a horrid situation. I regret to say it, but Jardine is a pig dog of the worst description and he should have never been sent as skipper. His tour of office has put the game back 50 years, and I know that Australians will never forget his criminal proceedings ... Percy Chapman and I ... agreed that Jardine was a rotter.'[25]

In light of the Australian Board's cable and the general hostility towards his team, Jardine – who had the Australian

dressing-room door shut in his face as he sought out Woodfull
– thought it only right to secure a vote of confidence from his
players. 'My reason for this was that there is a limit to the criticism
and hostility which can be borne by any individual or collection of
individuals,' he later wrote. 'I felt exceedingly strongly that unless
the team was whole-heartedly convinced of its own rectitude and
sportsmanship, the enjoyment of the tour … would have been
so seriously impaired that, solely for the sake of that efficiency, I
should have been prepared to consider the abandonment of leg-
theory.'[26]

The Australian press had been full of allegations about
internal strife among the tourists – Tate was alleged to have
thrown beer over Jardine – and when an article claiming further
dissension appeared in the middle of the Adelaide Test, Allen told
his father that it was true. Certainly, Jardine, like any tour captain,
had his detractors, not least for his exacting line on discipline.
He expected his players to look after their fitness, to drink in
moderation and go to bed early during the Tests. (He complained
about being woken up one evening when the team thought he'd
gone away for the weekend.) A stickler for the highest standards,
he admonished his senior players at practice if they displayed
flaws in their technique and he lambasted Voce when the latter,
fielding catches in the deep, turned his back and caught the ball
behind him. 'Imagine, Bill, if you'd done that in a Test match in
front of 80,000 people,' he said.

He irked the reserves by getting them all to change into
their whites before a Test, claiming it enhanced team spirit,
and he rounded on the 12th man if drinks weren't produced at
precisely the right time; he upset Brown by confiscating his golf
clubs following his reckless batting against Western Australia and

he also brought Sutcliffe to heel in the first Test when England needed one run to win in their second innings. 'I don't suppose, skipper, you will want me to go in now,' Sutcliffe declared, to which Jardine, drawing himself up to his full height, replied, 'Sutcliffe, when I want to alter the batting order, I will inform you.'

He alienated Tate by not playing him more often, especially after his previous success in Australia, and he had a fractious relationship with the ebullient Pataudi, who resented his omission from the Test team so soon after scoring a century at Sydney. Although this was primarily down to cricketing reasons, his relaxed lifestyle and his overt opposition to Bodyline didn't help. 'I see that His Highness is a conscientious objector,' Jardine coldly observed after Pataudi refused to field in the leg trap at Sydney. 'Before I left England several people told me that there were many qualities I'd like in Douglas,' declared Pataudi. 'Well, I've been with him now for nearly three months and I haven't found one yet that I care for.'[27] Years later he suggested another reason for their feud. 'I always felt Jardine, although a perfect gentleman and a great cricket captain, rather resented my inclusion in an England XI because I was an Indian and because, at that time, the Indian was a "damned good cricketer" provided, of course, he never tried to prove himself the equal of the sahib-loke.'[28]

Jardine also fell out with Larwood during the Melbourne Test when the latter's left boot split on the opening morning, forcing him to leave the field four times during the first innings, and, afterwards, by picking him for a minor match at Bendigo when he felt he was due a rest. He also incensed him before the Adelaide Test by hitting balls to exasperated fielders for nearly two hours in the gruelling heat. When Voce threw one in some 30 yards beyond Duckworth, Jardine barked, 'Just repeat that,

Voce, and I shall cancel the practice and address the team as a whole in the pavilion.' The next ball Voce threw even further beyond Duckworth and Jardine announced back in the pavilion that he would arrange for Voce's immediate passage home. 'Then you'd better arrange for me in the same cabin, skipper,' drawled Larwood, at which point Jardine backed down.

His moodiness was legendary. Bill Ferguson, the baggageman/scorer, wrote that he could be charming one minute and uncivil the next, and had a tendency to respond to greetings in stony silence. A more scathing assessment emanated from Allen, who, as a fellow amateur, spent the most time with Jardine off the field and who was constantly complaining about his moodiness. On the penultimate evening of the Adelaide Test, he informed his father that 'Douglas Jardine is loathed and, between you and me, rightly more than any German who ever fought in any war'. He continued: 'There is no getting away from it, Jardine is a perfect swine and I can think of no other word fit for mum to see which describes him well enough. Plum simply hates the sight of him and so does everyone else. I have never had a scene with him in public but I have had one or two on the quiet which not a soul knows; in fact, we are thought to be good friends.'[29]

Allen felt hard-done by Jardine because, Bodyline aside, he wasn't permitted to bowl against the lower order in the Tests – 'Douglas gives them to the pros to keep their support' – but despite these squalls, the captain retained the loyalty of his team. 'The players were solidly behind Jardine, and we all admired him tremendously,' recalled Duckworth, one of the few professionals he mixed with off the field, mainly at the bridge table, 'because he would never ask anyone to do a job, he would not tackle himself.'[30]

Even when Jardine relegated Duckworth to reserve wicketkeeper, the latter remained totally loyal and supportive.

On Bodyline, it was well known that the other amateurs disliked the tactics and that several professionals, such as Hammond, Ames and Verity, had their reservations, but aside from their desire to maintain team unity, their loyalty to Jardine precluded any dissent. 'Hedley was not 100 per cent behind the tour tactics,' wrote his biographer, Alan Hill, 'but he admired the courage and tenacity that Jardine showed in pursuing what he was sure was the only way to beat the Aussies.'[31] Most crucially, the northern contingent of Sutcliffe, Paynter, Duckworth, Leyland, Mitchell, Larwood and Bowes remained rock-solid behind him and his uncompromising desire to win. 'They backed Jardine to the hilt,' recalled Wyatt. 'Herbert never hesitated in his views about our bowling strategy. He did not see anything wrong about pursuing the tactics.'[32] To the Australians, Sutcliffe was the strongest advocate of Bodyline and used to encourage it by walking straight to his position. 'There was a mystifying action in the fifth Test which suggested that Sutcliffe, befitting his high professional post, held a strong arbitrary place in the team,' wrote Fingleton. 'Bradman had just arrived to bat. Jardine threw the ball to Allen to bowl. Sutcliffe hurried across, took the ball from Allen and threw it to Larwood.'[33]

'Jardine might have been unpopular with a few of the players,' said Larwood, 'but everyone respected and admired him and many of us liked him.'[34] While the captain tried to curb Larwood's post-match drinking by detailing two players to keep an eye on him and ensure he returned reasonably sober, he was prepared to overlook the occasional indiscretion. He also indulged his partiality for a beer at drinks intervals by arranging for a half pint to be discreetly placed in the middle of the tray, well camouflaged by the other glasses.

Such thoughtfulness was typical of Jardine's concern for his players. He arranged for Duckworth to see the pyramids on the voyage out; he offered the injured Larwood a free holiday in New Zealand and when Paynter won the fourth Test with a six, Jardine promised a signed England shirt to the boy who picked the ball up if he returned it so he could give it to Paynter, which he did. At Christmas he sent cards and presents to the players' families and at the end of the tour he gave all his players a silver ashtray – paid for out of his own pocket – and wrote private notes of appreciation, as this note to Verity's father indicates: 'Hedley has come through his first tour triumphantly, no mean feat to start with the stiffest tour, but particularly for a slow left-hander. On and off the field Hedley has been a real friend and grand help to me – you must be a very proud father and with very good reason!'[35]

Jardine also sent Allen's father a confidential copy of the report he'd written about his son:

'G.O. Allen set a truly magnificent example to the side, knocking off smoking and drinking – an excellent tourer in every way, and one who deserved every atom of success which came his way, and was, in fact – or so it seemed to me, in not having more success with the bat – a wonderful short leg.

'I can't say more than that for I mean every word of it – how pleased and justly proud you and Lady Allen will be to have him back.'[36]

It was a noble gesture, in contrast to the spiteful barbs which Allen wrote about Jardine behind his back.

At the crisis meeting, chaired by Sutcliffe in the absence of Jardine or the managers, on the penultimate evening of the

Adelaide Test, the players, while failing to mention Bodyline, unanimously supported their captain. A public statement to this effect buttressed his position but, smarting from the charge of bad sportsmanship, he continued to fret about the Australian Board's cable. 'Whether the team played another Test match or not did not rest with me,' he wrote, 'but after considering every point of view I was firmly determined that I should not lead them on to the field of play in another Test match, unless and until that charge had been withdrawn. I made no secret of this.'[37]

Allen later declared: 'I'll always remember Douglas saying to me, "Have you seen the cable?" And I said, "Yes, I have, and I think it's dreadful." He said, "I know they'll let me down at Lord's." I said, "No, Douglas, you're wrong. No one can call an Englishman unsporting and get away with it – they've lost the battle with the first shot they've fired." I can still see the smile that came over his face.'[38]

Allen's prognostication proved correct. Unable to grasp the gravity of Bodyline because of the subjective nature of the reporting and notes from Jardine himself, Lord's, recalling the damage inflicted on English cricket by Gregory and McDonald in 1921, replied in suitably lofty tones.

We, Marylebone Cricket Club, deplore your cable. We deprecate your opinion that there has been unsportsmanlike play. We have fullest confidence in captain, team and managers and are convinced that they would do nothing to infringe either the laws of Cricket or the spirit of the game. We have no evidence that our confidence has been misplaced. Much as we regret accidents to Woodfull and

Oldfield, we understand that in neither case was the bowler to blame. If the Australian Board of Control wish to propose a new Law or Rule, it shall receive our careful consideration in due course.

We hope the situation is not now as serious as your cable would seem to indicate, but if it is such to jeopardise the good relations between English and Australian cricketers and you consider it desirable to cancel the remainder of the programme we would consent, but with great reluctance.[39]

With Bodyline threatening the cancellation of the tour and a serious breach in Anglo-Australian relations, it needed the intervention of those in high places to pour oil on troubled waters. Foremost in these deliberations was Alexander Hore-Ruthven, the governor of South Australia and cricket enthusiast, who happened to be on leave in England at the time of the Adelaide Test. A retired soldier of great distinction, his tact and sensitivity made him a respected governor and when alerted to the growing mood of bitterness in Australia by his English-born secretary, Legh Winser, he contacted the Dominion Office.

At a meeting there on 1 February, presided over by Dominions Secretary Jimmy Thomas, and attended by Hore-Ruthven and a delegation from MCC led by the president Lord Lewisham, it was agreed that the word unsportsmanlike in the Australian Board cable should be withdrawn. On that same day, Warner had sent a telegram to the head of the British Mission in Canberra, Ernest Crutchley, asking him to use his good offices to help get the offending word withdrawn. Crutchley phoned the Australian Prime Minister Joseph Lyons, who quickly understood the gravity of the situation. Leading a coalition government committed to economic recovery, and sorely in need of a £17 million conversion loan on the London Stock Exchange, he had every incentive to resolve the cricketing impasse between the two countries. That same day he met Dr Allen Robertson, chairman of the Australian Board of Control, and asked him to build bridges. Lyons' intervention helped to do the trick. Confronted with MCC's uncompromising response and reluctant to cancel a tour which had captivated the public and filled their coffers, the Australian Board felt obliged to partially back down. On the day before the Brisbane Test, they sent MCC another cable withdrawing the word unsportsmanlike and reiterated that the tour would continue. Even this concession failed to satisfy Jardine. It needed a long, expensive phone call to Lord's before he was finally reassured.

Warner had played his part in restoring peace but his fractious relationship with Jardine, who'd objected to his original idea of a general statement signed by the two captains, had taken a severe toll on him. In a letter home on the day that peace was restored, he excoriated Jardine, calling him 'very trying' and 'a bundle of nerves', insisting that he should not captain again. 'He is most ungracious, rude and suspects all. He really is a very curious character and varies like a barometer. He is very efficient but inconsistent in his character and no leader. I ought to get a prize for Patience or Tact and good temper if not a Knighthood!! 75% of the trouble is due to D.R.J.'s personality. We all think that D.R.J. has almost made me hate cricket. He makes it war. I do hope the Test will go happily. I rather dread it.'[40]

After Adelaide the tour continued with a two-day match against Victoria Country XIII at Ballarat, an occasion marred by the crowd's hostile treatment of MCC and a verbal broadside from the acting mayor about the iniquities of Bodyline at an official lunch. In reply, Jardine was the soul of discretion. After expressing thanks for the welcome, he said: 'You, sir, are perhaps a brave man to debate one side at least of a subject which is *sub judice*, and it is not my place to debate it. I believe it has been said that a cricketer is easy money – you can't libel him. I would only ask you to consider this question – to look and see how many times Larwood has hit the wicket. It is a fairly familiar cry among Australian barrackers, "bowl at the wicket", and I think you might consider his record in that respect.'

Jardine missed the return match against New South Wales, but played against Queensland Country XI at Toowoomba, scoring an imperious undefeated 77 in the second innings. A greater trial awaited him against Queensland, since confronting him was Eddie Gilbert, the Aboriginal fast bowler with a dubious action who'd dismissed Bradman a year earlier with one of the fastest spells the latter had ever encountered. The local press had keenly anticipated the clash, but before Jardine did battle with Gilbert, he offended umpire John Bartlett following the dismissal of Queensland's wicketkeeper Len Waterman, who was run out at the bowler's end. The bail was knocked off and Jardine picked it up and kept hold of it as he walked down to the slips to confer with his men. When Bartlett approached him and asked him for the bail, Jardine looked at it before throwing it past point, forcing the umpire to retrieve it, much to his fury.

During the final stages of the Queensland innings, Larwood had annoyed the 10,000 crowd by bowling consistently short at the former Australia all-rounder Ron Oxenham, and they were in an unforgiving mood when Jardine came out to open during the day's closing overs. A wag cried out, 'Come on, Eddie. Give it to this bloke. His family took the land from your family a hundred years ago,' referring to Jardine's ancestors taking large land holdings on the Cape York peninsula in the previous century. Working up a great speed, Gilbert struck Jardine a nasty blow on the hip, much to the pleasure of sections of the crowd. In obvious pain, he saw out the rest of the over before returning to the pavilion as police held back the surging masses chanting, 'Bastard, bastard, bastard'.

'It was an experience that would have daunted many lesser men, but Jardine not least was a man,' recalled Bowes. 'With head held high, deliberately wearing his brightly coloured Harlequin cap, chin jutting forward and lips tight closed, he appeared neither to see nor to hear. Almost imperiously he walked through the gate of the barbed wire compound which brought privacy of a sort to the England dressing-room. His back was as straight as a ramrod as he mounted the few wooden steps to the dressing-room door. No centurion ever made a more dignified exit from the arena.

'He walked to the table in the centre of the dressing-room, ignoring the odd remark of "Well played, skipper" and looking straight ahead, asked if all but the England players and the masseur could leave the room. When this was done Jardine collapsed on the table and speaking through clenched teeth in agony, he said, "This hip. It's giving me hell," as a massive area of raw flesh had emerged. Guts! Not a spectator or an Australian friend knew how much he had been hurt. He certainly did not intend any opponent to get any satisfaction from it.'[41]

'That was real courage,' recalled Hammond. 'When a cricketer sees that spirit in his skipper, he remembers it always and tries to play on for his side as he can stand on his two feet.'[42]

After a day to recover, Jardine proceeded very cautiously to make 34 before he was bowled by Oxenham. MCC built a substantial total and went on to win by an innings.

With Voce unfit for the fourth Test, Jardine replaced him with leg-spinner Mitchell, who'd dismissed Bradman cheaply in the return game against New South Wales. In blistering heat and the greatest humidity that Larwood had ever known, Australia batted first on an even-paced pitch and enjoyed their best start of the series, reaching 251/3 by the close. That evening, concerned by the threat posed from Bradman, who remained undefeated on 71, Jardine took Voce to one side in the dressing-room and asked him to ensure that Larwood had an early night. Larwood was in his room at 9pm when a casual acquaintance rang him to invite him to a party. Having discussed it with some of his team-mates, he, Voce, Ames and Leyland crept out of the hotel, intent on going for an hour and drinking orange juice, but in time a crate of beer in the corner proved irresistible. After a convivial evening they returned in the small hours the worse for wear, especially Larwood, who began singing in the hotel foyer. They woke the next morning in a frazzled state, but Larwood won his bet with some journalists the previous evening that he would bowl Bradman by the end of his third over. As Bradman walked off, Jardine went across to Voce and said, 'Well done. Thanks for taking such good care of him last night.'

The fall of Bradman sparked a revival in England's fortunes as they overcame the conditions to take the last seven Australian wickets for 76. 'In almost unbearable heat Douglas handled his bowlers with wonderful judgement,' recalled Wyatt. 'Intuitively he seemed to know just how much he could ask of them while they were operating under such acute physical strain.'[43] As for Jardine, he attributed their success to a suggestion from co-manager Palairet that the bowlers should sample some champagne at the intervals to keep them refreshed.

Continuing the good work, Sutcliffe and Jardine, in his most fluent innings of the series, opened up with 99/0 by the close. It was a different story when the game resumed after the weekend. Before play began Jardine clashed with umpire Hele when the latter ordered the groundsman to cut short the rolling of the pitch because the players were entering the arena. Having informed Hele that he'd umpired his final Test, Jardine then took exception to be given out caught behind off O'Reilly for 46, one of several controversial dismissals that day. 'How have you got me out in your book?' he later asked scorer Bill Ferguson at lunch. 'Umpired out or cheated out?'

England's halting progress that afternoon and their unpromising position at 216/6 forced Paynter to the crease despite running a temperature. Taken ill on the second day with tonsillitis, he was examined by a doctor who advised his removal to hospital without delay. His illness elicited little sympathy from Jardine because he hadn't reported it before the match and on visiting him on the rest day, he told him they may well need him to bat. When Warner rebuked him for his insensitivity, Jardine, in allusion to the fighting spirit of the British Army during the Second Afghan War of 1880, replied, 'What about those fellows who marched to Kandahar with fever on them?'

On Monday afternoon, Jardine dispatched Voce to the hospital and as he and Paynter listened to England's plight on the radio, Paynter resolved to bat. Brushing aside the protests of the matron, he left for the ground in his dressing gown, changed on arrival and was soon walking to the wicket, wearing a panama hat. Fortified by frequent doses of brandy from the 12th man, he survived to stumps and returning to hospital he was met by the matron who asked, 'How's the little hero?'

He felt better the next morning and, batting with great resolution, scored 83, adding 92 for the ninth wicket with Verity, giving their side a first-innings lead of 16. Australia began their second innings confidently before a brilliant catch by Jardine at mid-off disposed of Richardson, and a shrewd field placement accounted for Bradman when he hit Larwood to backward point. With Woodfull and Ponsford also falling cheaply, the home side finished the day uneasily on 108/4. Even a full-blooded drive by McCabe which struck Jardine painfully on the knee, drawing guffaws from the outer, seemed scant consolation.

With Larwood, Allen and Verity taking the last six Australian wickets for 65, England required 160 to win. They soon lost Sutcliffe, and for the rest of the session Jardine and Leyland concentrated on mere survival, the former going over an hour without scoring, during which the spinners bowled wide of his leg stump before he succumbed to Ironmonger for 24. His innings had taxed the patience of the crowd and when O'Reilly complimented him on his batting after stumps, Jardine staring at him, replied, 'Really, Billy, really. Don't you think that I was like an old maid defending her virginity?'

With flags at half-mast on the final day to mark the passing of Archie Jackson from tuberculosis, England, with Leyland to the fore, quickly scored the remaining 53 runs needed to win by six wickets and regain the Ashes. Woodfull led his players into the England dressing-room to toast them in champagne prior to a reception at Government House, where Jardine, quoting Kipling, spoke modestly about his team's success. That evening they celebrated with a dinner at their hotel before attending a charity dance in its ballroom at which Jardine, elegantly attired in black tie, looked the soul of contentment as he waltzed a glamorous woman around the dance floor.

His leadership won near unanimous recognition. The *Daily Telegraph* in Sydney commented: 'The grim purposefulness with which Jardine led his men to success in the face of the most remarkable protestations in the history of the game stamps him as a born leader, indomitable, and giving nothing away, and as a man who allowed no obstacle to prevent him reaching his goal.'[44]

Now that the Ashes were back in English hands, Warner tried to persuade Jardine to abandon Bodyline for the final Test at Sydney, but he wasn't for turning. His desire to heap further humiliation on his opponents, and Bradman in particular, saw him refuse an ailing Larwood's plea that he be rested. 'I'm sorry, Harold, I can't grant you the favour,' he told him. 'We've got the bastards down there and we'll keep them there.'

Losing the toss yet again, England began well with Larwood dismissing Richardson, Woodfull and Bradman cheaply, but they failed to capitalise because of some fallible catching. Unimpressed with their sloppiness, Jardine read the riot act at lunch, only to fall prey to that same ailment afterwards, much to the concealed amusement of his team-mates. With the middle order, led by Len Darling with 85, Stan McCabe with 73 and Leo O'Brien with 61, effecting a solid recovery, Australia made 435, their highest score of the series. During a drinks break when Jardine carried a drink to O'Brien and presented it with a bow, his gesture prompted a voice from the Hill to call out, 'Be careful, O'Brien, taste it before you drink it!'

Throughout the series, Woodfull had refused to retaliate against Bodyline by resorting to similar tactics, but, at Sydney,

Australia gave a first cap to 'Bull' Alexander, Victoria's erratic fast bowler who'd riled MCC four years earlier by damaging the pitch with his follow-through. Unable to curb this tendency, he once again drew protests from both Sutcliffe and Jardine and was unfortunate to have the latter dropped twice before he fell to O'Reilly for 18. His dismissal revealed a rare weakness in his batting. In ten out of 16 Test innings in Australia, he was out to the spinners, six of those dismissals coming in 1932/33, chiefly because of his indeterminate footwork.

When Sutcliffe was out during the closing overs, Jardine infuriated Larwood by sending him in as nightwatchman after all his efforts with the ball. He survived a suicidal single to Bradman at cover and, still fuming the next morning, he attacked from the outset and raced to 98 before splicing a catch to mid-on, where Ironmonger, a maladroit fielder, took a neat catch. He returned to a hero's reception from the crowd, who acknowledged his battling qualities, and a complimentary word from Jardine, who met him at the pavilion gate.

With Hammond contributing a peerless century and Wyatt making 51, England finished with a narrow lead of 19. Larwood completed Richardson's pair before Bradman, in a thrilling cameo, left his stumps wide open to hit the attack through the vacant spaces on the off side. Later on, Larwood struck him a stinging blow on the upper arm before he pulled up lame with a swollen left foot, the result of constant pounding on Australia's rock-hard wickets. His serious condition, however, made little impression on Jardine, who, desperate to keep the pressure on Bradman, ordered him to finish the over. In agony, Larwood could only stand at the crease and swing his arm over and Woodfull, ever the gentleman, pushed the remaining deliveries back down the wicket. Even after he'd completed the over, Jardine insisted that Larwood stay on the field while Bradman remained at the wicket and placed him at short cover point. A few overs later he was put out of his misery when Bradman was dismissed by Verity's faster ball for 71 and he limped off behind him in silence, never to return to the Test-match arena.

Bradman's unorthodox approach of stepping away to leg to hit through the off side mystified Jardine, who thought he should have continued to hook, not least to disperse the inner field; it also drew criticism from revered old timers such as Monty Noble and Warwick Armstrong, who accused him of being reckless. Allen was even more scathing. 'Don Bradman made some incredible shots but he is a terrible little coward of fast bowling.'[45] His assessment, shared by Larwood, seems unfair. Appreciating that mere defence against such an attack achieved little, Bradman opted for defiance and although his series average dropped by nearly a half to 56, he remained the flagship of the fleet at which every missile was targeted in the knowledge that a direct hit would sap morale down the line. 'You know, we nearly didn't do it,' Jardine confided to John Arlott years later. 'The little man was bloody good.'

Woodfull and Bradman aside, Australia offered little resistance and England were left requiring 163 to win. Canny to the end, Jardine asked Wyatt to open instead of Sutcliffe, who looked jaded; he then incensed the crowd by drawing the umpire's attention to the way Alexander was running on the wicket. Hele spoke to the bowler twice and an irate Alexander, spurred on by the Hill, found an extra yard of pace. After several short balls he struck Jardine a sickening blow on the hip bone, the same one that Gilbert had smashed three weeks earlier. As the crowd laughed and cheered, a callous breach of protocol which drew fierce condemnation from English and Australian journalists alike, Jardine, while clearly winded, declined the assistance of the fielders and quickly resumed batting. Later when he returned to the pavilion, Wyatt saw blood running down his leg. His bravery, according to O'Reilly, was his most impressive act throughout the tour. 'We were all, to a man, appreciative of the fact that he had at last copped one, and that he could take it as well as dish it out.'[46]

Jardine resumed in defiant mood the next morning, upbraiding Wyatt for making a mountain out of a molehill, as the latter recalled. 'I got hit on the glove and I went down to tap the wicket. Douglas came charging down the wicket and said: "What the hell are you doing? You don't want to make it look difficult."'[47] Jardine was out for 24 soon afterwards, followed by Leyland without scoring, before an unbeaten partnership of 125 between Wyatt and Hammond guided England to an eight-wicket victory. Woodfull again visited their dressing-room to congratulate them on their success, but not one of the Australian team was present at the New South Wales Cricket Association's farewell dinner for MCC, or, on the quayside, to see them off when they sailed for New Zealand. 'It was a jarring reminder of the bitterness that had marred the tour,' wrote Laurence Le Quesne in his book *The Bodyline Controversy*, 'and it can have left the minds of few of the MCC party entirely at peace.'[48] 'At the end of that season the nerves of all the Australian batsmen had worn thin,' recalled Fingleton. 'I do not think there was one single batsman who played in most of those bodyline games who ever afterwards recaptured his love of cricket.'[49]

In face of all the vitriol, Jardine continued to defend Bodyline – or leg theory as he called it – thereafter, claiming it conformed very much to the letter of the law, while conveniently underestimating its intimidatory aspect. Constructed primarily to counter the threat posed by Bradman, the tactics proved highly successful, as the results indicate, but, according to Fingleton, it came at a great cost, prostituting the art of batting, fracturing relations between the two countries and endangering safety. 'I saw more bruises to square foot of flesh on batsmen that season than I saw during the remainder of my career,' recalled Vic Richardson.[50] 'My constant dread,' said George Hele, who umpired in all the Tests, 'was that a batsman would be killed.'[51]

Above all, Australians thought Bodyline flouted all canons of good taste and fine sportsmanship. 'That dreadful display of heartlessness was more than anyone could take without some show of discontent,' wrote O'Reilly in his autobiography. 'Sitting in the safety of the Australian dressing room I quickly summed it up then as the lousiest thing that I had ever seen in my cricket career. I still class it as such.'[52] He thought that the game which Jardine was presiding over had nothing to do with the game that Australians had been brought up to play. According to Bradman's leading biographer, Irving Rosenwater, the quiet Englishman who'd read Chaucer on the boat to Australia 'had become by far the most hated antagonist among all cricketers who had ever visited that land'.[53]

Attacks on Bodyline didn't just emanate from Australia. At the end of the tour Frank Foster, the leading proponent of leg theory in Australia in 1911/12, publicly denounced the England captain.

'Before Jardine left England, he came frequently to my flat in The St James, and secured from me my leg-theory placings.

'I had no hint that these would be used for bodyline bowling.

'I would like all my old friends in Australian cricket to know that I am sorry that my experience and my advice were put to such unworthy uses.'[54]

Hobbs, a staunch defender of Bodyline in Australia, changed tack once back home, publicly condemning it as being both unsporting and dangerous, a view later supported by Hammond, who was the victim of such tactics by West Indies in 1933. He wrote: 'No one was killed by bodyline, but that was good luck rather than a normal average. I do not think Jardine and Larwood had considered this sufficiently before they experimented with it.'[55]

According to Wyatt, there were arguments both for and against Jardine's tactics, but the crux of the matter was that this policy bred ill-feeling. 'For this reason, I regretted its introduction, although I felt many incidents which the Press chose to link with Jardine's uncompromising tactics were grossly exaggerated.

'It is perfectly true that Douglas made no attempt at any time to ingratiate himself with the Australian crowd. It was not his way, he never played to the gallery. By nature, he was aloof, to the Australian spectator he probably did give an impression of irritating superiority. But in totally ignoring hostile demonstrations against him when on the field he wanted to make one thing plain. Noisy opposition could never intimidate him. He considered Leg Theory a perfectly fair form of attack, and he was not going to be deterred from using it. I admired him for sticking to his guns.'[56]

Despite his mercurial personality and the controversy provoked by his ruthless approach, there could be no denying Jardine's exceptional leadership. J.C. Davis, the distinguished editor of the Sydney *Referee* and authority on Australian cricket, wrote: 'Let us divorce our thoughts from the bodyline element, and we must recognise in D.R. Jardine a captain of very high attainments. In the peculiar type of bowling, he has handled; in the uncommon medley of batting types; in the conditions of cricket in Australia so different, in some directions, from those in England; Jardine has handled his men, his team, with that infinite capacity for taking pains, for thinking clearly, and for acting instantly, which one of the poets tells us is akin to genius.'[57]

O'Reilly declared that his captaincy of a team under those conditions must rank as one of the finest examples of international captaincy ever known, and Fingleton wrote that there was something indefinably magnificent and courageous in the resolute manner in which he stuck to his guns.

A meticulous planner, Jardine made a detailed study of every Australian batsman, analysing their strengths and weaknesses and setting the appropriate field for them. Discerning that several of the batsmen – Kippax, Woodfull and Ponsford – tended to move across towards the off side, his strategy of getting Larwood and Voce to bowl a leg-stump line was vindicated by the number of times they were bowled leg stump. Deploying his bowlers in short bursts, he not only had someone fresh up his sleeve, he also ensured that the batsmen never saw too much of one of them. A firm believer in physical fitness, he encouraged every fielder to specialise in a particular position. A fine gully himself, he also was a fearless short leg and a committed outfielder who chased every ball frantically to the boundary. He instructed his batsmen to play in an attritional manner and although it didn't make for spectacular viewing, their tactics paid off with England scoring heavily in four of the five Tests.

*Wisden* wrote that he led the side superbly and *The Times* attributed England's success primarily to his captaincy. 'He has handled the bowling, batting, and fielding of his men with wonderful judgement and unflinching determination, and it may fairly be said of him that by adapting their play and his own to the conditions of Test Match cricket he has beaten the Australians at their own game.'[58] According to Bowes, he was the greatest man he'd ever known and a supreme leader – a sentiment similar to that expressed by his Yorkshire team-mates. Verity, who named his son after him, thought he was unrivalled as a captain, while Sutcliffe, who'd branded him a 'queer devil' on the previous tour to Australia, now saw him in a very different light. Aside from rating him unrivalled as a tactician and a fighter, he discovered a leader of supreme qualities. 'He planned for us, cared for us, and fought for us on that tour, and he was so faithful in everything he did that we were prepared on our part to do anything we could for him.'[59] In Hammond's opinion his courage, tenacity and tactical skill were rarely equalled, and even Warner, for all his reservations about Jardine personally, was fully admiring of his fortitude and absolute unselfishness. Indeed, Bodyline aside, it is difficult to think of any England captain in Australia winning such recognition from friend and foe alike for his leadership prowess.

**Endnotes:**

1  Kevin Perkins, *The Larwood Story*, p151
2  R.S. Whitington, *Time of the Tiger: the Bill O'Reilly Story*, p108
3  Fingleton, *Cricket Crisis*, Introduction
4  Ibid, p76
5  Ibid
6  Gilbert Mant, *A Cuckoo in the Bodyline Nest*, p68
7  E.W. Swanton, *Follow On*, p140
8  E.W. Swanton, *Gubby Allen: Man of Cricket*, p124

9  *Port Lincoln Times*, 27 January 1933

10  Douglas Jardine, *In Quest of the Ashes*, p207

11  Sissons and Stoddart, *Cricket and the Empire*, p22

12  *Truth*, 15 January 1933

13  Fingleton, *Cricket Crisis,* p85

14  *The Bulletin*, 14 December 1982, p72

15  Howat, *Plum Warner*, p113

16  Ibid, p109

17  Sissons and Stoddart, *Cricket and the Empire*, p72

18  Fingleton, *Cricket Crisis*, p2

19  Howat, *Plum Warner*, p118

20  *Daily News* (Perth), 19 January 1933

21  Quoted in Derek Birley, *A Social History of English Cricket*, p236

22  Ibid, p237

23  Bateman, Anthony (ed), *The Cambridge Companion to Cricket*, p77

24  Quoted in Peel, *Playing the Game? Cricket's Tarnished Ideals from Bodyline to the Present, p29*

25  Quoted in Frith, *Bodyline Autopsy*, p237

26  Jardine, *In Quest of the Ashes*, p151

27  Quoted in E.W. Docker, *Bradman and the Bodyline Series*, p57

28  *Times of India*, 20 September 1965

29  Rendell, *Gubby Allen: Bad Boy of Bodyline?* p37

30  *Birmingham Post*, 20 June 1958

31  Alan Hill, *Hedley Verity: Portrait of a Cricketer*, p62

32  Hill, *Herbert Sutcliffe: Cricket Maestro*, p187

33  Fingleton, *Cricket Crisis*, p64

34  Hamilton, *Harold Larwood*, p170

35  Hill, *Hedley Verity: Portrait of a Cricketer*, p62

36  Swanton, *Gubby Allen: Man of Cricket*, p136

37  Jardine, *In Quest of the Ashes*, p154

38  Frith, *Bodyline Autopsy*, p219

39  Quoted in Peel, *Playing the Game? Cricket's Tarnished Ideals from Bodyline to the Present*, p30

40  Howat, *Plum Warner*, p128

41  John Arlott (ed), *Cricket: The Great Captains*, p48

42  Mike Colman and Ken Edwards, *Eddie Gilbert: The True Story of an Aboriginal Legend*, p118

43  Pawle, *R.E.S. Wyatt: Fighting Cricketer*, p109

44  *Daily Telegraph* (Sydney), 17 February 1933

45  Derriman, *Bodyline*, p22

46  Bill O'Reilly, *Tiger: Sixty Years in Cricket*, p101

47  Alan Hill, *Hedley Verity: Portrait of a Cricketer*, p65

48  Laurence Le Quesne, *The Bodyline Controversy*, p92

49  Fingleton, *Cricket Crisis*, p56

50  Vic Richardson, *The Vic Richardson Story*, p67

51  Quoted in Fingleton, *Cricket Crisis*, p55

52  O'Reilly, *Tiger: Sixty Years in Cricket*, p92

53  Irving Rosenwater, *Sir Donald Bradman*, p185

54  *Smith's Weekly*, 18 March 1933

55  Walter Hammond, *Cricket My Destiny*, p89

56  Pawle, *R.E.S. Wyatt: Fighting Cricketer*, p113

57  *The Referee*, 1 March 1933

58  *The Times*, 17 February 1933

59  Herbert Sutcliffe, *For Yorkshire and England*, p117

# CHAPTER 8

# THE CONQUERING HERO

AFTER THE storm, the calm. MCC had alienated Australia by shortening their tour to add New Zealand to their itinerary for the first time and with this in mind they arrived there to the warmest of welcomes. At a reception hosted by the government in Wellington, Jardine alluded to a Christmas card he'd received from the New Zealand Cricket Council, which contained some verses from the poet Arnold Wall's *A Beautiful Game*, the last of which he proceeded to read out.

> A time will come, a time will come,
> When the people sit with a graceful heart,
> Watching the beautiful, beautiful game,
> That is battle and service and sport and art.
> A time will come, a time will come,
> When the crowds will gaze on the game and the green,
> Soberly watching the beautiful game,
> Orderly, decent, calm and serene.

'Australian papers please copy,' he added dryly to much laughter.

Large crowds attended the two Tests notable for the lack of Bodyline – Larwood was absent because of injury – and barracking. In the first Test at Christchurch, Jardine, greeted warmly by the crowd, batted in relaxed fashion for 45, adding 87 with Hammond, who went on to score 227 in England's total of 560/8 declared. New Zealand, bowled out for 223, were forced to follow on when rain brought proceedings to a premature end.

Rheumatism forced Jardine out of the second Test at Auckland, notable for Hammond's 336 not out – a Test record score, eclipsing Bradman's 334 at Headingley in 1930 – and the weather once again saving the hosts. No matter. The visit had been a great success. Jardine told his hosts how pleasant it was to come to a country 'where my forefather and parentage seem to be known' and in a gracious farewell he not only spoke positively about the future of New Zealand cricket, he also commended their crowds for their decorous behaviour.

Given a rousing send-off, MCC began their homeward voyage across the Pacific via Fiji, where Jardine was presented with a whale's tooth by the local chief, and Honolulu. Accompanying the tourists on their journey was the English actress Violet Vanbrugh, who was returning from a successful tour of Australia and New Zealand. She performed at the ship's concert, but made little impression on Jardine who read a book throughout and failed to applaud. 'For a Wykehamist whose school motto is "Manners Maketh Man", I thought it was an insulting public exhibition of rudeness, wrote Gilbert Mant, 'and it did not pass unnoticed by Miss Vanbrugh and the other passengers.'[1]

After disembarking at Vancouver, MCC travelled across Canada by train to Montreal, where they boarded the ocean liner *Duchess of Atholl*. On their first evening the players held a private farewell dinner at which Sutcliffe presented Jardine with a silver cigarette box engraved with the names of the team. Extolling his skill and courage, he expressed his confidence that D.R. Jardine ranked with any previous great captain and it was a privilege to play under his leadership. Moved by the acclamation, Jardine thanked the team for their loyalty.

Following a storm-lashed voyage across the Atlantic, the liner berthed at Greenock on the Clyde on 6 May. There they were serenaded by pipers on the quayside, and on receiving the congratulations of the welcoming party, Jardine expressed pride in his Scottish heritage. A quick dash to Glasgow, where 10,000 people awaited them, enabled them to catch the train south and when Jardine arrived at Euston with the rump of the party he was treated like royalty. 'Good old Jardine' rang in his ears as he greeted his parents and the MCC hierarchy. Thereafter, he became the focus of a cheering, back-slapping crowd which attempted to carry him on their shoulders. He managed to escape to the sanctuary of the Station Hotel, but in response to repeated demands for a speech he appeared at the window to express his thanks. 'We went out a happy band and we returned a happy and united band,' he told them. 'They have made themselves a great side in the face of difficulties which might quite excusably have broken up most sides.'

From the moment he stepped ashore, Jardine's homecoming was one of uninterrupted triumph, as thousands up and down the country celebrated the achievement of regaining the Ashes. He marked his return to cricket by captaining MCC against Jackie Grant's West Indians. Although the tourists were blessed with the warmest weather since 1921, they failed to do themselves justice. Deprived by the absence of the charismatic Constantine for the most part because of his contractual obligations with the Lancashire League side Nelson, they relied heavily on the batting of George Headley and the bowling of Manny Martindale. Constantine's availability for the match against MCC showed what a force they could have been as he and Martindale bowled with great ferocity. The opening batsmen were clearly unnerved by the barrage of bouncers, which generated much hostile comment in the press, and Hendren became the first batsman to wear protective headgear. Entering at 43/3, Jardine was cheered all the way to the wicket, with even the West Indians joining in the applause, but the felicitations didn't last because he was soon out caught at short leg off Constantine for 7. Chapman rallied MCC with 97 and Bryan Valentine with 60, but they still trailed by 63 on first innings. Needing 332 to win on the final day, a fourth-wicket stand of 81 between Hendren and Jardine appeared to have secured a draw, but after the latter was out for 44, the lower order sunk without trace and they lost by 152 runs.

Welcomed back by Surrey for their derby against Sussex at the end of May, Jardine, having missed several matches because of work, immediately proved his worth. Coming to the wicket at 18/3, he survived some anxious moments against Tate, but, mixing immaculate defence with some delicate leg-side shots, he played faultlessly for 75.

He went one better in the second innings by scoring an unblemished 105, sharing a third-wicket stand of 225 with Tom Barling. His declaration, however, seemed unduly cautious and Sussex, set 471 to win, comfortably played out time.

Jardine remained in the runs when Surrey travelled to Trent Bridge for the bank holiday game against a Nottinghamshire side in which Larwood played solely as a batsman because of his injured foot. After the home team made 267 on the first day, a vast crowd saw Surrey begin inauspiciously against Voce before Jardine came to the rescue with a masterly 67, and with Fender hitting a century, they had the better of a draw.

On the second evening, stumps were drawn 15 minutes early so Jardine could present Larwood and Voce each with a cheque for £388 from the proceeds of the Nottingham Newspapers Shilling Fund in recognition of their success in Australia. He was greeted with loud cheers and a rendition of 'For He's a Jolly Good Fellow'. Having raised a laugh by comparing the crowd favourably with Australian ones, he described the presentation as one of the proudest moments of his life. Calling both Larwood and Voce real men and true heroes, he paid tribute to the great mental courage they'd shown in Australia.

In reply, a nervous-looking Larwood admitted he found it difficult to express in words what he felt, describing Jardine as a magnificent captain, a great sportsman and a true friend. His words assumed a deeper meaning when, minutes later, in a private ceremony, Jardine presented each player with his own gift: an ashtray. According to Duncan Hamilton, 'The inscription on Larwood's ashtray – every word in capital letters – was heartfelt:

TO HAROLD FOR THE ASHES- 1932-33. FROM A GRATEFUL 'SKIPPER'.

'For Jardine, it was his way of articulating his gratitude to his fast bowler, something he was unable to do with the English language alone. Jardine paid for the ashtray out of his own pocket. The altruistic act was the final confirmation for Larwood that Jardine was one of the most exemplary human beings he had ever met: decent, fair, scrupulously loyal, staunchly committed to Larwood's own cause. While others tried to make him feel like a shabby failure, Jardine was steadfast, and a true officer. Larwood would have trusted him with his life, and the lives of his children too.'[2]

Jardine made 50 against Warwickshire and although he failed against Essex, he had the satisfaction of beating them by an innings. After Gover had bowled them out for 66 on a rain-affected pitch, he reluctantly consented to Fender's request that they swap ends because the latter thought he could exploit a worn patch at the other end. Fender then approached Jardine who, without seeking an explanation, granted him his request and Fender repaid the compliment by taking 8-29 in the second innings.

Jardine's triumph in Australia made his appointment as captain against West Indies in three three-day Tests a formality, but the side contained a number of changes from the winter. With Larwood and Wyatt injured and Paynter and Voce out of form, they were replaced for the first Test at Lord's by George Macaulay, Walter Robins and debutants Cyril Walters, the Worcestershire opening batsman, and Maurice Turnbull, the Glamorgan captain. After a heavily truncated first day because of the weather, England, resuming at 43/0, slumped to 155/6 before recovering to 296 all out thanks to an admirable unbeaten 83 from Ames. In the remaining time that day, West Indies suffered the worst of all starts and they staggered to 55/6 by stumps. On the final day, Jardine gave the ball to Robins and he mesmerised the tail, taking the remaining four wickets to finish with 6-32. Following on 199 behind, West Indies, despite 50 from Headley, performed little better in their second innings with Verity and Macaulay both taking four wickets. Although they'd disappointed with their spineless batting, critics were quick to lavish praise on Jardine for his attacking instincts, not least his close-in field. The *Daily Express*'s William Pollock wrote: 'Jardine is obviously a psychologist, as well as a great cricketer. He was exercising a moral effort on his opponents, and beat them all ends up. He has a navy-like efficiency in his side, and I believe he schemed every ball. It was 100 per cent captaincy.'[3]

Back with Surrey, Jardine, as was his wont, reserved his finest efforts for the ultimate challenge – against the county champions Yorkshire at Sheffield. Dismissed for 253, Yorkshire struck back through Bowes, and Jardine came out to bat on the first evening accompanied by a thunderous ovation from the 21,000 Bramall Lane crowd, who let him know what they thought of his efforts in Australia. Halfway to the middle he stopped. Then standing bolt upright, he faced each side of the ground, lifted his cap and waved his bat. The cheering broke out again when he reached the middle, an ovation so intense that it brought a tear to his eye. 'If anyone needed confirmation of what Yorkshiremen thought about our tactics in Australia, they were made apparent on that day at Bramall Lane,' declared Sutcliffe.[4]

Eleven overnight, Jardine was soon out the next day edging a good delivery from Bowes, who ended with 7-68. Leading by 119 on first innings, Yorkshire were soon 8/2 but Sutcliffe made 61 and Surrey required 315 to win. Again, they began poorly with Sandham and Barling dismissed in the opening overs. Fourteen for two overnight soon became 26/3, but Jardine joined Gregory and playing with rare diligence they took the score to 101/3 at lunch. Gregory and Fender departed soon afterwards but Jardine remained firm, totally in control, and only after his dismissal for 105 could Yorkshire be guaranteed victory. '"A captain's innings" may be a poor phrase,' declared *The Times*, 'but it at least conveys something of the courage and tenacity, to say nothing of the purely technical skill, of a truly great innings.'[5]

Jardine again played a lone hand against the Players at Lord's as the Gentlemen crashed to an innings defeat. All out for 309, the Players then took advantage of a helpful wicket to cause all kinds of trouble for their opponents. Even Jardine was tested in the conditions, scoring a mere six runs in 55 minutes, but with eight men out for 62 he opened his shoulders. Unleashing every weapon in his arsenal, he dominated a ninth-wicket partnership of 78 with Ken Farnes before he was lured out of his ground by left-arm spinner James Langridge and stumped for 59. *The Times* called him 'as great a fighting batsman as ever played in this great match', and the cricket historian Ronald Mason rated his innings the most brilliantly resourceful display he'd ever seen.[6]

For the second Test at Old Trafford, Wyatt, Langridge and 'Nobby' Clark, the tall left-arm Northamptonshire opening bowler, replaced Turnbull, Leyland and Allen. The West Indies, boosted by the inclusion of Constantine, batted first on a slow wicket and made 375 with Ivan Barrow and Headley both hitting centuries.

Resolved to give England a taste of their own medicine, Constantine and Martindale bowled Bodyline at their opponents, with Hammond in particular in the line of fire. Struck on the chin by Martindale following a blow on the back as he ducked from Constantine, he registered his disgust as he left the crease for repairs. He returned soon afterwards with two stiches and offered his hand to Constantine, only to be out to him soon afterwards, caught in the leg trap. When Wyatt departed at 134/4, England were in some bother. Jardine, however, stood firm. Singled out for the short-pitched bowling, he was equal to the challenge by drawing himself up to his full height and playing with soft hands to keep the ball down. It didn't make for compulsive viewing, as the crowd's impatience made clear in the hour before tea, but Jardine, as ever, was unmoved by such considerations. He added 83 with Ames and then after Langridge's dismissal, he was joined by Robins at 234/6. 'This is absolutely no problem,' he tried to reassure him about the short ball but, after ducking for a couple of overs, Robins said, 'It may be no problem for you up there at 6ft 3in, but you want to come down to 5ft 7in!'

Sixty-eight not out overnight, Jardine made light of the attack the next morning as he moved steadily towards his maiden Test century, a landmark greeted by hearty applause from the crowd. His seventh-wicket partnership with Robins yielded 140 and when he was caught low by Constantine in the gully for 127 – a dismissal he queried – he departed to the most tumultuous ovation Robertson-Glasgow had ever heard on a cricket ground. Although the wicket was easy-paced and the West Indian quicks lacked the speed and accuracy of Larwood, his innings drew praise from all quarters, not least from Constantine himself. According to *The Times*, 'he treated bodyline with typical determination and won the duel so completely that the West Indies abandoned the short stuff against him', and *Wisden* declared that 'he probably played the bowling better than any other man in the world'.[7] 'What a really great innings Jardine played at Manchester,' noted Sutcliffe. 'It was a classic and one of the best I have ever seen against such a magnificent attack which was sustained for an incredibly long time. There were scores of vicious bouncers, to which our skipper … found the right answer.'[8]

Losing their last three wickets in five balls, England were all out for 374, one run behind West Indies. They then turned their fire on their opponents when Clark bowled Bodyline at the start of their second innings. He dismissed Barrow for nought and struck Clifford Roach once, but the latter came out fighting and his belligerent 64, along with 64 from Constantine, earned them a draw. This was Clark's first match under Jardine's captaincy and he was more than put through his paces. 'Nobby was a pretty indifferent fielder,' recalled his Northamptonshire team-mate Dennis Brookes, 'but he had hardly been seen in that role, since he was virtually keeping one end going by bowling through the match.' As they came off the field at the end of the West Indies' second innings, Jardine said to Nobby, 'I want to congratulate you, Clark, on your improved fielding.'[9] Not surprisingly, West Indies were keen to retain Constantine's services for the third Test and they struck an agreement with Nelson, which would see Essex's Morris Nichols substitute for him. When Jardine heard about this, he allegedly defeated the plan by persuading the selectors to pick Nichols for England.

It was a match Jardine was forced to miss because of a nasty injury sustained against Kent at the Oval. Struck a painful blow on the wrist by Bill Ashdown when fielding in the gully in the first innings, he endured something worse in the second innings when the same batsman, one of the most powerful strikers in the game, hit him a terrible blow on the right shin. He was helped off the field in obvious pain and although nothing was broken it incapacitated him for the rest of the season. Wyatt took over the captaincy for the third Test and a new-look England side beat West Indies by an innings with Fred Bakewell scoring a century and debutant 'Father' Marriott taking 11 cheap wickets with his leg-spin.

On 10 July Jardine had been asked to captain MCC on their tour to India that winter, and although initially inclined to reject the invitation, Fender persuaded him to see it as a gesture of support which he should accept. On playing grounds he was the obvious choice, but, after the ructions in Australia the previous winter, MCC minuted the fact that the president Lord Hailsham and the treasurer Lord Hawke were to have a private word with him before departure, presumably to caution him about the use of Bodyline. In a letter to Alfred Wagg, Jardine's employer and godfather, seeking permission for him to be given leave, Hailsham admitted that he felt 'a little ashamed of the doings of our team last winter'.[10]

Jardine was keen to have Wyatt once again as his vice-captain, but Wyatt felt in need of a winter off and, apart from Verity, the side contained no one else from the Australian tour. Seven others – Walters, Clark, Langridge, Nichols, Marriott, Bakewell and Charlie Barnett – had played against West Indies that summer. In addition, the Derbyshire wicketkeeper Harry Elliott and his county colleague, Les Townsend, had previously won Test caps. Only the Yorkshire batsman Arthur Mitchell, the Kent captain Bryan Valentine, their wicketkeeper 'Hopper' Levett, the Surrey all-rounder Bob Gregory and the Cambridge University batsman John Human had yet to represent their country.

The manager, Major E.W.C. Ricketts, was a Wykehamist and Indian Army veteran with a deep knowledge of the country. He'd managed India's Olympic hockey team in 1928 and their cricket tour to England in 1932 and, despite suffering bouts of ill health, he won Jardine's trust for his exceptional competence in India, a striking contrast with his predecessor in Australia a year earlier.

**Endnotes:**

1 Mant, *A Cuckoo in the Bodyline Nest*, p129
2 Hamilton, *Harold Larwood*, p290
3 *Daily Express*, 28 June 1933
4 Hill, *Herbert Sutcliffe: Cricket Maestro*, p193
5 *The Times*, 5 July 1933
6 Ibid, 21 July 1933
7 *Wisden* 1934, p31
8 Hill, *Herbert Sutcliffe: Cricket Maestro*, p193
9 Michael Marshall, *Gentlemen and Players*, p110
10 Frith, *Bodyline Autopsy*, p360

CHAPTER 9

# INDIAN SUMMER

JARDINE'S RETURN to the land of his birth took place at
a turbulent time in the country's history. The tour, originally
scheduled for 1930/31 and then for 1931/32, had been postponed
because of civil unrest orchestrated by the Indian nationalist
movement under its leader, Mahatma Gandhi. Now with order
restored, the Viceroy, Lord Willingdon, a former Cambridge
and Sussex cricketer and leading patron of the Board of Control
for Cricket in India (BCCI), looked to the tour as a means of
improving Anglo-Indian relations. The initial signs weren't
propitious.

Although a telegram purporting to be from the BCCI and
expressing 'disgusting insult' at the selection of a second-string
side turned out to be a hoax, they did send a telegram, dated
17 August, reporting intense disappointment about the absence
of so many leading players. In order to guarantee the financial
and sporting success of the tour, they urged the inclusion of
luminaries such as Hobbs, Sutcliffe and Hammond. Nine days
later, a second telegram from the BCCI's president Grant Govan
clarified matters. While professing no right to question MCC's

judgement in the selection of their team, their essential message remained broadly the same.

With the BCCI inundated with appeals for matches from all over India, a gruelling itinerary of 34 games was drawn up, necessitating long rail journeys over a land mass similar to the size of Europe, often in blistering heat. The proposal to play on Sundays in a non-Christian country aroused grave concerns from religious bodies such as the London Missionary Society, the National Christian Council of India and the Lord's Day Observance Society, but despite representations from the Archbishop of Canterbury, the itinerary remained unchanged.

On 22 September the team left Tilbury on the SS *Mooltan* and on their arrival at Bombay on 12 October, they were given a rousing welcome. A microphone had been installed on the deck to enable Jardine to broadcast to All-India Radio, something he struggled to do as the crowd surged around him. Besides posing for photos in company with his former bearer, Lalla Sebastian, MCC's captain spoke of his delight to be back in the land of his birth. 'I was born in Bombay and, as St Paul, a great man from another place, said, "I am a citizen of no mean city"'. Alluding to the disappointment felt in India caused by the absence of many of their leading players, he assured his hosts that their replacements would become household names.

Although the quality of their opposition would vary enormously, Jardine was leaving nothing to chance. Ever a stickler for detail, he sent a telegram from the *Mooltan* to Karachi demanding to know details of local grounds in the city such as the length of the matting wickets, the height of the sightscreens and the state of the outfield. He also took a keen interest in the rolling of the pitch prior to each game, since this helped determine his decision of which bowler bowled from which end, and before taking the field he insisted the umpires inspect the ball to ensure it was the right size.

After draws in their first two games, both non-first-class, MCC gained their first victory against Sind, a match in which Jardine scored a chanceless hundred and Verity took ten wickets. Before the team left for Peshawar, they were accorded a civic welcome from the Karachi municipality. An address on embossed silk in a silver casket was presented to Jardine by the Mayor of Karachi and Jardine was visibly moved in his reply, appreciating in particular the friendliness shown to his team from all communities.

MCC were again in the runs against Southern Punjab following a scintillating hundred from the 22-year-old Lala Amarnath, who was to dominate Indian cricket over the decades as player, captain, manager and father of two Test cricketers. A protégé of Frank Tarrant, the former Victoria and Middlesex all-rounder who was employed as a coach by the Maharaja of Patiala, he was chosen for both Sind and Southern Punjab. Fortunate to be given an apparent reprieve by umpire Tarrant when on 3, Amarnath was approached by Jardine at the end of the over and asked if he'd hit the ball. 'There was definitely a sound,' declared Amarnath, to which Jardine retorted, 'The bloody sound could have been heard clearly in Sydney,' a none too subtle allusion to the nationality of the two Australian umpires, Tarrant and his 19-year-old son.

At a time when princely patronage of Indian cricket had reached its zenith, no one exerted a greater influence than the Maharaja of Patiala, a loyal friend of the Raj who'd contributed substantially to the Allied cause in the First World War. Although

Patiala used cricket to further his political ambitions, not least his resistance to Indian nationalism which threatened princely power, he nevertheless could claim to be a genuine lover of the game with a creditable playing record. In addition to leading the first Indian tour to England in 1911, aged 19, he helped found the BCCI in 1928 and employed many leading professional cricketers. Appointed captain of India on their tour to England in 1932, he later withdrew because of ill health and thereafter he began to lose influence within the BCCI because of his feud with Lord Willingdon, who, personal antipathy aside, disliked his resistance to his imperial reforms. Patiala saw Jardine's tour as an opportunity to recover lost ground with his lavish hospitality of the team, including a sumptuous banquet at his palace during his match against them.

On the best ground in the country, complete with magnificent pavilion and immaculate turf wicket, a large crowd, many arrayed in colourful turbans, and featuring a number of the Maharaja's wives, gathered to watch the game. It proved no spectacle. Against an attack which included the 52-year-old Tarrant, who took four wickets, Jardine continued his fine form with an accomplished 80, his forward play an object lesson in footwork. MCC made 300 but, led by 156 from Wazir Ali, Patiala's XI managed to secure a narrow first-innings lead when stumps were drawn prematurely on the final day to enable the tourists to go hunting at the Maharaja's lodge at Pinjore.

In order to repay the Maharaja for his hospitality, Jardine invited him to play for MCC in their next game against a Delhi District XI. As an MCC member, Patiala was within his rights but his inclusion was fiercely opposed by Willingdon, who had serious reservations about him. The previous year Patiala, a notorious philanderer, had been expelled from a ball at Simla for making a pass at the Viceroy's unmarried daughter, and in cricketing affairs he found him to be an unscrupulous schemer. The stand-off over Patiala didn't bode well for Jardine's stay, along with the other amateurs, at Viceroy House. 'We are being smothered with MCC cricketers who are staying with me at Delhi at the present moment,' Willingdon wrote to King George V in his monthly letter.[1] When the Viceroy asked Jardine to reconsider, the England captain merely refilled his pipe with tobacco and when Lady Willingdon tried something similar, he refused to budge. No one, however grand, would usurp his right to pick the side he wanted. Patiala duly played and made 54.

The contretemps over Patiala intensified Jardine's resolve to beat the Viceroy's XI, a team composed of five Europeans and six Indians. Played in a festival atmosphere, with parts of government closed down for the duration of the match and the band playing the national anthem, MCC nevertheless meant business. They began well, dismissing their opponents for 160 and when they slumped to 142/5 Jardine came to the rescue. Nursing an injured wrist and wonky knee, he proceeded cautiously but, in partnership with Valentine, he put the game out of reach before he was bowled by Tom Longfield, later Ted Dexter's father-in-law, for 93.

Before the start of the home side's second innings, the groundsman rolled the pitch for 20 minutes, greatly exceeding the statutory seven-minute limit, a breach of the rules which infuriated Jardine, who demanded an apology. One senior official warned him that if word seeped out about his attitude, British prestige would suffer, but the England captain wasn't for turning and with the Viceroy reluctantly caving in, he duly received his apology. 'I wouldn't have gone on to the field without it, even if the king of England was playing against me,' Jardine duly reflected.[2]

Following this altercation, he was in no mood to go easy on his opponents and unleashing the full force of his pace attack, they bowled out the Viceroy's XI for 63 with Nichols taking 5-14. It was an unfortunate end to what was meant to be a friendly fixture celebrating Corinthian values. 'The cricketers have left us for elsewhere thank goodness,' wrote Willingdon to his sister. 'I don't like Jardine and don't wonder at the Australians hating him. He is a fine cricketer and very good captain, but he is the most self-opinionated man I've ever met; full of wind and head, talks to all of us as if he and not we know much about India.'[3]

Jardine took time out from the next two matches to shoot tiger at Junagadh, the former fiefdom of Ranji, bearing a gun presented to him by Patiala. As a fine shot, he was only too happy to accept prestigious invitations to shoot game from maharajas by virtue of his social connections and his status as England captain. After three days up a tree in the Gir Forest, and with the aid of 30 beaters, he shot a lion and took the skin home.

He returned for the two-day fixture at Jamnagar, another game where stumps were drawn early so the team could hunt panther at Killeshwar. Weeks later he went on a tiger shoot at Gwalior and Dilawar and, judging by numerous photos, he enjoyed celebrating his various trophies, which by the end of the tour comprised one lion, two tigers, two panthers, one bear, three crocodiles and numerous stags. On one occasion when he wounded a tiger, he insisted that he walked after the wounded animal and put it out of its misery rather than allow the beaters to endanger their safety.

*Jardine and Cook House during his final term at Winchester. Jardine is seated second from the right.*

*The Oxford University and Australian sides prior to their game at Oxford, 1921, a game in which Jardine scored 96 not out in the second innings.*

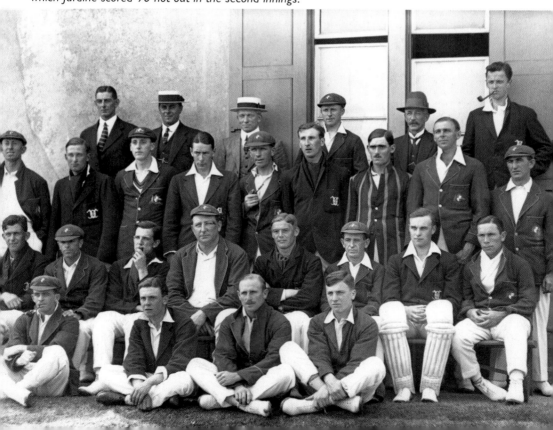

MCC in Australia 1928/29.
Jardine, the one player wearing
a cap, was a valuable member
of this Ashes-winning side.

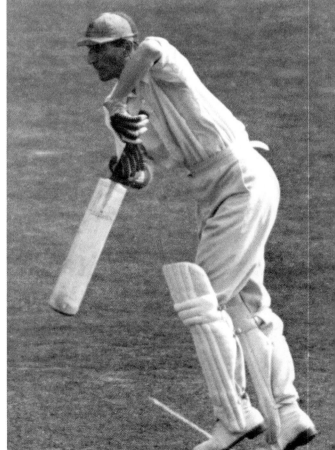

Jardine batting for the South of
England against the North at
Old Trafford, 1932.

Jardine, wearing his celebrated Harlequin cap, illustrated on a Player's Cricket Tobacco Card.

Mr D. R. JARDINE.          SURREY.

The MCC team on board the SS Orontes at Tilbury prior to their departure to Australia, September 1932. Jardine is second on the left.

*A confident captain on board the* Orontes.

*Jardine conferring with his players during the first Test against Australia at Sydney, 1932, a game which England won by ten wickets.*

*Jardine leads England on to the field for the second Test at Melbourne.*

*Jardine presents cheques to Harold Larwood [right] and Bill Voce [left] from a grateful Nottingham public in recognition of their success in Australia.*

*Jardine batting against Warwickshire at the Oval, 1933.*

*The 1933/34 MCC side to India on board the SS Mooltan.*

*Jardine with his rival captain, C.K.Nayudu, prior to the second Test at Calcutta, 1933/34. Both captains had a healthy respect for each other.*

*Jardine with his fiancée, Margaret Peat, 1934.*

Jardine opening the batting in a charity match, 1951.

Jardine captaining the Authors XI against the National Book League at Vincent Square, Westminster, 1956. It was one of his final games.

On returning to Bombay, Jardine spent time with his old bearer Lalla Sebastian, visiting his childhood haunts and climbing the hill to the Sewri cemetery so the latter could place a wreath on the grave of his late wife. On becoming unwell, Sebastian asked Jardine to go on ahead, declaring that he would catch him up. After his failure to appear, Jardine returned to find that he'd collapsed. He rushed him to hospital, but he died shortly afterwards of heart failure.

In their match against the Bombay Presidency, MCC quickly dismissed their opponents for 87, before gorging themselves on a flat wicket. Determined to make runs in his home city, Jardine took no chances but his crisp leg-side shots delighted the large crowd and his century was greeted with sustained applause. With the first Test in mind, he delayed the declaration to get some additional batting practice and although the home side escaped with a draw, MCC entered the first Test in fine fettle. Not only had Jardine, Walters and Valentine scored plenty of runs, the attack of Clark, Nichols, Townsend, Verity and Langridge had proved too powerful for their opponents.

At the same time, Jardine was having some trouble welding his new-look side together. While all touring parties contain their idiosyncratic, not to say temperamental characters, this one had more than most. Amid the amateurs, Marriott's age and insistence on keeping to an insufficient vegetarian diet weakened him in the field and made him unpopular off it, while Levett's high consumption of alcohol made him a liability. 'His social manner, combined with the failing noted above, were several times remarked on by those with whom he stayed during the Tour and by others who met the players at social functions,' remarked Ricketts in his end-of-tour report.[4] Preferring the company of the professionals to the amateurs, he set a bad example, especially on train journeys, when he, Bakewell and Mitchell consumed far more drink than was good for them, a fact that didn't escape the welcome parties. 'He was always most difficult to deal with as he would always rudely resent any attempt at a friendly word of advice, and could not be brought to see that conduct such as his was not only detrimental to the name of the MCC but even deserving of reproof.' Several times Jardine admonished him, once severely, which only increased his resentment that he was being unfairly victimised. Even at the end of the tour when Jardine asked him to drink in moderation on the voyage home, if only to protect MCC's prestige, Levett refused to offer any such assurance. 'In my opinion, a useless member of the side and a social menace,' the manager concluded.[5]

'Jardine didn't make life very easy for me,' Levett later recalled. 'If I had been to a university and got a Blue, he would probably have treated me differently. I had not been to Eton or Harrow. I rather felt he was a snob, one of those old la-di-dah, aloof men who preferred people who had been to university.' Believing that Jardine lacked good cheer and that he carried his aggression towards the opposition to excess, he continued: 'I wouldn't have cared to play a lot of cricket under him. I wouldn't have enjoyed my cricket. He wasn't my cup of tea.'[6]

Amid the professionals, Ricketts singled out Bakewell, Elliott, Mitchell and Clark for censure. Describing Bakewell as 'a rather unsatisfactory person' with an addiction to alcohol, he had cause to rebuke him at Delhi for deliberately disobeying Jardine. He pointed out that a repeat offence would probably see him sent home, but despite Bakewell's promise to improve, he lacked the strength of character to conform. 'I hope Levett, Bakewell and

Mitchell will behave on the way home,' wrote Jardine at the end of the tour. 'They haven't been good out here; the bottle makes too strong an appeal to them.'[7]

According to Ricketts, Elliott was not a happy choice as senior professional. 'His character seems to be entirely underdeveloped and he lacked the personality, presence and influence necessary of his position. He was influenced by others.'[8]

Clark was also problematic; moody, gauche and lacking in self-awareness. 'Jardine's main trouble is with Clark,' Ricketts wrote to William Findlay on the eve of the second Test: 'He has got the mind and outlook of a child of two and thinks he is about to die if he scratches his hand or gets a slight bruise and I think Jardine is afraid he will give up the ghost in the Test match and become a useless passenger – he is always moaning that he is ill and wants a doctor.' Nichols, in contrast, 'worked like a Trojan as a lot of hard work falls on him, especially when Clark shows the white feather as he frequently does.'[9]

Confronted with Clark's hypochondria, Jardine appears to have handled him pretty effectively, since Clark, no mean performer on the tour, ranked him the best captain he ever played under. 'Nobby told me that the secret of Douglas Jardine's success in getting the best out of him was that he knew when to pull his leg and when to crack the whip,' recalled Dennis Brookes. 'Nobby found it pretty hard work on some of the featherbed wickets, on which they had to bowl in India. He was always a temperamental performer who quickly got "sore shins" if things were not going his way. On one occasion, it was clear that he was not over-enthusiastic about continuing to bowl. "What's the matter, Clark?" asked his captain. "I've got a sore shin, Skipper," Nobby replied. Douglas Jardine just said, "You remember when we were out shooting the other day and we saw a buck wounded? What did it do then? "It got up and ran on three legs, Skipper," Nobby replied. "Well," said Jardine. "you can bloody well bowl on one leg."'[10]

Frustrated by the tepid efforts of some of his bowlers in the heat, Jardine fulminated on one occasion, 'Thank God we have one bowler in the side,' a reference to Verity, whom he so greatly admired.

The India team, captained once again by Nayudu, contained six players who'd toured England in 1932 and five debutants, including Amarnath and Vijay Merchant, both of whom had impressed against the tourists. Although they boasted a formidable pace attack in Mohammad Nissar and Amar Singh, their batting lacked depth and their fielding paled in comparison to their opponents. Their intention had been to play Lall Singh, an enterprising batsman who'd played against England in 1932, but Jardine objected to his selection on the ground that he was based in Malaya and he hadn't completed his residential qualification. The BCCI supported Singh's claim, but Jardine, taking his stand on the rules, refused to budge and he was backed by the Imperial Cricket Conference.

Because of its status as the hub of Indian cricket and the only city able to guarantee the 26,000 rupees demanded by the BCCI, it seemed appropriate that Bombay staged the country's inaugural home Test. The venue, the Bombay Gymkhana, although formed exclusively for Europeans, and flying only the MCC flag and the Union Jack, relaxed its regulations to allow the Indian side to use its facilities. A capacity crowd of 50,000, crammed into makeshift stands and tents, saw India bat first and progress tentatively against a lively attack led by Clark and Nichols. Only Amarnath and Nayudu managed to break the shackles and it needed a deft bit of captaincy by Jardine to separate them. Noting Nayudu's penchant for attacking the off side, he moved a man from square leg to cover point, whereupon the Indian captain tried to play a ball from Clark to the vacant space on the on side, missed and was adjudged lbw.

India were all out for 219 and England, profiting from several missed chances, were comfortably placed at 143/3 when Jardine came to the wicket. He began confidently, stroking three boundaries past mid-on, and although he soon lost Langridge, he found a willing partner in the debutant Valentine. Together they took the score to 294/4 at the close with Jardine on 53.

On the Sunday, the demand for tickets was so great that thousands were locked out of the ground and seats were eagerly snapped up at five times their proper value. Jardine only added seven to his score before losing his off stump to Mohammad Nissar, India's best bowler with 5-90, but Valentine continued to attack and his swashbuckling 136 was primarily responsible for England's total of 438. India started their second innings badly, losing both openers to Clark for 21, but Amarnath was in sparkling form, reaching his fifty in as many minutes with ten boundaries. Seventy not out at tea, he continued to flog the bowling to all parts, so much so that Jardine struggled to set a field. Well supported by Nayudu, who was handicapped by a painful left hand, he reached his century before the close. As the ground descended into pandemonium, Nayudu, having completed a single, left his crease to congratulate Amarnath, overlooking the fact that the ball wasn't yet dead. The ball was returned by the outfielder to wicketkeeper Elliott, who took off the bails and was about to appeal when Jardine signalled to him to desist.

There were amazing scenes at the close. After being congratulated by Jardine, Amarnath was mobbed by hundreds as he reached the pavilion. Responding to the crowd's repeated demand for an appearance, he eventually emerged to acknowledge the cheers and a gold cup was presented to him in commemoration of his great feat by the Hindu Gymkhana.

At 159/2 overnight, India were confident they could save the match. Another large crowd watched Amarnath and Nayudu take the score to 207/2 before both were out in quick succession, the former to a brilliant diving catch at fine leg by Nichols. His departure opened the floodgates, and the rest of the batting was swept away by the destructive force of the England attack led by Nichols, who returned match figures of 8-108.

Although England needed only 40 to win, Jardine was taking no chances. Observing the deterioration in the weather, he instructed his opening batsmen to play a few shots and, led by Barnett, they duly delivered, winning by nine wickets. Nayudu was dignified in defeat, declaring his team had learnt a lot, while Jardine was equally diplomatic in return. Not only did he play a personal tribute to the 'able charming captain of the Indian team, Major Nayudu', he also waxed lyrical about the sportsmanship and impartiality of the large crowds.

From Bombay Jardine missed his team's game in Poona to enjoy several days shooting. *The Times of India* devoted considerable coverage to his hunting exploits and the compliments he received from many distinguished European and Indian spectators when he returned home with a prized trophy.

His absence in Poona caused considerable resentment with the locals. That resentment in many ways reflected the extreme disappointment at missing out on his presence, since MCC without Jardine was akin to the Indian nationalist movement without Gandhi.

Like Bradman in England, Jardine's cult status was such that he attracted vast crowds all over India, be it in the street, at practice or in the middle. The esteem he inspired was manifest in the warmth of the reception accorded him whenever he went in to bat. The fact that a singular man like Jardine could cope with all this attention was helped by his genuine love of India and its cricketing culture of decorum and deference, in stark contrast with the rough and tumble of Australia. (His experience of these two countries proved similar to that of one of his successors, Mike Brearley.) Appreciating that India had some way to travel on their cricketing odyssey, Jardine encouraged them at every stage, the sincerity of his words being such that he avoided the risk of sounding patronising.

India's defeat at Bombay and the dropping of five players for the second Test laid bare all too clearly the divisions within Indian cricket. After dissatisfaction with his leadership in the first Test, there was an attempted coup against Nayudu's captaincy in favour of Wazir Ali, and the absence of any Bengali representation in the Calcutta Test led to many spectators boycotting the match.

Winning the toss, England recovered from a shaky start with three batsmen being hit to close at 257/5, Langridge making 70 and Jardine, batting in his most obdurate style, 42 not out. He was dismissed for 61 the following morning, one of three wickets to fall in quick succession, before a ninth-wicket stand of 70 between Verity and Townsend restored their fortunes. A total of 403 looked all the more formidable when Clark and Nichols once again troubled the Indian batsmen, taking three quick wickets and forcing Dilawar Hussain, the big, bald wicketkeeper, to retire hurt after the latter struck him on the head. He returned swathed in a large bandage to make a rumbustious 59 before he was caught by Jardine, one of three catches he held in the innings.

All out for 247, India were forced to follow on. Needing to bat through the final day on a wearing pitch with all their wickets intact, they looked destined for defeat at 88/4. Merchant and Nayudu dug in either side of lunch in the face of Jardine's constant bowling changes till a smart catch off Verity by the England captain disposed of the former and Verity trapped the latter lbw. Once again, the home side were indebted to another adventurous fifty from the valiant Hussain, so that by the time they were all out for 237, they were safe.

From Calcutta, MCC travelled by train to Benares to play the Maharajkumar of Vizianagram's XI. Vizianagram was a minor chieftain who left his home in southern India and moved to Benares in Uttar Pradesh following a quarrel with his nephew. A bitter rival of the Maharaja of Patiala, he rose to prominence by organising a tour to Ceylon and parts of India in 1930/31 and underwriting the tour to England in 1932, a rise sealed by his friendship with Willingdon. A Machiavellian schemer, he was appointed vice-captain of the 1932 tour to England, despite his limitations as a cricketer, and although he later withdrew, he sealed his ambition when named as captain of the 1936 tour of England.

Arriving at Benares after a 12-hour journey, MCC were expecting a day off only to discover that the match was due to start at midday against a side containing the best of India. Fielding first on a matting wicket, Nichols, Clark and Townsend were soon into their stride, causing mayhem among the home team before Jardine took Clark off, the one time he eased up all tour, quite possibly to save the blushes of Vizianagram, who, batting at No.7, made 17. Recovering from 67/7 to 124 all out, his side struck back by bowling MCC out for 111, Mohammad Nissar taking 6-60 in a spell of sustained hostility. Only Valentine with a dashing 53 looked comfortable.

Batting again, Vizianagram's XI made 140 in damp conditions which affected the bowlers' run-ups, but when Jardine called for sawdust there was none available. Requiring 154 for victory, MCC suffered another poor start, losing their first three wickets for 23. Jardine and Human survived to stumps and, after a night of excessive hospitality, the captain continued in defiant mood the next morning till given out lbw to Nayudu for 36, one of three contentious decisions given by Frank Tarrant. With Nayudu taking 4-24, MCC slid to defeat by 14 runs, their first and only loss of the tour.

Delighted with the result, Vizianagram never ceased reminding everyone thereafter that he was the only Indian to beat Jardine, who looked the soul of disappointment amid the celebrations. His refusal to come out of the pavilion to acknowledge the cheering crowds may well have reflected his dissatisfaction with the staging of the match. According to Ricketts, the accommodation was disgraceful, the atmosphere unpleasant and the conduct of the Maharaja selfish, especially his unwillingness to play local players, contrary to the expressed wishes of the BCCI.

Prior to the third Test at Madras, Jardine caused ructions by objecting to the appointment of Tarrant as umpire. At issue was his performance in MCC's games all tour, and the feeling that he was biased against them, either because he was an Australian or because he'd coached many Indian players. (He also had lucrative links with a number of the Indian princes through his dealings in high-priced race horses.) Reluctant to have him officiating in the first Test, the tourists' mood darkened when, in the games against Vizianagram's XI and the Nawab of Moin-ud-Dowlah's XI, an inordinate number of lbw decisions were given against them. In the latter match, Ricketts reported that they'd been deprived of victory 'by the amazing conduct of the umpire [Frank Tarrant] who altered his watch during the tea interval with the obvious intention of allowing the home side to save the match which it did, the last wicket playing out time'.[11]

In addition to these concerns, Tarrant came into conflict with Jardine in the second Test. Alarmed by the physical damage posed by Clark's bouncer, he warned Jardine that unless his fast bowler desisted from bowling short, he would stop him bowling. In response Jardine told him he would stop him umpiring and he did precisely that. He notified MCC of his dissatisfaction with Tarrant and the BCCI replaced him with the former Worcestershire player John Higgins – Jardine didn't trust Indian umpires – much to Tarrant's disgust. 'Where are the sportsmen of 1934, if the captain of the MCC cannot take lbw decisions with good grace?' he said in an interview with *The Times of India*. 'A world-renowned cricketer does not, while umpiring, give decisions against his better knowledge. He has a reputation to protect.'[12] According to the *Sind Observer*, an Indian nationalist paper, Tarrant's suspension was symptomatic of the spirit in which Jardine conducted his captaincy. He seemed to feel that he was an imperial general on a conquering expedition.

Jardine further inflamed matters when he publicly disputed Tarrant's claim that he was a world-renowned cricketer, declaring that no cricketer merited such a description if they hadn't played in a Test match. His comment, and one from a European, which referred to 'Nayudu and his band of assassins who followed Jardine over the country', alienated the Indian team enough for them to absent themselves from a dinner hosted by the Madras Cricket Club, the hosts for the final Test.

Winning the toss yet again, England were given a perfect start with an opening stand of 111 by Walters and Bakewell, and they appeared well set at 170/2 before Amar Singh, uninterested for much of the series, suddenly perked up. Aided by a responsive pitch, his swing played havoc with the middle order, and at 208/7 England were floundering. Had Verity been caught on 2, they would have struggled to score 250; as it was, he survived in partnership with Jardine till stumps and the next morning they took their partnership to 97, Jardine scoring 65 and Verity 42, out of their total of 335.

For the second match in succession, India suffered a nasty injury early in their innings when opener Naoomal Jeoomal was hit over the left eye by a short ball from Clark. Bleeding profusely, he was carried off on a stretcher to play no further part in the match. The injury riled the crowd who barracked Clark whenever he pitched short and, later, when fielding out in the deep, a large stone was thrown in his direction. At the end of the over, the volatile Clark walked towards the boundary as an anxious Jardine looked on, but on reaching it he merely placed the stone on the ground before returning to the middle.

There was further tension when the young Yuvraj of Patiala was forced to take evasive action against Clark and Merchant took a nasty blow on the chin from Nichols. Jardine allowed him to retire to have stiches inserted, but on his return, he quickly recalled his fast bowlers. Unsettled by pace, India succumbed to Verity, who took 7-49, and were all out for 145.

Electing to bat again, England, through a century from Walters and an unbeaten 35 from Jardine, were able to declare at 261/7, setting their opponents 452 to win. Once again, Jardine placed his faith in Verity and Langridge and they duly responded by taking nine wickets between them as England emerged victors by 202 runs to complete a 2-0 win in the rubber.

With these injuries to the Indian batsmen in mind, MCC sailed to Ceylon under something of a cloud. They won their first match against Ceylon by ten wickets, but their victory was marred by an unpleasant incident in the home side's second innings when Marriott's peculiar run-up evoked some ribaldry from the students' enclosure. Taking exception to these comments, Jardine at once stopped Marriott from bowling and asked the umpire to speak to the crowd. Both the umpire and the opposing captain appealed to their sense of sportsmanship, but, a few overs later, when Clark was bowling a mild form of Bodyline, there was more barracking. After the tea interval a posse of police was stationed in certain parts of the ground, and eight of the alleged offenders were ejected, provoking hostile editorials in the island's press. Black flags greeted the team as they drove from Colombo to Galle in antiquated taxis for a one-day fixture. The vehicle carrying Jardine and three others repeatedly broke down and because he refused to change cars, the 11am start was postponed to 2pm when a furious MCC captain came face to face with a restless crowd. The match was later abandoned as a draw.

There was further trouble in the match against a Ceylon and India XI at Colombo, where the MCC flag was hauled down from the pavilion. After the tourists were all out for 155 in their first innings, they fought back, taking four wickets for 62 by the close, but the dismissal of Vernon Schokman, who hit his wicket after being struck on the jaw by a Clark bouncer, angered the crowd.

Having established a lead of 51 on first innings, MCC then subsided to 78 all out. With their last pair at the crease, Clark raised eyebrows when he damaged the pitch by digging his heel into the same spot where a good length ball would pitch. His antics earned him a rebuke from the umpire and at the end of the innings Valentine, leading the side in Jardine's absence, visited the opposition dressing-room to apologise to his opposite number, admitting that he'd never seen anything like it before.

Needing 130 to win, the home side reached 81/2 at the close and appeared on the cusp of victory. Crowds celebrated a likely triumph in the street but their optimism proved premature, since the next day MCC showed all their fighting quality. In front of a capacity crowd, Clark, Nichols and Verity – thrust into the attack at the behest of Jardine, who sent Valentine a note from the pavilion – proved so dominant that they bowled their side to an eight-run victory. 'I am glad in every way that we are cutting short our stay in Colombo,' Jardine wrote to Findlay on the eve of the team's departure from the island. 'The CCA [Ceylon Cricket Association] has just fallen into the hands of the Ceylonese and the treatment generally accorded to us has annoyed the Europeans very much. A great contrast to India.'[13] The Clark incident, he reported, was unfortunate but the locals weren't friendly before that and too much was made of it.

The team returned to India to conclude their tour with a special charity match at Bombay for the Viceroy's Earthquake Fund following the Quetta earthquake. The match not only petered out in a dull draw, it failed to attract public support amid Muslim and Hindu anger that the local team was monopolised by Europeans, and they boycotted a banquet in Jardine's honour. Jardine's speech at the Taj Mahal Hotel drew sustained applause as he paid glowing tribute to his opponents, calling Nayudu the most amiable captain he'd played against and Merchant the soundest batsman in India. He also predicted that Indian cricket would lead the world in another decade, and when that day came he would ask his hosts to pause for a moment and look gratefully to the MCC, whose proud boast was that they taught others to play cricket better than themselves.

Despite the tour's failure to make any real profit because of the huge cost in staging fixtures, especially in the provinces, it had been successful in placing the game in India on firmer foundations and cementing imperial links. According to Ricketts, the civic welcome on MCC's arrival was the first one accorded to Europeans for a very long time and they were given civic receptions in all the larger cities. Delighted to be back in the land of his birth and fêted wherever he went, Jardine cut a more relaxed, approachable figure than in Australia the previous winter. 'In India the tour, if I may say so, has been a very great success – my mailbag is extraordinary and amusing,' he wrote to Findlay at the end of it.

'From the European secretary of a leper settlement to Congress leaders a chorus of praise has gone up and not one single nasty letter (shades of Australia!) We have been told time and again that we have been worth far more than all the round table conferences – this is not very high praise but is intended as such.

'Their Excellencies are extraordinarily good to us and perhaps they should not be named if it is likely to give the least flavour of politics to the tour – disoriented Indian opinion is apt to say that anything which goes down well is a political stunt!'[14]

A passionate believer in the imperial ideal, Jardine found much to admire about India, not least the conduct of his opponents and the sportsmanship of the crowd, in strong contrast to Australia. He marked Amarnath's century in the first Test with a warm handshake, he congratulated P.S. Ramachandran for his bowling for Madras Federation with a pat on the back, he invited Patiala to play for MCC and commended Vizianagram for his leadership prowess, which in reality was very limited.

Yet for all his warm words, Jardine's transition from warrior to diplomat went only so far. Not only did he remain an uncompromising adversary on the field with his ruthless will to win, he continued to speak his mind when necessary. In addition to his tussles with the Viceroy, the umpires and the Ceylonese crowd, two other instances stand out. At a ball held in honour of the Governor of the United Provinces, Sir Malcolm Hailey, Jardine refused to have the first dance with Lady Hailey, the beautiful daughter of a Russian count, waltzing off with someone else instead. When reproached by the military secretary for this breach of protocol, he replied haughtily that in all his travels around the world he'd never been ordered to dance with anybody. Then, in response to a comment from the president of the Nagpur municipality that MCC was better able to foster Anglo-Indian relations than the Round Table Conference, a series of peace conferences called by the British government to discuss the future constitution of India, Jardine raised a laugh with his barbed reply. Noting that a team of Round Table Conference delegates would in all likelihood draw a good gate, he doubted whether they could accept the umpire's decision.

Although their opponents had failed to live up to expectation, MCC's experimental side had acquitted itself well, winning the Test series comprehensively and losing only one match on their 34-match tour. Batting with commendable consistency, Jardine stood out as the premier batsman on either side and he led with his usual authority without quite inspiring the same devotion from his team as in Australia the previous year. At Madras, like a general at war, he inspected the spikes and even the laces of each cricketer's shoes and before the game he was seen issuing orders to his players who stood in a single file like troops on a mission. According to Jack Hobbs, who covered the tour for *The Star*, its greatest highlight was Jardine's magnificent captaincy; he protected his pacemen by not over-bowling them, he set his fields with great foresight and excelled as a fighter, but he expected a tad too much from his team. To Walters, whose sloppy fielding made him a particular target for his captain's ire, he came across as rather soulless and lacking in warmth. 'I never understood the fellow,' he told David Frith years later. 'During the tour he seemed always to have a large book tucked under his arm. When the Indian officials and others lined up as he walked into a reception, one of those in the group was an uncle. You could tell, too, for he had the same huge nose as Douglas. Douglas just walked straight past him.'

Walters recalled another gripe against Jardine. Against Amar Singh, who cut the ball at speed off the matting pitch, Walters was playing off the back foot with great determination. Uncharacteristically, Jardine was upset and was bowled second ball, lunging forward. 'He said he was sick of watching me play back all the time,' said Walters with something of a smirk.[15]

His singular personality diminished his captaincy, according to Levett. 'Douglas Jardine had got used to the idea of demanding and receiving support from his fast bowlers in leg theory when dependent upon the exceptional accuracy of people like Larwood, Voce and Bowes. When we went to India, he failed to appreciate that a bowler like Morris Nichols was a natural in the sense that he could swing the ball both ways but he could not be sure which way the ball would move. As a wicketkeeper, I could see the problem which Jardine created by insisting that Morris should bowl on one side of the wicket all the time whereas, if left to his own devices, he could cause the batsman difficulty precisely because he varied his attack. Jardine didn't take kindly to it when I pointed this out to him.'[16]

In Arthur Mitchell's opinion, the captain had little time for the lesser bowlers. 'He would set fields for the second-string bowlers and say: "Bowl to that." He did not take them quietly on one side, talk tactics with them, and make the most of their talents … He was quite intolerant of the second best.'[17]

In contrast, Valentine wrote that Jardine was 'an absolutely dedicated cricketer and to me the best tactical leader I've played under. As a leader of men, he expected everyone in the side to do exactly as he wanted them to do. I don't think he understood that every person or player has different characteristics; some need a bit of encouragement, others have to be driven to get the best out of them. I was fortunate as I had a good tour and got on very well with Jardine.'[18]

Another to sing his praises was John Human, who often was billeted with him. 'To me Douglas was a wonderful man and a credit to Winchester and Oxford. He was always writing to my parents letting them know how I was getting on …

'On the field I have never known a better skipper who could sum up the opposition very quickly and could instruct his bowlers where to bowl. It took at least a month to know Douglas and being with him all the time I always thought he suffered from an inferiority complex to strangers or it could be shyness. Although he had many critics, I was one of his supporters.'[19]

From an Indian perspective, Amarnath later called him the best captain he ever met, while Nayudu found him a tough fighter, a shrewd tactician whose knowledge of the game was very profound. 'With a height of six feet two inches, he was a commanding figure on the field. He was a strict disciplinarian and would not tolerate any opposition, defiance or nonsense. He was aloof and unsentimental. He commanded loyalty rather than won it.'[20]

While the team sailed from Bombay for home on 10 March, Jardine stayed on in India for another six weeks to hunt game in Mysore, Benares and Nepal with Vizianagram, knowing full well that he'd played his last game for England.

## Endnotes:

1  Lord Willingdon to King George V, 19 November 1933, Royal Archives, Windsor PS/PSO/GV/C/P/522/373

2  Mihir Bose, *A History of Indian Cricket*, p83

3  Ramachandra Guha, *A Corner of a Foreign Field*, p210

4  *Manager's Report of MCC Tour to India 1933-34*, MCC Archives

5  Ibid

6  Bose, *A History of Indian Cricket*, p89

7  Douglas Jardine to William Findlay, 9 March 1934, MCC Archives

8  *Manager's Report of MCC Tour to India, 1933-34*, MCC Archives

9  E.W.C. Ricketts to William Findlay, 1 March 1934, MCC Archives

10 Marshall, *Gentlemen and Players*, p112
11 *Manager's Report of MCC Tour to India 1933-34*, MCC Archives
12 *Times of India*, 12 February 1934
13 Douglas Jardine to William Findlay, 28 February 1934, MCC Archives
14 Ibid, 9 March 1934
15 Quoted in Frith, *Bodyline Autopsy*, p390
16 Marshall, *Gentlemen and Players*, p112
17 Alan Hill, *Hedley Verity*, p78
18 Douglas, *Douglas Jardine: Spartan Cricketer,* p175
19 Ibid, p176
20 Quoted in Guha, *A Corner of a Foreign Field*, p220

# CHAPTER 10

# THE RETREAT FROM BODYLINE

ALTHOUGH JARDINE'S use of Bodyline had made him a hugely divisive figure in Australia, he returned to a euphoric reception from those who'd appointed him. At a celebratory tour dinner at the Dorchester that July, the new president of MCC, Lord Hailsham, called his leadership in Australia magnificent. 'Jardine is probably the best captain in the world today and his gallant band of sportsmen has worthily upheld England's reputation.'

Days after Jardine returned from Australia, he went to Lord's, dressed in top hat and tails, to submit his tour report; later he, along with Larwood, Voce and Warner, was interviewed by the sub-committee set up to investigate the tour. His account, rather than Warner's, formed the basis of MCC's reply of 12 June to the Australian Board's attempt to amend Law 48 outlawing deliveries intended to intimidate or injure batsmen. According to MCC, the Australian Board's use of the term Bodyline was misleading – it was merely fast leg theory – and they rejected any term implying a deliberate attack by the bowler on the batsman. They also dismissed the idea of a new law as impractical, since it placed too much authority in the hands of the umpire and expressed their concern about barracking. Unless it was stopped or greatly modified, it was difficult to see how representative matches could continue.

MCC's rebuke followed a bitter interview given by Larwood to the *Sunday Express*, in which he castigated the venom of Australian crowds and the failure of the Australian Board to control them. His comments touched a raw nerve there, not least the implication that Bradman lacked courage against fast bowling, and enhanced the Board's determination to press their case for a change in the law. Their hopes lay in the capable hands of Sir Alexander Hore-Ruthven and Dr Robert Macdonald, the residual representative of the Australian Board in England.

On his return to Australia from leave, Hore-Ruthven wrote to the Dominions Secretary J.H. Thomas in June 1933 to inform him of the deep sense of injustice felt there about the reporting of Bodyline in the British media. 'I confess that until I arrived out here, I was under the impression that the Australians' attitude with regard to Jardine and Larwood was not altogether warranted, but since I have been back and have had opportunities of discussing the question with sound, reasonable men, I am forced to the conclusion that the Australian case had far more justification than one would have been led to suppose at the other side of the world.'[1]

Having alluded to the near-unanimous view that England had flouted the spirit of the game, he continued: 'It is also felt that the initial mistake lay in the selection, as Captain, of a man of Jardine's temperament and reputed antipathy towards Australia which had not escaped notice in the previous tour, and that it is

213

hardly "cricket" on the part of the MCC to allot Australia all the blame for the trouble which subsequently arose as a result of their unfortunate selection.'[2]

He concluded by appealing to Thomas to help end the growing anti-English sentiments in Australia by encouraging the British media to adopt a more balanced view.

Thomas's response isn't entirely clear but, as an imperialist keen to keep Australia onside, it seems likely that he would have conveyed the gist of Hore-Ruthven's missive to his cabinet colleague, Lord Hailsham, the Secretary of State for War and president-elect of MCC. Hailsham in turn would probably have acquainted his colleagues on the MCC committee with these sentiments as they subsequently strove to make peace with Australia without letting down Jardine too badly.

Macdonald, the former Queensland captain, had a great deal to do with shaping the final settlement. Dismayed by MCC's unbending response of 12 June, he subsequently discovered in conversations with Findlay that the MCC secretary was unaware of Jardine's switch to Bodyline in the immediate aftermath of Woodfull's injury in the third Test. 'If that incident at Adelaide had been published here, Jardine's mentality and ruthlessness would have been remarkably revealed to the English people,' he wrote. 'The veil of silence was drawn over it by the English press.'[3] Sensing that the British government was keen to heal the rift with Australia and conscious of the likely financial losses accruing to English cricket should the Australian tour of 1934 be cancelled, Macdonald resolved to adopt an uncompromising position with MCC over Bodyline. He was helped by the change of opinion towards Bodyline as its physical damage became more evident during the summer of 1933.

Aside from the West Indians, Constantine and Martindale, the main exponent of Bodyline was Bowes. Having infuriated the crowd at Cardiff by hitting Glamorgan's Maurice Turnbull and J.C. Clay, a tailender, at the end of May, Bowes caused further uproar by knocking Lancashire's Frank Watson senseless at Old Trafford, followed by Nottinghamshire's Walter Keeton at Trent Bridge. Apart from the human cost, these injuries discredited the cause of Bodyline, especially since England claimed in Australia that their object wasn't to hit the batsman. 'Poor old Johnnie Clay woke up in severe pain the morning after the Yorkshire match and read in the morning paper that Douglas Jardine had been cheered in a match at Lord's because he had brought the Ashes back,' declared Turnbull at a dinner of the London Welsh Society. 'But the way he brought them back was to introduce Bodyline, and that more than rankled a bit.' His words won him a standing ovation and it was partly down to his dislike of Bodyline that he declined an invitation to tour India under Jardine that winter.

In the Varsity Match at Lord's, Cambridge fast bowler Ken Farnes, bowling Bodyline, hit several of his opponents, including Peter Oldfield, the Oxford No.11, bowled off his jaw, and opener David Townsend, who broke his wicket after being struck on the neck. Seven MCC members, including the cricket journalist Sir Home Gordon, wrote to *The Times* to denounce such tactics – even Larwood hadn't bowled Bodyline at the lower order – and warn that they risked destroying the spirit of the game.

Three weeks later, during the second Test against the West Indies at Old Trafford, public opinion took a further turn when Constantine and Martindale bowled Bodyline, injuring Hammond in the process. *Wisden* called this kind of bowling 'objectionable' and Arthur Gilligan confessed that after watching Bodyline for two days, he was sick and tired of it. Warner, no longer a Test selector, also spoke out. Writing to the *Daily Telegraph*, he regretted that West Indies had resorted to Bodyline, which he described as intimidation that often gave rise to serious injury. He accepted that Bodyline was legal, but questioned its value if it generated controversy and bred ill-feeling, as it had between England and Australia. Should it continue, the courtesy of combat would disappear from the game and would be replaced by anger, hatred and retribution.

Equally significant was the attitude of Nottinghamshire captain Arthur Carr. Having announced his intention in pre-season to use Bodyline against other counties, he began to have second thoughts when facing Leicestershire's Haydon Smith at the end of July. Subjected to a barrage of fearsome bouncers, one of which hit him, and fearing that someone might be killed, he and his opposite number, Eddie Dawson, mutually agreed to a Bodyline pact.

When Jardine's account of the 1932/33 tour, *In Quest of the Ashes*, appeared in August, his refusal to accept that Bodyline posed any harm to the batsman's safety brought a sharp riposte from Neville Cardus.

'Jardine does not face Australia's bodyline case that at least one ball in every over from Larwood was aimed at the body/head.

'Jardine maintains that Larwood bowled at the leg stump, but omits to explain why he set only two fieldsmen on the off. He also evades the important question of why Hobbs regarded bodyline as venomous, and why thousands in Australia – not all hooligans – should have mistaken a ball on the leg stump for a high kicker at the batsman's head.

'Jardine meets Australia's charges against Larwood with an accent of contempt, and merely dismisses them as unthinkable. Jardine does not realise that the recent unprecedented intensity of barracking was provoked because the crowds, rightly or wrongly, regarded Larwood as bowling at their favourite batsmen's bodies.'[4]

Having previously encountered Sir Stanley Jackson, the president of MCC, on 11 July and discovered that he strongly opposed both Bodyline and Jardine's leadership, Macdonald met him again at Lord's on 31 July, along with his colleagues Hailsham, Hawke and Findlay. There, in pivotal deliberations, he informed them that Australia would only tour in 1934 provided MCC guaranteed in advance that any form of intimidatory bowling of the 1932/33 variety would be outlawed. Yet appreciative of MCC's need for a face-saving formula by which they could renounce Bodyline without disowning Jardine, he advised the Australian Board to avoid the word Bodyline when they replied to MCC. His advice was readily accepted and the moderation of the Australian Board's cable of 22 September allowed MCC in their reply of 9 October to comply with their request that bowling which directly attacked the batsman wouldn't be used in England in 1934. 'The terms of settlement are such as to leave no sore feeling on either side,' pronounced *The Times* … 'It is clear then that MR JARDINE, who is once again leading a team on their behalf, retains their full confidence. On the other hand, the particular kind of fast leg bowling that has been the source of controversy is likely to be dropped.'[5]

At a joint meeting of the Advisory County Cricket Conference and the Board of Control for Test Matches, attended by the county captains, that November, MCC accepted that any direct attack by the bowler upon the batsman would be declared an offence against the spirit of cricket. The Australian Board, perturbed perhaps by Larwood's continued threat to bowl Bodyline in 1934, pushed for something stronger, but the most that MCC would countenance was a formal understanding that the Ashes series of 1934 would be played in the right spirit. The Australian Board, now under the moderating influence of their new chairman, Aubrey Oxlade, accepted the reality of the situation and confirmed by an 8-5 majority on 14 December that their players would leave Australia on 9 March.

The other contentious issue that needed resolving was the future of the England captaincy. No fan of Jardine, Macdonald told Findlay in a letter in October 1933 that if he continued as England captain the Tests would be played as a 'veiled vendetta'. He described Bodyline methods as wholly Teutonic and linked Jardine's win-at-any-costs mentality with Attila, the marauding leader of the Huns.

Macdonald had an ally in Hore-Ruthven who'd come to fully appreciate the lasting damage wrought by Bodyline. Desperate to restore Anglo-Australian relations, he wrote to Warner in confidence in November to ask him to use his influence with MCC to ensure that Jardine wasn't appointed captain for the 1934 series.

Warner replied to him on 3 January 1934, thankful that the rift between MCC and the Australian Board had been settled. 'The Press and Public will give the team a good reception. The real trouble is Jardine. Is he to be captain? At present I say "No" unless he makes a most generous public gesture of friendliness and then I am not sure I would trust him. He is a queer fellow. When he sees a cricket ground with an Australian on it he goes mad! He rose to his present position on my shoulders, and of his attitude to me I do not care to speak. It is hoped he may retire at the end of the Indian Tour, but in many quarters here – where they do not know the truth – he is a bit of a hero. If he is captain in the First Test and is not friendly, he will not capt. in the 2nd but I would not have him at all, as I do not believe in honouring a man who has done untold harm to cricket and its spirit and traditions. His book is full of contemptuous and disparaging remarks of Australia and Australians, and in his chapter on the IVth Test, at Brisbane, he actually has the impertinence to justify his questioning of the umpires' decisions; and he the captain of England!! But, please, keep my own opinion on DRJ to yourself.'[6]

Hore-Ruthven wrote again in a letter marked *Private* and *Personal* on 5 February.

My Dear Plum,

The Jardine question is very important and from what I can see of the signs out here the only thing that could disturb the harmony which players and public are all anxious to maintain, would be to put Jardine in charge again. The whole atmosphere will be altered at once if he is made Captain. The players will go on the field with the feeling of irritation and suspicion, and it will play into the hands of the extreme element here who wanted to demand guarantees that Jardine would not be Captain and that body-line bowling would not be allowed, and they will at once say that 'Gentlemen's Agreements' are no good to them, and in future we must have the written guarantees. And, moreover, the sensational section of the Australian Press will make the most of it and start the controversy all over again.

I know the difficulties of not appearing to let him [Jardine] down, but the question is so vital, not only from the point of view of cricket, but of the friendly feeling between the two countries, that some excuse must be found for leaving him out. As, once the sore is opened again it is going to be very difficult to heal, and all the soothing syrup we have administered of late will be wasted.

We can't get away from the fact that the root of the trouble was the selection of a man of Jardine's temperament as Captain, so why go on pouring sand into the machine until in the end you smash it up?

You may think that I am exaggerating the feeling which Jardine's captaincy would give rise to, but it has been my business to make a careful study of Australian mentality for the last six years and I have no doubt as to the repercussions this would cause on men's minds out here, and these are not only my personal opinions, but are shared by many who are far better judges than I. So I think it is best to speak one's mind openly, and I hope you will forgive me for being so frank.[7]

Before Hore-Ruthven's second letter reached him, Warner conveyed his concerns to Findlay on 22 February.

Of course, if Jardine were captain, it might be awkward, but your conversation the other day led me to understand that Jardine would be required by MCC to give certain guarantees which would appreciably ease the situation. I believe that you realise that I was his best friend and supporter. I have no axe to grind and my objections to his methods and manners was because I considered them contrary to the ideals and interests of cricket and the prestige of MCC. I believe that history will find me guiltless of a wrong appreciation of the situation. I do not consider that Jardine – on his Australian form – can produce the friendly relations and happy spirit which MCC so urgently desire in the coming Test matches and which are so very vital for the good of the game.[8]

Others within the MCC hierarchy felt more or less the same. On 16 February Lord Belper, a member of MCC's advisory committee, publicly denounced Bodyline at the Nottinghamshire County Cricket Club dinner, and assured his audience that it wouldn't be used that summer against Australia. Prior to this, Sir Stanley Jackson, presiding over Yorkshire's annual meeting and alluding to his recent trip to India to watch MCC, denounced the closeness of the leg-side fielders to the batsman, since they upset his attention. 'Had I been the batsman,' he averred, 'I would not have stood it.'

Sir Stanley spoke out again when addressing the Press Club dinner in mid-March. Admitting to some anxiety about the forthcoming Australian tour, he said it was absolutely crucial that cricket in 1934 showed that the recent misunderstandings and differences had been consigned to history. 'We must also show that the former friendliness, good fellowship and goodwill are re-established. Without that cricket is not worth playing.' The fact that Jackson, a leading MCC powerbroker, was about to be appointed chairman of selectors strongly suggests that had Jardine been chosen as captain against Australia, his appointment would have come with strings attached.

MCC's reservations about Jardine's ongoing feud with Australia weren't unfounded. His account of the Bodyline tour, while more measured than Larwood's, did little to soothe bruised egos down under. In typically forthright fashion he defended Bodyline as legitimate, criticised the Australian batsmen's technical deficiencies playing it, and decried the Australian crowds for their crude partisanship. He also berated the Australian Board for failing to curb the rowdiness and for calling his tactics unsporting, comments that inevitably jarred. Bradman spoke for many by declaring Jardine's account biased. He overlooked the ecstatic reception the Sydney crowd gave to Larwood for his 98 in the fifth Test and he failed to realise that his own unrelenting attitude did much to provoke the crowd's hostility. 'If the MCC wants offensive barracking to cease in Australia, it has the remedy in its own hands,' wrote Arthur Mailey. 'Don't send Douglas Jardine out again.'[9]

His spat with the Australian Frank Tarrant and the other controversies at the end of the India tour exacerbated the reservations against him. 'Jardine is a wonderful captain and a great leader, but both here and in England much satisfaction will be expressed if he does not lead England in the forthcoming Tests,' wrote former Australian batsman Charlie Macartney in *Truth*.[10] At the farewell dinner for Woodfull's team, Bill Kelly, the manager of the 1930 Australian tour to England, lambasted Jardine for his tactics and when a large crowd gathered at Sydney railway station to give the players a rousing send-off the suggestion from one fan that they cheer Jardine was met with silence.

As press speculation about Jardine's future continued to mount during the latter part of the Indian tour, he kept his own counsel, but, according to Arthur Gilligan in the *News*

*Chronicle*, he'd indicated before departing for India that he wouldn't captain against Australia in 1934; then the following February he apparently wrote to MCC to confirm this – just when he'd decided to extend his stay in India to go hunting, which meant that he would miss the start of the English season. In early March he cabled Surrey to inform them that because of his limited availability for the coming season he would resign the captaincy, and, on 31 March, he sent a cable to the *Evening Standard*, declaring that he had 'neither the intention nor the desire to play cricket against Australia this summer'.

Despite Warner's scheming, there is no evidence to show that Jardine was about to be deposed, but the terseness of his press statement reflected his bitterness at the way MCC had caved in to Australian demands over Bodyline. Again, there is no positive proof that Jardine would have been forced to abandon Bodyline, but that seemed the logical assumption behind MCC's assurance to the Australian Board that the 1934 series would be played in the right spirit and the subsequent comments by Belper, Jackson and Findlay. The latter told Warner that MCC would want guarantees from Jardine before reappointing him against Australia and for a proud man such as Jardine, who continued to believe in the legitimacy of Bodyline, that would have been a humiliation too far.

That said, Jardine's decision to retire wasn't simply the result of Bodyline. On a wider front there was his disillusion with the growing commercialisation of Test cricket. Although he played cricket as hard as any professional, he was essentially a traditionalist who revered the game's rarefied character – its pastoral setting, its close-knit friendships, its lavish hospitality and its aristocratic code of courtesy. Much less appealing were the disturbing new trends of the inter-war era: the greater emphasis of money, the raucous partisanship of the crowds, especially in Australia, the intrusive power of the mass media and the cult of the individual above the interests of the team.

There were also personal considerations. With marriage looming, the constant absences from home seemed less enticing, and with an ambitious father-in-law who expected his daughter to be kept in some style, the need for financial security was paramount. A lucrative £5,000 contract to write for the *Evening Standard* on the forthcoming Anglo-Australian series wasn't to be dismissed lightly.

The manner of his resignation failed to impress Warner who thought his cable – written for public consumption – was in direct contradiction of MCC's so-called promises to Australia. 'Everyone is entitled to his own opinion and is, of course, a free agent in regard to the employment of his spare time, but we greatly regret the tone of Mr Jardine's cable to the *Evening Standard*,' he wrote in *The Cricketer*. 'The MCC have assured the Australians of a warm welcome and an enjoyable visit and on the eve of the Australians' arrival Mr Jardine thinks fit to send a message which, to say the least of it, is discourteous to our visitors and in direct opposition to the wishes publicly expressed by the Club of whose Cricket and Selection Committee he is a member.'[11]

Others were more sympathetic. Raymond Robertson-Glasgow, no advocate of Bodyline, wrote: 'I hope Jardine resigned on his own accord. It would be degrading to think that he was shuffled out from his claims by the miserable show of inconsistency and faintheartedness on the part of Marylebone, which is indicated. The MCC defended his tactics in a bitter controversy, and thus morally pledged themselves to regarding him as the proper and natural choice for captaincy. If pressure has been exerted on him to secure his resignation it is tantamount to a betrayal of his cause, and hoodwinking of the public who followed them in backing Jardine, and upon whom they must rely for financial support.'[12]

According to Bruce Harris in the *Evening Standard*, no other leader combined Jardine's great abilities as a player and captain. 'Jardine's absence will be deplored by tens of thousands of English cricket lovers. It can hardly be doubted that the effect of the so-called bodyline trouble has been to deprive England of her best captain, whose presence in 1934 would have given England a moral advantage over her opponents.'[13]

Similar sentiments were shared by *The Times* cricket correspondent: 'Not so good was the announcement that D.R. Jardine does not see his way to play in any of the Test Matches. He has had a busy, and not a particularly happy, time as captain of England, and he is a free agent to determine how best he may spend what leisure he has. But the fact remains that the game will lack one of the best cricketers in this country, a man of strong personality, and that we would all like to have seen him playing again.'[14]

Even in Australia, the target of Jardine's bitter resignation statement, the reaction was broadly one of disappointment. 'It is a pity, too, because England loses the services of a finished batsman, a splendid fieldsman, and an astute leader,' commented Eric Barbour, the former New South Wales all-rounder, in the *Sydney Mail*. 'Jardine's retirement is inevitable, because his peculiar personality and his methods have clouded the reputation of English cricket, not only in Australia, but in India and in the West Indies.'[15]

'Douglas Jardine will not be captain for the first Test match and putting aside all controversial ideas, Australia should regret his absence,' declared an editorial in *Truth*. 'Jardine, despite all criticism – partial and impartial – is without doubt a great cricket leader, and England can ill afford to lose him.' These words were amply borne out by the fact that it would be another 19 years before the Ashes, lost in 1934, would be won back by England.[16]

While Jardine rarely spoke about his treatment by the MCC, his daughter Fianach later claimed that he felt fully abandoned by them. 'He was never angry about the furore over Bodyline, but, yes, there was this distinct air of sadness more than anything else in that father believed he had done what the MCC had agreed to. He felt that having said one thing, when the going got really difficult the MCC made him the fall-guy.'[17]

Getting to the truth is difficult, since the MCC files on Bodyline disappeared mysteriously during the Second World War. Suspicion fell on Warner, who was in charge at Lord's at that time and who, as chairman of selectors and manager in Australia, had much to conceal; certainly, this was the view of Larwood.

It is true that Warner's diplomatic charm belied his thirst for victory and that, knowing the particular challenge posed by Australia and Bradman in 1932, he sought refuge in someone of Jardine's steely determination to take up the cudgels on behalf of MCC, so much so that when Jardine procrastinated about accepting, he asked Jardine's father to intervene.

Not only that. With victory in mind, Warner gave Jardine the fast bowlers he wanted, including Bowes whom he'd publicly lambasted for intimidatory bowling days earlier at the Oval. Gerald Howat, Warner's biographer, wrote: 'What a fast bowler with a packed leg-side could achieve, he well knew. He had seen it, for instance, when W.B. Burns of Worcestershire had bowled against Middlesex in 1910 … Foster had employed a similar attack in the 1911-12 tour of Australia in which Warner was captain. This much is not in dispute.'[18]

More debatable is whether Warner knew about Jardine's intention to bowl Bodyline in Australia. According to Howat, probably not. 'When the storm broke, his letters to his wife … indicate a surprise which was not feigned.'[19] Gubby Allen claimed that Warner hated Bodyline and tried to persuade Jardine to abandon it, but his refusal to condemn it throughout the tour upset his hosts.

As for the MCC committee, there is little evidence one way or the other to indicate whether they were party to Jardine's plan – probably not is the likely conclusion – but once the alarm bells sounded any scruples they might have had were muffled by the exhilaration of victory. 'Splendid, well played all. My heartiest congratulations,' the president of MCC cabled on hearing of the retention of the Ashes. 'Well Bowled. Congratulations. Marylebone. From the Club.' Throughout the exchange of cables with the Australian Board in 1933, MCC persistently refused to condemn Bodyline and at the Ashes celebration dinner that July, their president, Lord Hailsham, complimented Jardine on his wonderful captaincy in Australia and the team for worthily upholding England's reputation.

These accolades soon looked incongruous when MCC changed tack and excoriated Bodyline. Given the need to clean up the game, restore relations with Australia and ensure that the 1934 tour went ahead, it could be argued that they had little choice, but it is easy to see why Jardine and Larwood felt abandoned by a fickle establishment that appeared devoid of principle.

## Endnotes:

1 Swanton, *Follow On*, p144

2 Ibid, p145

3 Quoted in Ric Sissons and Brian Stoddart, *Cricket and the Empire*, p120

4 *The Guardian*, 17 August 1933

5 *The Times*, 11 October 1933

6 Frith, *Bodyline Autopsy*, p376

7 Howat, *Plum Warner*, p143

8 Ibid, p144

9 *The Sun*, 13 June 1933

10 *Truth*, 18 February 1934

11 *The Cricketer*, 5 May 1934, p1

12 *Liverpool Post*, 2 April 1934

13 *Evening Standard*, 1 April 1934

14 *The Times,* 18 April 1934

15 *Sydney Mail*, 11 April 1934

16 *Truth*, 29 April 1934

17 *Daily Telegraph*, 1 December 2006

18 Howat, *Plum Warner*, p109

19 Ibid, p111

# CHAPTER 11

# OUTCAST

WITH ENGLAND hosting Australia in the first rubber since Bodyline, the *Evening Standard,* appreciating its news value, signed both C.B. Fry and Jardine as cricket writers. With Fry concerned that the recruitment of Jardine might diminish his own role, the editor stipulated that they should produce two very different columns. While Jardine would provide conventional coverage of the Tests, Fry would write a features column which brimmed with classical allusions, literary quotations and sparkling wit and which helped to revolutionise sports writing. Their views received wide coverage, not least in Australia – Jardine also gave a daily seven-minute summary for an Australian radio station on the Tests – helping to increase the paper's circulation. Although outspoken on occasions, especially in his defence of Bodyline and Larwood, Jardine proved admirably impartial in his assessment of the two sides.

In his first article, he criticised the omission of Fingleton and Ironmonger from the touring party, declaring that he'd never met an Australian cricketer with cause to congratulate the Australian Board of Control on its work, least of all its tact.

England, however, had problems of their own, for, aside from Jardine's absence, there was clearly a reluctance by the selectors to pick Larwood and Voce. Weeks before the first Test, Larwood had been summoned to see Sir Julien Cahn, a wealthy Nottinghamshire businessman, philanthropist and cricket enthusiast, who told him that he must apologise to MCC for his bowling in Australia if he wanted to be selected for the Tests that summer. Resentful of the Lord's establishment for their lack of gratitude towards him, Larwood refused and absented himself from the first Test – which England lost – supposedly on grounds of fitness.

   He then added fuel to the fire by writing a ghosted article for the *Sunday Dispatch* in which he attacked those in authority, especially their disowning of Bodyline, and vowed not to play against Australia that summer. His stance was supported by Carr, his county captain, and Jardine, who advocated his return for the second Test. Declaring that much of the comment written about him amounted to ignorance and sensationalism, he expressed the hope that a charming fellow and a great cricketer should get a fair deal to which anyone was entitled under any rules of elementary fairness. 'To my mind, there is a genuine danger of Larwood being forced into a grossly unfair position, saddled with a responsibility which, whose ever it may be, is certainly not his. It is not enough to ask Larwood to play in a Test match. He must know in advance if any conditions are attached to the invitation.'[1] When Warner contended that Larwood's selection should be conditional upon an apology for his outburst, Jardine retorted that any suggestion of victimising the decade's best bowler would leave a nasty taste. There was a danger of some people losing their sense of perspective as the Australians had in 1932/33. It wouldn't be fair to pick Larwood and then refuse him the field he wanted.

Larwood's feud with the establishment was further inflamed when Nottinghamshire met Lancashire days later at Trent Bridge. On an easy-paced wicket, the visitors, batting first, were dismissed for 119 by Larwood and Voce who took all ten wickets between them. While the former dropped his pace, the latter bowled at his most aggressive and hit a couple of batsmen. Although Lancashire went on to win the match, they objected to Nottinghamshire's tactics and protested to Lord's, the instigator being their chairman, Tommy Higson, who happened also to be one of the Test selectors and an opponent of Bodyline – yet another example to Larwood of the establishment's chicanery.

Larwood's absence at Lord's was barely noticed, since Verity exploited a drying pitch to perfection to take 15 wickets as Australia slid to an innings defeat. Always a great admirer of Verity, Jardine twice sent notes to the England dressing-room to compliment him for an exhibition of bowling which, in terms of accuracy, he thought had never been surpassed. Lambasting the Australians for their impetuous batting, especially in the second innings, he singled out Bradman for particular censure. 'Bradman must bear a share – a heavy share – of blame for the unnecessary manner in which he got himself out. He must be well aware of the effect he has on his team-mates.' Jardine accepted that his day would come, 'but a player of his class and calibre should suit his style to the situation or make some effort to do so.'[2]

The third Test was a high-scoring draw and the fourth Test at Headingley saw Bradman return to form with a magisterial 304. As he neared his triple century, a spectator looked up to the press box and exclaimed, 'We want you out there, Jardine.'

Critical of Bradman's buccaneering approach in the first three Tests, Jardine now wrote: 'Fortunately for his captain, his side and himself, he ultimately abandoned this creed. The instantaneous success which rewarded his return to his more normal methods at Leeds, served not only to place him on his former pinnacle, but to convince him himself of the error of his previous ways.'[3]

With the England batting failing for a second time in the game, a heavy defeat loomed until the weather came to their rescue. Acknowledging their good fortune since they'd been outplayed, Jardine pilloried the selectors for their folly of playing only one fast bowler, Bowes, and once again pressed for the return of Larwood and Voce for the final Test. The selectors instead chose Allen and Clark in addition to Bowes, but, on a flat Oval wicket, Australia, led by 266 from Ponsford and 244 from Bradman, took complete control. During their 451-run partnership, Sutcliffe, collecting the ball from the boundary from another Bradman stroke, asked the crowd whether anyone had any suggestions. Arthur Carr in the press box certainly did – he thought that Jardine, Larwood and Voce should be on the field. 'I wish I had been on the field, too,' was Jardine's recorded comment to Carr.

After their win by 562 runs, Jardine readily conceded that Australia were worthy winners of the series, since they had been superior in all departments. Examining England's plight, he thought that financial and other considerations had shaped the selectors' thinking over the laws and principles of the game. 'Sir Stanley Jackson's influence on Yorkshire cricket is as well-known and recognised as Mr Higson's in Lancashire. When the selection committee was formed, both were known to oppose the leg-theory. Maybe, it is pertinent to inquire why Mr Higson never raised a protest so long as Lancashire had the Australian

E.A. McDonald, to bowl leg-theory, nor Sir Stanley Jackson when Bowes bowled with a leg-side field.[4] He remained bitter about Voce's treatment, but, given Australian sensitivities regarding Bodyline, his exclusion was understandable.

In the game against Nottinghamshire prior to the final Test, Australia came face to face with Voce bowling Bodyline. He took 8-66 in their first innings and when he began their second innings with another bombardment, Woodfull told the Nottinghamshire secretary that if Voce took the field the next day, Australia would refuse to play, an ultimatum with which the county complied, much to the crowd's fury. Jardine later wrote: 'The action of the Nottinghamshire Committee in withdrawing Voce from further participation in that game on account, it was alleged, of sore shins, created the only unpleasant demonstration by the crowd throughout the tour. To compare the treatment of the Australians on that occasion, at the hands of a few thousands of justly disappointed spectators, with the hostile demonstrations meted out to the last Marylebone Cricket Club team at the hands of tens of thousands upon every Test Match ground in Australia is to compare a molehill with a mountain.'[5]

Nottinghamshire did resort to one final salvo of Bodyline against Middlesex at Lord's, Voce knocking Len Muncer, a lower-order batsman, unconscious. Appalled by such pugilism, the Middlesex committee protested vehemently and joined Lancashire in declaring their refusal to play against Nottinghamshire the following year.

Confronted with such hostility, the Nottinghamshire committee apologised to MCC and dismissed Carr, their captain, whose support of Larwood and Voce had remained staunch, a decision which caused mutiny in the ranks. A vote of no confidence in the committee was carried at a special general meeting in November, leading to their resignation.

Two months later, the decision was rescinded at the Annual General Meeting. As far as Jardine was concerned, Nottinghamshire had been needless victims of an organised hypocrisy. 'It seems abundantly clear that Lancashire and Middlesex applied financial pressure. Middlesex's methods of playing fast bowling in recent years have caused mirth or despair to their supporters, while Lancashire's views of fast bowling were very different when they had Tyldesley or a McDonald to bowl for them. Their drawing power, however, is not such that Notts would feel the loss of their fixtures unduly.'[6]

Prior to this, Jardine suffered another reverse when MCC finally convinced themselves that legislation was necessary to outlaw Bodyline. An amendment was made to Law 43 banning 'persistent and systematic bowling of fast short-pitched balls at the batsman standing clear of his wicket'. The umpires would be the arbiters of direct attack.

Addressing the Club Cricket Conference in January 1935, Jardine took aim at the new lbw law, in which a batsman could be dismissed lbw even if the ball pitched outside off stump – provided he was in line with the wicket. While the law was altered to deter the growing emphasis on pad play, Jardine feared it would not only erode the artistry of batting, especially classical off-side play, but would also encourage the off-spinner at the expense of the leg-spinner.

For a man deemed rather standoffish in company, Jardine enjoyed a varied and fulfilling social life away from cricket, attending shooting parties, dances and club dinners. Handsome, intelligent and extremely charming when the occasion merited it,

Jardine was never short of female admirers. In the mid-1920s he became very close to Margaret Frazer, the sister of his great friend Jack Frazer, whose family he often stayed with in Sussex. Much taken by this vivacious beauty, he proposed marriage to her under a bridge in Scotland, a proposal she rejected. Later that decade, he briefly courted Marjorie MacIntyre, the attractive daughter of his friend Ian MacIntyre, a former Scottish rugby international, prominent Edinburgh lawyer and Conservative MP. A budding actress studying at the Royal Academy of Dramatic Arts, Marjorie showed little interest in cricket and she disliked long and tedious afternoons at the Oval 'watching distant people in white flannels doing not very much'. Feeling herself ignored at one of Jardine's parties, she turned to the nearest person who happened to be the revered C.B. Fry and said brightly, 'I do hope you're not another of those awful cricket bores.' Aware that she and Jardine were ultimately incompatible, she returned to Scotland in the early 1930s and later married the renowned writer, Eric Linklater.

After Jardine was briefly engaged to a woman called Edith Nielsen in 1930, he became close to Joy Branson in New Zealand when he stayed with her family during a fishing trip there in March 1933. There was talk of an engagement to an Australian beauty called Joan Badgery in April 1934, but the rumours proved hopelessly inaccurate for one very good reason: Jardine was already secretly engaged. In 1932 he was invited to a shooting party in Norfolk by his good friend Sir Harry Peat, the senior partner in Peat Marwick Mitchell, an international accountancy firm. There at his home, Hockwold Hall, he met Peat's younger daughter Margaret, whom Jardine called Isla. When he expressed his boredom with the attention of people who discussed only cricket, Isla said to him, 'Please don't be frightened, I am not going to talk about cricket as I am not frightfully interested in it.' Instead, they discovered a mutual love of fishing and hunting, and a dislike of large, formal gatherings. Taking a shine to each other immediately, they were engaged before Jardine left for India in October 1933, but, in compliance with Sir Harry's wishes, they kept their engagement secret till he returned the following May.

The wedding took place at St George's Church, Hanover Square, on 15 September 1934, a society occasion which featured surprisingly few cricketers: just Raymond Robertson-Glasgow, Gubby Allen, Percy Fender and Richard Palairet. Disdaining his traditional solemnity, Jardine's face lit up as he peered at his bride advancing down the aisle with her father, and when the happy couple emerged from the church they were met by a plethora of flashbulbs. After a reception at the bride's home, 16 Bruton Street, and honeymoon in East Africa hunting game, they returned to live in Airlie Gardens, Kensington. Their flat was rented from Sir Herbert Olivier, one of the official First World War artists, and his wife, who was Isla's aunt. Olivier later painted Jardine's portrait that now hangs in the Members' Bar of the Lord's pavilion.

Following the birth of their eldest child, Fianach – named after one of his favourite fishing lochs in Scotland – the family bought The Crofts at Shinfield, near Reading. With Jardine reluctant to continue working in the City and unable to provide for his growing family on his salary from journalism, there was a need to supplement the family income. On the advice of his best man, Arthur Child-Villiers, who was 17 years his senior, Isla was encouraged to put her horticultural expertise to good use by turning their 30 acres of land into a market garden. The enterprise was only partially successful and so Jardine felt compelled to seek employment with Cable and Wireless. Unsuited to the job of a travelling salesman, he left to work for a coal-mining company before returning to the press box in May 1939 as the *Daily Telegraph*'s cricket correspondent.

In 1935 Jardine had continued to work for the *Evening Standard* when England hosted South Africa. After an unsuccessful tour to the West Indies the previous winter, in which they lost 2-1, the return of Warner as chairman of selectors placed Wyatt's future as captain in some jeopardy, especially since Warner was a known admirer of Gubby Allen. On 12 April Jardine wrote to Wyatt: 'I hope you will be quite fit early in the season. Poor Bob! Warner's efforts on behalf of Gubby and Leveson Gower's on behalf of Errol Holmes bid fair to make the season interesting! Let me know if there is anything I can do at any time, for you know how essential I feel it to be that that skipper should be worth a place in the side himself as a cricketer.'[7]

Contrary to Jardine's expectation, Wyatt rather than Allen was invited to captain England in the Test series. Delighted with his appointment, Jardine wrote to congratulate him and advised him to assert himself, especially against Warner and Higson. The advice went unheeded. The South Africans, under H.F. Wade, confounded expectations by winning a Test in England for the first time to take the rubber 1-0. 'The South Africans should be enthusiastically grateful to the selectors who played 25 people in the five Tests,' Jardine wrote at the end of the series. 'The selectors are too old and hopelessly out of touch with what is a relatively young man's game.'[8]

The following year brought Jardine much sadness with the death of his mother, two years after the passing of his maternal grandmother, who'd latterly lived with his parents in Cornwall Gardens, South Kensington. Writing to a friend to decline an invitation to play in a friendly, he expressed a reluctance 'to take on any additional interest in cricket'. That summer India toured England which gave him the opportunity to renew his friendship with their captain, the Maharajkumar of Vizianagram, an eccentric appointment given his lack of talent. Besides being part of the official welcoming party on their arrival, he attended a reception for them by the Secretary of State for India, and was present, along with seven other former England captains, at a dinner hosted by Vizianagram at the Carlton Hotel. Later that summer he was the guest of honour of the High Commissioner of India at a reception for India's hockey team, winners of the Olympics tournament in Berlin weeks earlier.

The year also saw the publication of Jardine's booklet, *Cricket: How to Succeed*, sponsored by the National Union of Teachers, in which he explains the rudiments of the game. Aside from stressing the importance of physical fitness and advising coaches to lay off captains on matchdays, his most interesting thoughts concerned the priorities of any captain. To him the cardinal rule was never to ask any member of the side to do anything which he wasn't prepared to try himself; followed by the need to take chances and accept responsibility when things went wrong. According to Charles Bray of the *Daily Herald*, it was one of the best textbooks on cricket that he'd ever read, a view endorsed by Johnnie Moyes, who thought it excellent. Later that year Jardine's coaching book, *Cricket*, was published, a book in which he discussed all aspects of the game with characteristic thoroughness, sticking religiously to the canons of orthodoxy – his stance aside – that had served him so well.

In light of Jardine's continued defence of Bodyline, the possibility of his return to Australia as a journalist to cover the

MCC tour of 1936/37 weighed heavily on Sir Alexander Hore-Ruthven, now Lord Gowrie, Governor of Australia. As early as March 1936, he wrote to Warner to ask him to use his good offices to stop this possibility. 'I cannot conceive anything more calculated to revive the friction and ill-feeling that existed here three years ago than the presence of the gentleman that you mention and the style of articles which he would presumably contribute,' he wrote.[9]

He suggested that Warner meet up with Stanley Bruce, the Australian High Commissioner in London, to discuss the matter, since reservations expressed from an Australian point of view would count far more than a British one. Alluding to the splendid atmosphere generated by an MCC tour to Australia in 1935 under the Surrey captain Errol Holmes, he reckoned 'it would be a tragedy if the whole thing was upset by the presence of this individual'. As Gerald Howat has stated: 'We cannot automatically assume that Gowrie was alluding to Jardine … as he was careful never to mention a name in the letter, although it is a more than reasonable supposition.'[10]

Jardine remained in England but, even 10,000 miles away, he was still capable of raising Australian hackles. Addressing the English-Speaking Union in January 1937, he declared that international cricket had outlived its usefulness. 'As a money spinner, Test cricket is grand. Without Anglo-Australian tours, English county cricket would cease to exist, because two-thirds of the counties would be in queer street. Australia has lost the dignity of the game because of barracking. At first it is funny, but when one hears the four stock-in-trade cries of the barrackers through five months, they cease to be funny. It would be a tragedy if barracking ever came to English cricket.' Cricket was the best game in the world to play and talk about but the place to play it was the village green. He concluded by asserting that he was now more interested in big-game hunting than cricket.

His attack on Australian crowds provoked a predictable reaction. 'It is comforting to reflect that Mr Jardine is playing pretty much of a lone hand in the bitterness of his attack upon Test cricket ...' averred the *Brisbane Telegraph*.[11]

'The pessimism of Mr D.R. Jardine about the future of the game of cricket is rather tiresome,' commented the *Melbourne Argus*. 'Most people will agree that barracking is improper and that irritating and persistent barracking, which tends to affect the nerve of the player, is grossly unjust. Nevertheless, Mr Jardine's preoccupation with an old grievance is out of place. He should reserve his remarks until there is occasion to justify them.'[12]

Jardine's disillusionment with the first-class game probably helped him adapt to the relaxed atmosphere of wandering club cricket, which might well have appeared alien to someone of his competitive temperament. In 1937 he scored 50 and 47 for the Free Foresters against Cambridge University, then a first-class fixture, and, the following year, 74 for I Zingari against the Lords and Commons at the Oval. His team-mate R.L. Arrowsmith, a well-known Charterhouse schoolmaster, noted the sensitive manner in which he dealt with Lord Ebbisham, a cricket enthusiast still bowling at 70. Rather than trying to banish him to all parts of the ground, he contented himself by taking a single off each ball he faced from him.

In addition to his games with Free Foresters, I Zingari and the Harlequins, Jardine was happy to turn out for his father-in-law on occasions and he ran the annual Butterflies fixture against Winchester. In 1939 the college captain Tony Pawson, later the cricket correspondent of *The Observer*, managed to upset him when he told him that if he would take an early tea, he would declare in half an hour. Jardine, a stickler for the proprieties of the game, disapproved of such machinations, but he quite approved when Pawson batted on and left the Butterflies a couple of hours to make a near-impossible total.

In 1938 Jardine captained a press team, which included S.F. Barnes, one of England's greatest-ever bowlers, and his former Surrey team-mate E.M. Wellings, against the News Agencies at Wembley. The latter stood at first slip for the 65-year-old Barnes's first two overs before Jardine joined the cordon and said, 'Move over, I want to watch him too.' That afternoon Barnes took 7-35 and neither slip could see any difference in his finger movement which caused the deflections.

That year Jardine was employed by *The Observer* to write a few articles of the Australian tour to England. Although the respective captains, Hammond and Bradman, were both giants of the game, it wasn't a vintage rubber, since, weather aside, the bat dominated over the ball. The first two Tests were high-scoring draws, the third was abandoned without a ball bowled and the fifth – a massive England win – was ruined as a spectacle because of injuries to Bradman and Fingleton, which prevented them from batting in either innings. Only the fourth Test was a classic and Jardine admired Australia's fighting qualities which won them the game by five wickets. Any pleasure he derived from Hutton's record-breaking 364 at the Oval was tempered by his reservations about a wicket which was so flat that it reduced bowlers to impotence.

Aside from cricket, Jardine concerned himself with a number of contemporary issues, one of which was the abdication of King

Edward VIII in 1936 so that he could marry Mrs Wallis Simpson, an American divorcee. Several books have alluded to Jardine's support for the king and his disillusionment with the Church of England because of its refusal to tolerate a divorced woman as queen. If this was true, it might well have reflected Jardine's sympathy for a fellow leader shunned by the establishment for what he deemed to be spurious reasons, but I can find no evidence to link the abdication with his subsequent hostility to Christianity. Could it be that previous writers have confused him with the Reverend Robert Anderson Jardine, an eccentric parish priest from Darlington, whose admiration for the king led him to defy the Church of England by officiating at Edward and Wallis Simpson's marriage in France the following year? It is certainly true that Jardine became disillusioned with Christianity and he stopped going to church – although he insisted his children attend – but this seems overwhelmingly the result of his growing interest in the Hindu religion and Eastern mysticism, prompted by his time in India during the war. 'His main preoccupation, in the years when I knew him both in a City office and in my own home, was Hindu philosophy,' recalled a cousin. 'He had a speculative mind, intent on ethical and religious problems. Kindly and high-minded, he had in those years an antipathy to Christianity, to which he always referred as "Rewards and Fairies", equal to Gibbon's. Nor, in his manner and bearing, was there the faintest trace of the stern, aloof, decisive cricket captain. He was slow and hesitant in speech, and, as it seemed to us, in thought; he chewed things over and came to cautious and tentative conclusions, except when attacking "Rewards and Fairies". Then he could be trenchant, and we realised how this mild-mannered philosopher could have been the instigator of bodyline bowling.'[13]

He became a member of the Oxfordshire, Buckinghamshire and Berkshire area committee of the National Fitness Council, set up by the government in 1937 to oversee a national health campaign for young people. He also did philanthropic work at Eton Manor Boys' Club, founded in 1909 by his godfather Alfred Wagg and three other wealthy Old Etonians to provide leisure and sporting activities for the boys of Hackney Wick, a notoriously deprived part of east London. For many years the leading figure behind the boys' club was Jardine's best man, Arthur Child-Villiers, an eccentric aristocrat who happened to be the much-loved uncle of Frank Pakenham, later Lord Longford, as well as a keen sportsman and a director of Barings Bank. Using his many connections, he encouraged Jardine, alongside other luminaries, to visit the club, and consequently, Jardine not only helped out with some coaching, he also took a side to play against them and contributed generously to club funds.

Later he volunteered his services to the Earl Baldwin Refugee Fund, which was set up to provide aid for refugees from Nazi Germany, where anti-Semitism was becoming increasingly rife. The inter-denominational Refugee Fund was launched by the former prime minister Stanley Baldwin in a national radio broadcast on 8 December 1938; then the following month Jardine was appointed assistant secretary of the Fund's executive committee.

Part of his remit was to travel around the country pleading the cause of the refugees. At Guildford in February 1939, the mayor introduced him at a public meeting as the man who brought the Ashes back from Australia, to which an old lady in the audience was heard to whisper to her neighbour, 'Who was it that died in Australia?'

At Nottingham in May, in response to some hostility about the Fund, Jardine explained what it was doing for refugees. He wished to dispel the idea that it was purely a Jewish problem. The refugee crisis contained over half a million people who didn't call themselves Jewish. He paid tribute to those members of the unemployed who'd contributed generously to the Fund, then standing at some £500,000, and categorically denied the charge that refugees were taking British jobs. The truth was that they'd created employment for 15,000 native workers.

Despite Jardine's renown in Nottingham through his links with Larwood and Voce, his presence failed to generate great interest in the meeting, so much so that its chairman, Bishop Neville Talbot, expressed embarrassment for the poor turnout.

In May 1939 Jardine was appointed cricket correspondent of the *Daily Telegraph*. He began by reigniting his old feud with Plum Warner, who'd recently quit after a second spell as chairman of selectors. Welcoming his successor, Percy Perrin, the former Essex batsman, Jardine wrote that his presence would guarantee that England caps would not be distributed by way of experiment on the lines of the lyricist W.S. Gilbert's monarch King Goodheart, who generously distributed favours.

Unable to resist rising to the bait, Warner was quick to respond in a letter to the *Telegraph*. 'In fairness to my colleagues on the selection committee from 1931 to 1938 and to the captains of England teams – Jardine was one – whom the committee coopted it would be interesting to learn from Jardine the names of the cricketers who were awarded what he describes as Gilbertian caps.'[14]

Back came Jardine: 'I cannot understand why my enthusiasm for Perrin's elevation to the chairmanship should rally Sir Pelham to the defence of his colleagues. As Sir Pelham mentioned, they included myself, but he does not mention that they include Perrin, who I am delighted to honour.

'If Sir Pelham, in seeking a cover for his head, sees by implication, a crown lying about, and is casting himself for the part of King Goodheart, he must not blame me if it is a misfit.'[15]

In a second letter Warner wrote: 'I do not seek to cover my head but on the contrary, I am standing in the open and asking Jardine to come out and answer who were the cricketers awarded Gilbertian caps which is the point at issue between us?

He ended with a stinging rebuke. 'Jardine was at a great school, and when he replies to me, I hope he will do me the courtesy, this time, of approximating more closely than on May 5 the motto of that famous school.'[16] In a three-Test series against West Indies, England were the better side but the tourists, inspired by the batting of the inestimable George Headley, recovered from a rocky start to compete on even terms. They lost the first Test at Lord's by eight wickets, with only Headley, with two centuries in the match, performing to expectation. They competed on even terms in the draw at Old Trafford, a match ruined by rain, and had the better of the draw at the Oval. While Jardine admired the consistent batting of Hammond, Hutton and Compton, he lamented the shortcomings of the England attack, especially once Verity was injured. 'The dearth of high-class English bowlers is indisputable,' he wrote at the end of the summer. 'Goddard and Wright have been repeatedly tried, but the problem remains unsolved.'[17] It remained an ongoing problem in the immediate post-war era before an explosion of talent in the 1950s.

## Endnotes:

1 *Evening Standard*, 13 June 1934

2 Ibid, 26 June 1934

3 Rosenwater, *Sir Donald Bradman*, p228

4 *Evening Standard*, 23 August 1934

5 Douglas Jardine, *Ashes and Dust*, p29

6 *Evening Standard*, 16 January 1935

7 Howat, *Plum Warner*, p157

8 *Evening Standard*, 21 August 1935

9 Howat, *Plum Warner*, p161

10 Ibid

11 *Brisbane Telegraph*, 29 January 1937

12 *Melbourne Argus*, 29 January 1937

13 *The Times*, 24 June 1958

14 *Daily Telegraph*, 4 May 1939

15 *Daily Telegraph*, 5 May 1939

16 Ibid, 9 May 1939

17 Ibid, 22 August 1939

# CHAPTER 12

# REDEMPTION?

WHEN WAR broke out in September 1939, Jardine was offered a good job in the coal industry in Sheffield, but there was no question of him avoiding military service. A lieutenant in the 5th Battalion, the Queen's Regiment, at university, he resigned in 1924, but, with war looming, he was commissioned into the 4th Berkshire Regiment in May 1939. The regimental cricket side quickly signed him up and he played several times for them in Depot Week that June, scoring 83 against the Royal Engineers, Aldershot.

That August he commanded the Wokingham Territorials on camp at Lavant, near Chichester, and on his return, he was promoted to captain, days before Britain declared war on Germany on 3 September.

After four months' training at Newbury, the regiment sailed for France in January 1940. There they underwent further training at Tourmignies until they were deployed to combat the German spring offensive westward, which led to the surrender of France – a surrender which Jardine bitterly resented, thinking she had hoisted the white flag all too readily.

He was sent to Belgium in May to join his platoon, only to find that it had been wiped out. Stranded, he commandeered a troop carrier and drove back through enemy lines to Boulogne, where, despite an injured foot, he volunteered to hold Calais, but his CO refused. Only single men were to remain. He was one of the last men to be evacuated from Dunkirk. During the confusion on the beaches, he became separated from his batman and prior to evacuation, the batman got off the last destroyer to look for his officer. At last, he found him and as they came aboard, he said to Jardine, 'We're bound to be all right, now, sir; she's called after your favourite cricketer.' The pair sailed home safely on HMS *Verity*. Sadly, the story didn't have a happy ending, since Verity, serving with the Green Jackets, was severely wounded in the Allied invasion of Sicily in 1943 and was captured by the Germans. Taken to the Italian mainland, he died on the operating table in Caserta and was buried there with full military honours.

Hearing of his captivity, Jardine wrote to Verity's mother. 'I know something of your well-justified pride in him and his in you. It may be of some consolation in your anxiety to know that there are so many folks like myself the world over grieving with you and sharing your anxieties and hopes. I hope you will soon have better news of the cricketer and man I most admired.'[1]

Returning to more familiar surroundings, Jardine attended the London Counties–British Empire match at Lord's in the uniform of an army captain. As he walked around the ground unnoticed, two Australian soldiers saluted him without recognising him. Knowing the War Office, Jardine used to joke, his next posting would be as Liaising Officer with the Australian Army. In reality he was stationed at St Albans as a staff captain responsible for arranging transport for troops joining newly formed regiments, coming across as polite and friendly, if a touch aloof, to his fellow officers. On one occasion the Jardine of 1932/33 reasserted himself, as recalled by G.N. Gurney of Colchester. 'Part of our large rectory was requisitioned by the Army for billets, and it must have been about 1941 when a Captain Jardine arrived and introduced himself to my father, who replied, "I suppose you are no relation to the famous cricketer?" This was returned with the loud, unsmiling response, "Sir, I am the famous cricketer." There must have been a dozen people living in the house at this time, but we had only one bathroom. Jardine sent his batman to sit in the locked bathroom in order to reserve it for his use. My mother responded to this by removing the bath plug, but it made no difference for Jardine then blocked the hole with a handkerchief and continued as before. I well remember approaching him for his autograph. This he at first refused but later he had a change of heart.'[2]

In 1942 Jardine returned to India as a major in the Central Provisions Directorate. 'Father was sent then to the North West Frontier to places we had never heard of, and had, as they say, a lovely war,' recalled his eldest daughter Fianach. 'He used to send the most marvellous letters home which were so fascinating that even though he wasn't around for a long time it always felt as though he were there in our midst.'[3]

On the boat out, he beat Dr James Houston, an eminent physician, in the bridge final. Based first at Quetta and then at Simla, his father's birthplace, he felt very much at home amid the colonial architecture and breathtaking scenery. He became fluent in Hindustani, renewed his latent interest in mysticism and Eastern philosophy and mixed in easily with his fellow officers. He formed a close attachment to the actor and comedian Dennis

Castle who'd been sent to Simla as Entertainment Officer. They met after Jardine had given him the bird during a troop revue in the Gaiety Theatre, the centre of hill-station life during the Raj. As Castle stood beside the double bass he'd lugged on to the stage preparing to 'tune up' with the orchestra, a drawling, sardonic voice asked from the Royal Box, 'What guard do you want?'

'I blinked,' he later recalled. 'One never expected to be heckled by the Raj, least of all from a Royal Box, but I knew at once the speaker's identity. "Middle and leg," I countered, "but no Bodyline."'[4]

After Castle finished his act, Jardine came to his dressing-room. Although he'd been in Simla for months no one had dared mention Bodyline to his face. When he found Castle was a cricket buff, however, he did volunteer a curt but informative version of Bodyline, stating that if he could play it why couldn't the Australians?

Thereafter, they played snooker together in the United Services – Jardine proving something of a dab hand – and discussed the world of Edwardian variety together over evening drinks. 'We became friends,' Castle wrote, 'although it always amazed me that I held the same rank as he, for I felt his wiles would have been better employed combating Rommel in the desert than handing out military provisions in that Kipling backwater.

'In Simla he was reserved rather than aloof, and was popular in the best way possible with the ladies of the Raj. He liked my company because I belonged to the theatre, in which he was extremely well-versed. He would send up my tinselled world with a sly smile but never lost his affection for it.'[5]

Jardine travelled around the country lecturing to troops on anything from cricket to fishing and big-game hunting, and was invariably an inspiration to those who met him. He also played some cricket. Having scored 67 not out and 0 for the Punjab Governor's XI, captained by Patiala, against Punjab University at Lahore in November 1942, he led a Services XI against All India, organised by the Cricket Club of India, in aid of charity in February 1944. Dickie Dodds, later an all-rounder for Essex, but then the only debutant in a strong team of Test and county players, recalled the occasion. 'My impression of Jardine was of a man with whom you had to have either a good or a bad relationship. He was not neutral. He sort of came at you and began to probe your character. After our final practice session, he sat beside me in the dressing-room. I was impressed by the nonchalant way he peeled off the vast amount of plaster that appeared to be holding together his ageing muscles. Then he said, "Well, Dodds, what are you going to bowl and how do you plan to get these men out?" I had very little idea, which was probably what he wanted to find out.'[6]

Batting first on a good wicket, Jardine rolled back the years with a solid 43 before he was run out. His side made 308, only then to toil long and hard in the field while the opposition amassed 502/7 declared. After Dodds's leg-breaks came in for heavy punishment from Mushtaq Ali, who scored 190, he asked Jardine if he could move a fielder to the boundary, a request Jardine refused. 'Dodds, you and I are amateurs,' he barked. 'It is only professionals who ask to have their field shifted when they are hit for four.'

Despite a fighting century from Nottinghamshire's Joe Hardstaff and 81 from the future Indian batsman, Hemu Adhikari, who derived lifelong inspiration from Jardine's uncompromising approach, the Indian XI won by five wickets with minutes to spare.

At the end of the war, Jardine returned home to very different circumstances. At the beginning of the war, he and his family had moved to Drayton Manor, a wisteria-draped house, complete with a large garden and paddock, on the edge of a sleepy Somerset village. Yet for all its rural charm, Isla found bringing up four children – Euan was born in 1940 and Marion in 1943 – in a dilapidated house without much help a trial and in 1943 she suffered a breakdown. Consequently, with the return to peace they sold the house and moved to Radlett in Hertfordshire. There they kept a low profile. Even allowing for Jardine's strong links with the local cricket club, almost nothing was known about his personal life.

Devoted to his wife and family, Jardine spent much time in their company, reading to the children, playing games with them and taking them on outings. 'Father was shy, reserved, a terribly gentle man with a strict sense of fair play who wouldn't dream of stretching the rules during a family game of Ludo, never mind on the cricket pitch,' recalled Fianach. 'He had impossibly high standards if you were a child – standards, I have to say, that I failed to meet on numerous occasions. He had a lovely dry sense of humour, however, and used to love reading Kipling's *The Jungle Book* to my brother, two sisters and myself before we went to sleep at night.'[7]

He taught them to fish and shoot at the regular family gatherings at Hockwold Hall and at Cross Craig's House, the Perthshire estate on the southern shore of Loch Rannoch, which Sir Harry Peat used to rent each summer.

He also instilled in his two elder daughters a lifelong love of cricket and they often accompanied him to Lord's. 'If you grew up as I did, then it would be difficult not to be seduced by cricket,' declared Fianach, 'and I have never forgotten the influence that my father had on me and everybody who came into contact with him feels the same.'[8] He used to come and watch his two eldest daughters play for their school first XI at St Margaret's, Bushey, and Fianach recalled the occasion when they were both out within five minutes, whereupon he turned on his heels in complete disgust muttering 'Jesus'.

Euan, in contrast, was physically frail and wasn't expected to survive into adulthood. That he did says something about his resolve, inherited from his father, but his condition caused his parents much concern and brought out the best of them, their occasional exasperation tempered by general compassion. No scholar or sportsman, Euan struggled at school until his parents discovered Allhallows School in Devon, which catered for those with learning difficulties.

With a large family to support, Jardine was appointed company secretary of the paper manufacturers Thomas Owen, the forerunner of Wiggins Teape, a firm that employed a number of renowned cricketers including Len Hutton, Bill Edrich and Maurice Leyland. He then became chairman of the New South Wales Land Agency, a sheep-farming concern, and a director of the Scottish Australian Company after they took over the former in 1953.

In May 1946 Jardine played for an Old England XI against Surrey at the Oval as part of Surrey's centenary celebrations. On a day when the sun shone, the band played and King George VI attended, with 15,000 others, Surrey batted first and made 248/6. Old England began badly before 94 from Hendren, 62 from Woolley and a polished 54 from Jardine ensured a draw.

The visit of the Indians that year enabled Jardine to renew old friendships. At a lunch organised by the leading Indian cricket writer Berry Sarbadhikari at the Hyde Park Hotel, he and his father talked of nothing but India in an entirely natural way free of condescension. He also stressed to P.B. Datta, a future Cambridge Blue and captain of Bengal, Hammond's greatness as a batsman and that he was better than Bradman.

The following year Malcolm Jardine died, aged 77. *The Times of India* declared that he would be affectionately recalled by many of the older generation of lawyers in Bombay and *The Fettesian* wrote: 'A most lovable character in himself, those who came into contact with him could not fail to be attracted by his qualities of head and heart, or to appreciate his deep sense of honour.'[9]

That same year Jardine wrote to *The Times* about a matter which had taxed him for some time: the decline of the game as a spectacle because of the general fall in standard of top-flight bowling. His solution was the substitution of a smaller ball commonly used in prep schools for the present full-sized ball. 'In a man's hand this small ball, from the additional swerve and spin which can be imparted to it, should be capable of righting the present maladjustment between bat and ball.'[10]

Furthermore, he continued, it should encourage the development of bowling artists as opposed to overworked hacks. He accepted that there were disadvantages to his plan, but asked that the experiment be tried during the latter part of the 1948 season in all first-class matches. The counties did experiment with a smaller ball in 1955 but chose to stay with the status quo.

In 1948 Jardine wrote some articles for the *Evening Standard* on the Australian tour. Bob Wyatt recalled driving away from Old Trafford one evening during the Test when he noticed Jardine walking past and offered him a lift to his hotel. With some reluctance Jardine accepted, but he remained evasive about his destination. Eventually he said to Wyatt, 'Drop me at the next corner and I can walk from here,' but Wyatt insisted on driving him the whole way. It was only then that Jardine told him that he was going to stay at the home of an elderly nurse who had been kind to him while he was in a military hospital during the war. 'The old girl is in a bad way financially and I'm going there as a PG.' He was doing the nurse a good turn and he didn't want anyone to know about it.

Later that summer Jardine came out of retirement to lead an All-England XI against the county champions Glamorgan at Cardiff. Batting at No.6, he made a laboured 10 in the first innings and 23 not out in the second, but wasn't quick enough to force a win.

In 1950 he bade farewell to Harold Larwood when the latter, disillusioned by life in England, chose to emigrate to Australia. Before his departure, Jardine hosted a farewell lunch for him at a London club. At the end of it he presented him with a gold and brown pencil that Jack Hobbs had given him in 1925 after Hobbs had scored his 100th hundred. When Larwood wondered whether Hobbs would approve, Jardine assured him that 'Jack will be thrilled to know you have it.' The next day, as Larwood boarded the SS *Orontes* at Tilbury, he was handed his final telegram. It read: 'Bon voyage. Take care of yourself. Good luck always. Skipper.'

In 1953 Jardine returned to journalism to report on the Ashes series for *The Star,* telling Arthur Mailey that he had decided to forget about his business and concentrate on cricket for the summer, since he was becoming too detached from the real things of life. 'When I started writing about cricket,' recalled John Woodcock, the renowned cricket correspondent of *The Times,* 'Jardine was in the press box, a much more staid place than it is today, and his manner was more one of self-consciousness than superiority.'[11] Unlike Lord Hawke, who deplored the idea that a professional should ever captain England, he was highly supportive of Hutton who'd become England's first professional captain the previous year, declaring that he was the best man for the job, a view borne out by subsequent events. With more than a touch of gamesmanship in the Jardine tradition, Hutton led England to a narrow series win over Australia to regain the Ashes after 19 years, an achievement Jardine enjoyed celebrating at a special dinner that autumn.

That same year he became the first president of the Association of Cricket Umpires. Frank Higgs, who worked at Winchester College, went to the inaugural meeting at Lord's, and Jardine, on hearing of the presence of a member from Winchester, introduced himself. 'By a coincidence,' he said, 'I was at the College recently, dining with the warden.' 'I know, sir,' replied Higgs. 'I was the butler!'

Jardine worked hard for the association in its efforts to raise standards, winning the respect of Frank Lee, one of England's leading umpires, and on becoming president of Oxford University Cricket Club in 1955, he gave freely of his time and money.

He continued to take a great interest in his old school and having watched Winchester beat Eton in 1955, the first home victory in 'Eton match' since 1920 and only the second since 1904, he wrote to Graham Doggart, a former Cambridge Blue, whose son Hubert was now running the cricket at Winchester.

Dear Graham,

I felt I must write a few lines on Saturday's triumph.

Winchester may have many vices, but worship of games is not and never been one of them – yet many of us who love everything about the School, do get an uplift of heart when all too seldom we beat our daughter School.

I thought the boys played such good cricket – will you pass on some nice words and a large pat on the back for such an auspicious start to your son?

Yours sincerely,

Douglas R. Jardine[12]

It was through his friendship with Radlett captain Eric Parker that Jardine joined the local cricket club in 1949. He mixed in seamlessly and scored freely in the games in which he played, once driving a six over the pavilion, a feat yet to be emulated since. Chris Dexter, a Radlett team-mate of Jardine's, recalled the privilege of batting with him, or just watching him from the pavilion. In one match against West Herts, one of the strongest clubs on the local circuit, the opposition had the redoubtable Ted Hawes leading an accurate seam attack, but Jardine, after a few overs sizing him up, stroked the ball to the boundary with felicitous timing, however much the field was adjusted. Dexter noted that even Hawes began to lose control in his exasperation at Jardine's cultured drives and leg glances. He went on to score about 60 before deliberately getting himself out. 'It was when he returned to the pavilion that we learned why he no longer played the game regularly,' Dexter continued. 'He told us that, from the effects of a tropical disease he had had, he found that his hands swelled up, making it painful to grip his bat handle if he batted for an hour or more. So, he played no more long innings.'

His captain Parker once asked him to have a bowl, but Jardine the leg-spinner declined, saying he was, like German women, 'rather loose and very expensive'.

When Jardine joined the club, his team-mates found that, contrary to his fearsome image, he came across as mild-mannered and very self-effacing, quite content to be called by his Christian name. 'Despite his austere reputation,' declared Dexter, 'I can only say that I found him to be a very pleasant and friendly person, albeit in the later years of his life. If we asked for cricketing advice, he was quite ready to give it.'[13]

He continued to play in a limited number of friendly matches, most notably in the annual fixture between the Authors and Publishers at Vincent Square, Westminster. On one occasion in the early 1950s, *The Observer* journalist Michael Davie was fielding at slip when Jardine came in to bat looking grey with age. Facing his first ball – on a goodish length just outside off stump – Jardine, with effortless timing, stroked it past extra cover to the boundary, turned to the wicketkeeper, smiled and made some agreeable comment. 'For the rest of the day I watched him closely, unable to connect this sociable, if slightly remote figure with the haughty and brutal architect of Bodyline.'[14]

In the 1954 fixture he was photographed by *The Times* going out to bat with Philip Snow, a well-known colonial administrator in Fiji and dedicated cricketer, both of them scoring fifties. 'Douglas Jardine couldn't have been a more pleasant captain,' recalled Snow.[15] He found him a surprisingly large man, not only tall but big boned, and much larger than he appeared for pictures, although he'd seen him playing in the 1930s.

# REDEMPTION?

He was also a witty and popular speaker at cricket club dinners, often sharing the stage with his friend Dennis Castle, who later wrote: 'When he was present, I always recounted his favourite story. When I was playing for the Concert Artists Association Club in the mid-1930s an opponent came in to bat wearing a mock Harlequins cap. Obviously it was hand-made but the little man adjusted it importantly, marked his guard with a bail, had the screen moved, and surveyed the field imperiously. He then proceeded to use a cross bat, possessed no timing or footwork, and within three balls had given two chances in the slips and ran out a well-set partner. As we crossed at the end of the over, one of our comedians pointed to the cap and said, "He must be Jardine's butler."

'Like the actor he really was, Jardine, although he had heard the anecdote a dozen times before, would laugh, head back, as though it was entirely new to him!'[16]

Geoffrey Copinger, a stalwart of the Cricket Society, recalled his kindness at their Winter Luncheon at Lord's in January 1956. 'Neville Cardus was stricken with influenza and cried off the day before. Jardine was to me a first-class speaker with a dry sense of humour, which was much appreciated. It was quite clear that he had mellowed over the years since the controversial Bodyline tour.'[17] It was a view echoed by the cricket writer Irving Rosenwater, who arrived early for the lunch and had a long chat with Jardine. He was impressed by his easy friendliness and the gist of his talk – to keep cricket a simple game free from scientific legislation. 'There was,' Jardine declared, 'going to be a great deal more talk about light meters for umpires.' Miracle cameras that recommended the minute misdemeanours of fast bowlers were not, in his opinion, in the best interests of the game.

259

The following year saw a number of experiments with the County Championship. The reasons for their introduction were the subject of a talk by Gubby Allen, who was accompanied on the platform by Jardine. There had been a limit, 75 yards, to the maximum size of boundaries. Umpires had been given great powers to speed up play and there were bonus points for scoring runs more quickly. However, the most controversial provision had been the limitation of leg-side fielders, an unpopular measure even with those who had recommended it. It was, said Allen, the 'best of a bad lot', given that something had to be done to combat negative bowling. Jardine was not convinced. 'Be very careful how you monkey about with the Laws of Cricket,' he said. It was all prompted by treasurers saying, 'Look at our accounts.' Faster pitches, one and all seemed to agree would get the turnstiles clicking again.

With the passage of time, Jardine's image underwent a remarkable transformation to many Australians. Bill Brown, who toured England three times between 1934 and 1948, found him delightful company. On the 1948 tour, Jardine invited Arthur Morris and Keith Miller to dinner in London and came across as both interesting and charming as they talked about everything except Bodyline. He repeated the invitation five years later when he entertained Miller, Lindwall, Fingleton and O'Reilly at Balliol College during Oxford University's game against the Australians. While O'Reilly marvelled at Jardine's nonchalance in serving his chilled champagne in pewter pots, Fingleton recalled the dinner with pleasure as their host told interesting stories in a droll manner and Miller induced great laughter when the conversation turned from bumping races on the river to bumpers. 'Now, Douglas, talk about bumpers,' he said. Jardine was non-committal but praised Lindwall to the hilt.

On that Australian tour, O'Reilly, now a colleague of Jardine's in the press box, discovered a different man from the pugilist of Bodyline. 'I was overjoyed to find that Douglas Jardine was human, even shy. I was thunderstruck. Surely this was not the same bloke I knew in Australia in the summer of 1932/33. It looked like him: long, angular and forbidding. The conformation and the colour of the face, the high cheekbones and large pointed nose of America's Hiawatha were just as much in evidence. Yet there had been a strange but moving change. I liked him, I told him so.'[18]

During the Lord's Test of 1953, Jardine was one of 50 guests entertained to a grand dinner in the River Room of the Savoy Hotel by Australian prime minister Robert Menzies, his presence a source of fascination to Hassett's side. 'Being from Australia I'd been brought up on stories about what a bastard Jardine was,' recalled all-rounder Ron Archer. 'But now I was across the table from him he was just this charming, interesting, aristocratic Englishman.'[19] When Menzies rose to speak, he said in self-deprecatory tones, 'As you all know, I am the man in Australia who has most often had the legitimacy of his birth queried,' to which Jardine turned to O'Reilly and said, 'I say, Bill, I hate to disagree with your prime minister but surely I still have claims to that title.'

In November 1953 Jardine travelled to Australia for a six-week trip to visit property stations on behalf of the Scottish Australian Company of which he was a director. It was his first trip back since Bodyline and he wondered what kind of reception he would get, but Fingleton, who'd encouraged Larwood to emigrate to Australia, assured him he had nothing to worry about. Because the visit was arranged at short notice, Australians were caught off guard by Jardine's arrival and he slipped into Sydney without fanfare. By the time they learned of his presence, he was ensconced in Queensland, travelling long distances by car and plane.

When Jardine touched down in Sydney a week later, he was surrounded by flashbulbs and reporters who started quizzing him about the Australian cricket team. Looking rather bewildered by all the attention he was attracting, he eventually said, 'You've got the wrong Jardine, chaps. I'm W.J.R. Jardine of Melbourne Manufactures, on my way home from Europe.' Hours later the real Jardine arrived to participate in a national broadcast as the Australian Broadcasting Corporation's *Guest of Honour*. In a wide-ranging discussion, he expressed pleasure at the warm welcome given to Larwood on emigrating to Australia, a happy ending to a controversy which could scarcely be found outside story books. 'Though they may not hail me as Uncle Doug, I am no longer a bogeyman,' he commented. 'Just an old so-and-so who got away with it.'

Turning to current events, Jardine deplored the change to covered wickets in Test matches, a move made out of a greed for gate money. Uncovered wickets not only produced better batsmen, it kept alive the slow left-armer.

Alluding to Australia's recent tour of England, Jardine called Hassett's side a good one but not a great one. Unfortunate to lose the Ashes, he said the Australians had won golden opinions wherever they went, excellent ambassadors both on and off the field.

Hearing about Jardine's presence in Australia, Arthur Mailey launched a nationwide plea in the Sydney *Daily Telegraph* to locate him, since he wanted to invite him to lunch. Jardine was surprised when a shearer at an outback station showed him a copy of the paper. 'Gosh,' he said, 'Mailey never in my memory asked anybody to lunch. I am not going to miss this invitation.'

Contact was duly made and Mailey hosted a lunch at Sydney's Pickwick Club, to which Charlie Macartney, Warren Bardsley, Johnny Taylor, Bertie Oldfield, Robert Menzies and Harold Larwood were also invited. In a convivial meal they roamed over battles past with Macartney and Taylor claiming they would have dealt with Bodyline had they been playing. After it was over, Jardine, taking Larwood's hand, said, 'Goodbye, Harold. It has been lovely to see you,' to which Larwood replied, 'Come back and see me again, Skipper.' He neither saw nor spoke to him again.

In a final gesture of reconciliation, Jardine was an honoured guest of the Melbourne Cricket Club at Hassett's testimonial match, to which he contributed two guineas to the fund.

Yet for all his mellowing in middle age, there were limits to Jardine's change of heart when it came to confronting the old enemy. The renowned Australian broadcaster Alan McGilvray, who'd formed such a dislike of Jardine when meeting him in 1932/33, had the opportunity to play golf with him in England years later. Finding him to be affable company, he asked him whether he had any regrets about Bodyline, to which question Jardine drew himself to his full height and glaring at him, retorted, 'None. None whatever. I did what I had to do. I won the Ashes for my country, and if I offended people that's unfortunate. We had to prove we could defeat Bradman and we did.' In that frame of mind, he turned up at Tilbury in September 1954, by now something of a stooped figure, to see off Hutton's side and to give some uncompromising advice to his fellow Oxonian Colin Cowdrey: 'When you get to Ceylon, Cowdrey, have a hit and get your eye in. Then, when you reach Australia, just remember one thing. Hate the Bastards!'

It was this intensity from battles past that continued to taint Jardine's relationship with Bradman, never a man to forget a grudge. In his first autobiography, *My Cricketing Life,* published in 1938, Bradman blamed Jardine for Bodyline, and, ten years on, his resentment hadn't abated. Peter Wilson of the *Daily Mirror* recalled attending a beginning-of-tour reception for the 1948 Australians.

'As my taxi drew up outside Australia House two others arrived simultaneously. Out of one stepped my cousin on my mother's side, Douglas Jardine, out of the other Don Bradman. We entered the building and walked up the stairs together, myself in the middle.

'Douglas chatted to me, asking about my mother, but his Red-Indian style profile never inclined a fraction of an inch in the direction of Bradman who, face as clenched as a conker, ascended the steps as though neither of us had been there, or even existed at all.'[20]

Fingleton recalled that the room fell silent when an official announced the arrival of Jardine. Most of the Australians were happy to engage him, since they hadn't been part of Bodyline. Australian journalist Andy Flanagan was talking to Jardine when an English friend of Jardine's came up to him and asked if Bradman had ever given him a copy of his book *How to Play Cricket.* 'No, he didn't,' Jardine replied. 'What's more, I've never read it.'

The Australian bowlers Doug Ring and Bill Johnston met Jardine at one reception and took a liking to him. 'We had a chat for quite some time and we thought he was a pretty decent sort of fellow, pretty affable and he invited us out to dinner,' Ring later recalled. Needing their captain's approval for any private invitation, they wandered over to him and told them about Jardine's offer. 'And he looked at us and he said, "You like him?" "Oh yes," we said, "he seems a pleasant sort of guy." He said "Well, you can't go." He said, "Make your own excuses, but you're not going." So that was that. There was obviously a deep-seated enmity arising from the Bodyline series.'[21]

Needless to say, a farewell lunch for Bradman at the Savoy hosted by *The People*, and attended by eight other England captains, excluded Jardine from the guest list. Reflecting on a series that Australia won 4-0, Jardine judged their batting to be outstanding and their bowling good, if not up to the level of the 1921 side, but gave little credit to Bradman's leadership. 'To suggest that the fielding or captaincy was brilliant or inspired would be flattery but both were adequate or more than adequate.'[22]

The publication of another Bradman autobiography, *Farewell to Cricket* in 1950, kept the feud going with the author firing a few broadsides in Jardine's direction over Bodyline. Disputing Jardine's contention that Bodyline was mere leg theory, Bradman wrote that nobody was in the slightest danger from leg theory, whereas with Bodyline the physical danger to the batsman became his chief consideration. Reviewing the book for the *National and English Review*, Jardine, while reasonably restrained, chided Bradman for comparing his critic Fingleton's low scores against Bodyline with his more sustained efforts and dismissed his chapter on captaincy as trifling. The two of them met up again, this time in the press box during Australia's 1953 tour of England, with Bradman covering it for the *Daily Mail*. Placed next to each other during the Headingley Test, they'd greeted each other every morning with 'Good morning, Mr Bradman,' (conveniently ignoring his recent knighthood) 'Good morning, Mr Jardine,' the near sum of their exchanges till their evening farewells. 'I even sat next to Douglas Jardine all day in the Press Box without the slightest form of disagreement,' Bradman informed his Adelaide readers one day.[23] It was the closest he ever came to complimenting him. 'It was a difficult period,' Bradman later told Charles Williams, one of his biographers. 'He's a Scotsman and we sat next to each other 20 years later and didn't talk.'[24]

In the last year of Jardine's life, a Sydney reporter interviewed him in his London office. Three times the reporter mentioned Bradman and not once did Jardine show a flicker of recognition. When he was asked who was the greatest batsman he encountered, he replied, 'Oh Jack Hobbs, because of his brilliance on bad wickets.' 'Is that why you put him above Bradman?' his interviewer said. Jardine gazed out of the window and replied absently: 'Hobbs, yes,' leaving the interviewer with the impression that Bradman didn't exist. Months later, when Jardine died, Bradman was asked for his reaction. He refused to comment and for the rest of his life he continued to denounce him. Mike Denness, England's captain in Australia in 1974/75, recalled trying to talk to Bradman about Bodyline. 'I deduced that he didn't really accept the tactic that Jardine put in place and that was confirmed to me when he told me: 'You're a far more acceptable Scotsman than the last one who captained England here.'[25]

In contrast to his reaction to the death of Jardine, Bradman was much more generous over Larwood's passing in 1995. 'Although we were arch enemies on the field, this was because of Jardine's tactics,' he commented. 'There was no personal animosity between Larwood and me and we always remained good friends,' he continued slightly implausibly.[26]

To his dying day Bradman, who outlived all his contemporaries, found it hard to forgive the one man who made him look vaguely mortal on the cricket field and whose oil portrait hangs besides his own in the pavilion at Lord's.

In 1956 Jardine played for the Authors XI, along with Fingleton, Arthur Morris, Hutton and Fender, umpired Amersham's centenary match against Ian Peebles's XI and was an usher at C.B. Fry's memorial service at St Martin-in-the Fields. He was also the guest once again of Robert Menzies at the Savoy, along with Miller, Mailey and Denis Compton, during the Lord's Test, and he had his final encounter with Australian cricket when he proposed their toast during the Headingley Test, proving delightful company, according to Richard Whitington.

Too frail to play for the Authors XI the following year, he watched instead, and in late September he was present at a dinner at the East India Sports Club in honour of England captain Peter May. Two months later, Jardine travelled to Southern Rhodesia to inspect some property he owned there, accompanied by his daughter Marion. While he was there, he contracted tick fever and with no obvious improvement on the boat journey home, he was admitted to the Hospital of Tropical Diseases. They cleared up the tick fever, but discovered an advanced form of lung cancer, although he'd only been a light pipe smoker. Seeking relief from severe breathing difficulties caused by radiotherapy, the hospital sent him to a clinic at Montreux, Switzerland, at the end of May, but there was little they could do for him, especially now that the cancer had spread to his stomach. He died there on 18 June, aged 57. Given his previous good health, his daughter Fianach wondered whether his cancer might have been stress-related. 'Perhaps the pressure and strain of everything was a contributory factor to the cancer too. Cancer does tend to feed on worry, doesn't it?' she said.[27]

Jardine's passing, while hardly an occasion for national mourning, was marked in the appropriate manner. The day after his death, the flags were lowered at Lord's during the England– New Zealand Test and a minute's silence was observed in The Parks, where Oxford were playing Sussex. Dennis Castle, on duty at Lord's as a telephonist for Bill Bowes, who was covering the Test for the *Yorkshire Evening Post*, later wrote that amid the fall of wickets reporters made frenzied reference to *Wisden* for the now urgent obituaries. 'I recall Sir Len Hutton, then on duty for the London *Evening Post*, saying resignedly: "What can I say about Jardine? I never knew him,"' an interesting comment from one ex-England captain on another.[28]

Although the tributes naturally made considerable reference to Jardine's part in the Bodyline controversy, friend and foe recalled his many qualities of leadership. 'Australian sportsmen will mourn the loss of a great cricketer and captain,' reflected Bill Woodfull, Plum Warner remembered him as a very fine captain both on and off the field and *The Times* called him a great England captain.

At his memorial service at St Michael, Cornhill, in the City of London, his old Wykehamist friend, Sir Hubert Ashton, unpicked many parts of a complex figure. Beyond a gruff, austere exterior, he declaimed, there lay a man of kindness and loyalty, as well as his outstanding physical and moral courage.

Debarred by MCC from scattering his ashes in the Memorial Garden at Lord's – such a privilege was reserved for the fallen in two world wars – Jardine's family took them to the summit of Cross Craigs, a mountain overlooking Loch Rannoch, where he loved to shoot and stalk. Fianach recalled that, 'Although it was July, it was really quite cold and cloudy until the moment came to scatter father's remains when the sky turned blue and a brilliant sun came out.'[29]

Jardine's death dealt a devastating blow to his family. His grief-stricken wife sold the house and many of his cricket possessions and moved to West Wittering in Sussex, prior to becoming a tax exile in Malta and Guernsey. (Her husband left an estate of just over £71,000 which would have been worth more than £1.25 million in today's values.) Euan was taken out of school and sent to work as a farm labourer; then, after working as a chef at a hospital near London, he settled in South Africa, marrying a local woman and raising her daughter and niece as if his own. He also became a committed supporter of the African National Congress; he died of cancer in 1997. Marion devoted herself to social work in two of London's most deprived boroughs before her retirement in Kent, and Iona gave up her work as an air hostess to look after her mother. She still lives in Guernsey.

The most well-known of the children was Fianach. A graphic designer, she worked for Ruari McLean Associates, moving to Scotland with the firm in 1973, and she later lectured part-time in publishing at Stirling University. Although religiously indifferent as a child, she later developed a firm faith and, after training for the ministry, she became one of the first women to be ordained a priest in the Scottish Episcopal Church. Attached to St James the Great, Dollar, Clackmannanshire, she worked tirelessly, not least on behalf of the inmates at Glenochil Prison, where she was much loved.

Separated from her husband, Peter Lawry, she produced Jardine's only grandchild, Isla, the pet name her father gave her mother, and retained her lifelong love of cricket. As interest in her father continued throughout her life – she died in 2013 – she zealously guarded his reputation. 'For too long, he has been traduced as this win-at-all-costs Englishman, but that is simply nonsensical,' she told the *Sunday Times* in 2005. 'He was ferociously proud of his Scottish heritage and we have all done our best to carry on that tradition. All that I am really asking for is a fair assessment of the man I loved.'[30]

Fairness is a quality often absent amid the storms of passion aroused by controversies such as Bodyline, but time and perspective have lent a more sympathetic interpretation of Jardine's life; I hope this book has played a small part in achieving this.

**Endnotes:**

1  Hill, *Hedley Verity: Portrait of a Cricketer*, p141
2  G.N. Gurney to David Frith, 14 November 1982
3  *Daily Telegraph*, 1 December 2006
4  *The Cricketer*, September 1980, p52
5  *Wisden Cricket Monthly*, March 1983, p37
6  Dickie Dodds, *Hit Hard and Enjoy It*, p27
7  *Daily Telegraph*, 1 December 2006
8  *The Sunday Times*, 8 December 2007
9  *The Fettesian 1947*, p47
10  *The Times*, 5 July 1947
11  Ibid, 3 December 2007
12  Douglas Jardine to Graham Doggart, 27 June 1955, Winchester College Archives
13  Charles Randall, *125 Years of Radlett Cricket Club*, p2
14  Michael Davie, *Anglo-Australian Attitudes*, p110

15  Philip Snow, *A Time of Renewal*, p33

16  *Wisden Cricket Monthly*, March 1983, p37

17  Randall, *125 Years of Radlett Cricket Club*, p4

18  O'Reilly, *Tiger: Sixty Years in Cricket*, p101

19  Gideon Haigh, *The Summer Game*, p74

20  Peter Wilson, *The Man They Couldn't Gag*, p94

21  Margaret Geddes, *Remembering Bradman*, p118

22  *The Star*, 18 September 1948

23  *Adelaide News*, 24 July 1953

24  Charles Williams, *Bradman: An Australian Hero*, p458

25  *The Times*, 3 December 2007

26  *The Independent on Sunday*, 23 July 1995

27  Hamilton, *Harold Larwood*, p323

28  *The Cricketer*, September 1980, p52

29  *Daily Telegraph*, 1 December 2006

30  *The Sunday Times*, 10 July 2005

# DOUGLAS JARDINE

DOUGLAS JARDINE was one of cricket's most complex and controversial characters, best recalled for his leading role over Bodyline, but despite the reams of coverage devoted to that tour, he remained something of an elusive figure with little known about his early years, his professional work, his private life and his part in the Second World War. Although he wrote several books about cricket, he never wrote an autobiography, rarely discussed his contemporaries or courted publicity. This isn't entirely an accident since he was a shy, self-effacing person, very different from the fanatical leader on the cricket field. According to Gubby Allen, Jardine was 'a Jekyll and Hyde character. He had a very charming side. But when the Test matches were on, he was insane, utterly determined to win at any cost.'[1]

A Victorian in bearing, manners and morality, he personified in extreme form that era's rather paradoxical approach to sport. While an adherent to cricket's amateur code – the separation of the classes, his attachment to wandering clubs and his idealisation of the village green – he played as hard as any professional, the upshot of his wartime education at Winchester, where manliness was king. Although the cult of athleticism which took root in Britain's elite public schools in the 1850s was based on ethical principles, the reality was often very different. According to the sports historian J.A. Mangan, 'The playing fields were the place where public schools put into practice their own distinctive brand of Social Darwinism; in games only the fittest survived and triumphed.'[2] This paradox between sporting ideal and reality was later re-enacted on many a foreign field. Imperialists saw cricket as a means of civilising the Empire and reconciling the natives towards British rule, but its high moral tone concealed a more ruthless competitive streak. 'Beneath the stuffy, benign image of public service cultivated by British imperialism lay a more strident belief in the mission of the English people,' wrote Richard Holt. 'Sports were not just the source of high-minded ideals, they were inseparably associated with the more down-to-earth, assertive and patriotic Englishness.'[3]

If W.G. Grace was the personification of a sporting John Bull in the 19th century, then Jardine was his successor in the 20th, just when the game was becoming more competitive, a trend accentuated by the growth of a more robust nationalism after the First World War and the development of the mass media. For some time, leg theory and short-pitched bowling had been on the rise as bowlers tried to restore the pendulum which had swung disproportionately in the batsman's direction and it was with Bradman in mind that Jardine displayed his own brand of Social Darwinism.

For a man who saw cricket – ironically – as a great chivalric contest in which the values of physical and mental endurance prevailed, he bitterly resented the charge of unsportsmanlike behaviour that was levelled against him and his team in Australia.

His claim that Bodyline was perfectly legitimate cannot be questioned – no umpire ever objected to it – and he later found support from Australian captain Ian Chappell, whose grandfather Vic Richardson had played in that series. Chappell thought that Jardine was an astute captain who, in his efforts to tame Bradman, had every right to pursue a strategy that was within the Laws of the game and that the real villains of Bodyline were the administrators who framed those Laws.

The growing acceptance of persistent short-pitched bowling in the 1970s has also blurred the lines. In today's more competitive milieu when cricket has shed much of its Corinthian ethos, the case against him isn't quite so clear-cut. 'Jardine certainly did cricket no favours in his time,' wrote Alan McGilvray. 'But perhaps he was ahead of his time. Many of his attitudes would hardly raise a ripple in the more abrasive world of today.'[4] Allan Border, captain of Australia between 1984 and 1994, avers that he has been judged too harshly. 'As a tactic, Bodyline bowling was brilliant. It was a very professional decision taken because England had a problem with a particular batsman, Bradman, who had hammered them in the previous series. Intimidation is part of a fast bowler's armoury. I had no problem with the West Indians going for the body either. Jardine copped a fair hammering over the years for the huge ruckus he caused, a little unfairly.'[5]

Border's views are endorsed by Ian Botham, England's great all-rounder of the late 1970s and 1980s: 'Jardine didn't do anything illegal and used a game plan to beat a phenomenal force in Bradman. Like or dislike the tactics, at the end of the day, you've got to say, "smart work". He won the series.'[6]

'I have no doubt that Jardine was right to say that if England had used it to less effect, there would have been very little opposition,' wrote Mike Brearley. 'If Australia had won, the offence would have been minimal. If it had been used as an occasional variation, no one would have made a fuss. Does this exonerate him? Not exactly. For there is something about the relentlessness of Jardine that set him apart.'[7]

While taking his stand on the law, Jardine conveniently ignored the fact that by encouraging intimidatory bowling he was flouting the ethos of fair play that the British had propagated across broad swathes of the Empire, and which had found a loyal following among many Australians. Hence Woodfull's devastating response to Plum Warner during the Adelaide Test when he accused England of not playing the game.

Jardine proved a poor advocate of his case by the petulant manner in which he set out his defence in his book *In Quest of the Ashes*. According to Brearley, one of the features of Jardine's concept of chivalric cricket was the lack of arrogance in the winners. 'However, what Jardine shows no sign of appreciating is the extent to which he came across to Australians (and to some others) as superior, unbending and arrogant.'[8] The antipathy he bore them from his previous visit was understandable in part because of the undue hostility his slow batting had aroused in the crowd that was patently more vociferous and partisan than he was used to back home. Yet returning to Australia in 1932 with preconceived notions of animosity and non-cooperation towards his hosts hardly suggested the flower of English chivalry in full bloom. By deliberately offending the press and many others in a country deep in the throes of depression and uncertain about its future place in the world, Jardine undid much of the enormous goodwill that greeted his team on their arrival. His failure to treat his opponents with the respect they were entitled to, not least during the torrid

Adelaide Test, served only to fuel the crowd's indignation and prompted many of the offensive comments he so objected to.

Jardine's position is further undermined by the unease which a number of his team felt about his tactics. When those same tactics were seen back on home soil the following summer, not least by the West Indian fast bowlers against the England batsmen, the mood soon began to change. The fact that MCC, unwaveringly loyal up to then, legislated against Bodyline bowling in 1934 could be seen as a belated admission that Jardine had indeed acted in an unseemly manner. It was a decision that dismayed him and cast a shadow over the rest of his life. His daughter Fianach wrote that he never recovered from the stigma of Bodyline and that he was badly affected by the criticism that was hurled in his direction. Following a dispute with his party, a Labour MP, threatened with the withdrawal of the Whip, received a letter from Jardine which read: 'I have only met you once and I am opposed to you in politics. But I cannot go to bed tonight without wishing you well for tomorrow. I know how you must feel. I have been through it all myself.'[9]

Jardine's association with Bodyline has detracted from his prowess as a captain and batsman. If lacking the creative intuition and flair of his good friend Percy Fender, he combined a shrewd brain with a dominating personality who led very much from the front. 'I have never played under a better tactician than D.R. Jardine,' wrote Herbert Sutcliffe, 'and I have never played under a better fighter. His method of studying the game set every member of his side working on similar lines, and his fighting power was a wonderful sense of inspiration to us all.'[10] Sutcliffe's opening-partner-turned-critic Jack Hobbs was equally complimentary: 'I cannot help thinking that Jardine in his day was a great captain and had a cricketer's brain. He studied batsmen, their methods and their strokes. He had the key to all situations; he knew how to save runs and how to make batsmen fight for every run they got. Some of his moves were very clever.'[11] According to Arthur Mailey, he proved himself one of the finest strategists that Australia had seen. He knew the shots of every one of his opponents and placed his field accordingly. Only during the later stages of McCabe's great innings in the first Test did he appear lost for answers. Even Warner – no friend of Jardine's after 1932/33 – placed his captaincy on the highest of pinnacles. 'Jardine was a master of both tactics and strategy, and was especially adept in managing fast bowlers and thereby preserving their energy. He possessed a great capacity for taking pains, which, it has to be said, is the mark of genius. He left nothing to chance, and he never asked anyone to do anything which he would not have done himself. As a field tactician and selector of teams he was, I consider, surpassed by no one and equalled by few, if any.'[12]

A mark of Jardine's captaincy came after the Adelaide Test in January 1933 when the furore over Bodyline became so intense that both the MCC and the Australian Board, not to mention the politicians, became involved. Even those of his team who disapproved of his tactics stood solidly behind him and the majority continued to revere him for the rest of their days, not least those from backgrounds very dissimilar to his own. While much of their respect was based on his reputation as *victor ludorum*, it also had much to do with the depth of his personality. Behind the chilly exterior they found a man of integrity and kindness who fought hard for their interests. Asked what he thought of his captain, Larwood replied simply, 'I loved him.' He didn't inspire quite the same loyalty among his new-look team in India the

following winter, partly because some players weren't prepared
to abide by his high standards, but the same qualities of courage
and guile, apparent to so many Australians, won over many an
Indian. 'Of all the English cricketers who played in India before
the Second World War, it was Douglas Jardine who was most
admired,' wrote the Indian historian Ramachandra Guha. 'He left
an impression because of his dogged batsmanship, his masterful
captaincy, and not least, he treated Indians with a respect he had
previously withheld from the Australians.'[13]

A schoolboy prodigy, Jardine gave notice of his immense
talent at Oxford without quite living up to expectations, not
helped by the severe knee injury he sustained in his third year.
With his patrician bearing, immaculate technique and unruffled
temperament, not least against fast bowling, Jardine exuded a
real presence at the crease. Playing with intense circumspection,
he could read almost any bowler and many of his innings were
faultless. Switching from opening to No.5 on joining Surrey, he
found this position to be ideal and after several years of steady
improvement, he took a great leap forward in 1927 – a season
when he was only periodically available – by topping the national
batting averages with 91. He repeated the feat again the following
year, the season he made his Test debut, with an average of 87
and for the rest of his career he remained a batsman of the highest
class. Always an immense trier, he reserved his very best for the
big occasion, most notably for Surrey against Yorkshire and for
the Gentlemen against the Players. While the crux of his game
remained based on his solid defence, he could force the pace
with the best of them, his traditional strength on the leg side
supplemented by his classical off-drive and his power off the back
foot, most notably his rasping square cut.

Making his debut against West Indies in 1928, he immediately looked at home in the Test arena and his dogged batting in Australia that winter, although too cautious for some, proved central to England's 4-1 triumph. (Few players can claim Jardine's record of eight wins and two losses against Australia in Australia.) His absence for the next two years because of business commitments was keenly felt, a fact confirmed when he returned as captain in 1931. Only in Australia in 1932/33 did his batting disappoint, a fate which befell many a subsequent England captain there such as Hammond in 1946/47, Hutton in 1954/55, Denness in 1974/75, Brearley in 1978/79, Andrew Flintoff in 2006/07 and Alastair Cook in 2013/14. He returned to his best the following summer with a flawless century against West Indies at Old Trafford when he played the short ball better than any of his team-mates.

He continued in prodigious form against India in his final series. The leading batsman on either side, his retirement, thereafter, was a severe loss to English cricket. Had he played for another few years he would surely have continued to prosper and gain greater recognition for his achievements. As it is, his Test average of 48 is exceeded by very few of his countrymen – Hobbs, Sutcliffe, Hammond and Paynter among his contemporaries – discounting those who have inflated returns from a minimum number of innings. According to Hobbs, 'England never had a better number five; you could put him in when things were going wrong and be almost certain that he would stop a rot successfully.'[14]

Jardine's life in retirement was lived in the shadows, shunned by the cricket establishment and denied a UK national honour that was all but obligatory for an England captain. Although he never recanted on his use of Bodyline, the sadness that haunted him leads one to speculate that were he able to live his life again he might have acted differently.

No longer possessed of that Calvinist zeal which had driven him on the field, Jardine achieved little of note post-cricket commensurate with his gifts for leadership. That said, he won recognition as a devoted family man, a fair-minded columnist, a committed philanthropist, a valiant soldier and a popular after-dinner speaker. As he mellowed with age, the hidden depths of his personality became more apparent, his warmth and generosity enabling many a former adversary to view him more sympathetically. Any reappraisal of Jardine's life and character cannot erase the trauma of Bodyline, but it can allow him to take his rightful place in the pantheon of great England cricketers and, quite possibly, its greatest captain.

**Endnotes:**

1   *The Bulletin*, 14 December 1982, p70
2   J.A. Mangan, *Manliness and Masculinity*, p244
3   Richard Holt, *Sport and the British,* p263
4   Alan McGilvray, *Captains of the Game*, p79
5   *The Advertiser* (Adelaide), 7 November 2002
6   Ibid
7   *The Times*, 3 December 2007
8   Mike Brearley, *On Cricket*, p55
9   Information supplied by David Frith
10  Sutcliffe, *For Yorkshire and England*, p116
11  Jack Hobbs, *My Life Story*, p255
12  Pelham Warner, *Long Innings*, p204
13  *The Hindu*, 5 March 2000
14  Hobbs, *My Life Story*, p255

# BIBLIOGRAPHY

Altham, Harry and Swanton, E.W., *A History of Cricket* (London: Allen and Unwin, 1962).

Amarnath, Rajinder, *Lala Amarnath, Life and Times* (York: Sportsbooks, 2007).

Arnold, Michael, *The Bodyline Hypocrisy: Conversations with Harold Larwood* (Worthing: Pitch Publishing, 2009).

Arlott, John (ed), *Cricket: The Great Captains* (London: Pelham Books, 1971).

Bateman, Anthony (ed), *The Cambridge Companion to Cricket* (Cambridge: Cambridge University Press, 2012).

Birley, Derek, *A Social History of English Cricket* (London: Aurum Press, 1999).

Bonnell, Max, *Dainty: The Bert Ironmonger Story* (Melbourne: Melbourne Cricket Books, 2019).

Bose, Mihir, *A History of Indian Cricket* (London: Andre Deutsch, 2002).

Bowes, Bill, *Express Deliveries* (London: Stanley Paul, 1949).

Brearley, Mike, *On Cricket* (London: Constable, 2018).

Brodribb, Gerald, *Maurice Tate: A Biography* (London: London Magazine Editions, 1976).

Cashman, Richard (ed), *The Oxford Companion to Australian Cricket* (Oxford: Oxford University Press, 1996).

Colman, Mike and Edwards, Ken, *Eddie Gilbert: The True Story of an Aboriginal Cricketing Legend* (Sydney: ABC Books, 2002).

Constantine, Learie, *Cricket in the Sun* (London: Stanley Paul, 1946).

Davie, Michael, *Anglo-Australian Attitudes* (London: Pimlico, 2001).

Derriman, Philip, *Bodyline* (Sydney: Collins, 1984).

Docker, E.W., *A History of Indian Cricket* (London: Macmillan, 1976).

Docker, E.W., *Bradman and the Bodyline Series* (Sydney: Angus and Robertson, 1978).

Dodds, Dickie, *Hit Hard and Enjoy It* (Tunbridge Wells, The Cricketer Ltd, 1976).

Douglas, Christopher, *Douglas Jardine: Spartan Cricketer* (London: Allen and Unwin, 1984).

Evans, Richard, *Teddy: The Life of Major E.G. Wynard* (Sheffield: Chequered Flag Publishing, 2018).

Fender, P.G.H, *The Turn of the Wheel* (London: Faber and Faber, 1929).

Ferguson, W.H., *Mr Cricket* (London: Nicholas Kaye, 1957).

Fingleton, Jack, *Cricket Crisis* (Melbourne: Cassell, 1946).

Fingleton, Jack, *Brightly Fades the Don* (London: Collins, 1949).

Fingleton, Jack, *The Ashes Crown the Year* (Sydney: Collins, 1954).

Firth, John, *Winchester College* (London and Glasgow: Blackie and Co, 1936).

Frith, David, *Bodyline Autopsy* (London, Aurum, 2002).

Geddes, Margaret, *Remembering Bradman* (Melbourne: Viking, 2002).

Gibson, Alan, *The Cricket Captains of England* (London: Cassell, 1979).

Gover, Alf, *The Long Run* (London: Pelham, 1991).

Grant, Joan, *Time Out of Mind* (London: Arthur Barker, 1958).

Growden, Greg, *Jack Fingleton: The Man Who Stood Up to Bradman* (New South Wales: Allen and Unwin, 2009).

Guha, Ramachandra, *A Corner of a Foreign Field* (London: Picador, 2003).

Gideon Haigh, *The Summer Game*, (Sydney: Text Publishing Company, 1997).

Haigh, Gideon, *The Big Ship* (London: Aurum, 2001).

Hamilton, Duncan, *Harold Larwood* (London: Quercus, 2009).

Hamilton, Duncan, *The Great Romantic: Cricket and the Golden Age of Neville Cardus* (London: Hodder and Stoughton, 2019).

Hammond, Walter, *Cricket My Destiny* (London: Stanley Paul, 1946).

Harris, Bruce, *Jardine Justified* (London: Chapman and Hall, 1933).

Heald, Tim, *Jardine's Last Tour: India 1933-34* (London: Methuen, 2011).

Hele, George, *Bodyline Umpire* (Adelaide: Rigby, 1974).

Hill, Alan, *Hedley Verity: A Portrait of a Cricketer* (London: Kingswood Press, 1986).

Hill, Alan, *Herbert Sutcliffe: Cricket Maestro* (London: Simon and Schuster, 1991).

Hobbs, Jack, *Fight for the Ashes 1932-3* (London: Harrap, 1933).

Hobbs, Jack, *My Life Story* (London: The Star Publications Department, 1935).

Hollis, Christopher, *Oxford in the Twenties* (London: Heinemann, 1976).

Howat, Gerald, *Plum Warner* (London: Unwin Hyman, 1987).

Jardine, Douglas, *In Quest of the Ashes* (London: Hutchinson, 1933).

Jardine, Douglas, *Ashes and Dust* (London: Hutchinson, 1934).

Jardine, Douglas, *Cricket* (London: J.M. Dent, 1936).

Kay, John (ed), *Cricket Heroes* (London: Phoenix House, 1959).

Larwood, Harold, *Bodyline?* (London: Elkin Matthews and Marrot Ltd, 1933).

Lemmon, David, *Cricket Heroes* (London: Queen Anne Press, 1984).

Lemmon, David, *Percy Chapman: A Biography* (London: Queen Anne Press, 1985).

Le Quesne, Laurence, *The Bodyline Controversy* (London: Secker and Warburg, 1983).

MacDonald, H.F. (ed), *A Hundred Years of Fettes* (Edinburgh: T.& A. Constable, 1970).

Mailey, Arthur, *And Then Came Larwood* (London: John Lane, 1933).

Mant, Gilbert, *A Cuckoo in the Bodyline Nest* (New South Wales: Kangaroo Press, 1992).

Marshall, Michael, *Gentlemen and Players* (London: Grafton, 1987).

Mason, Ronald, *Ashes in the Mouth: The Story of the Bodyline Tests 1932-33* (London: Hambledon Press, 1982).

McGilvray, Alan, *Captains of the Game* (Sydney: ABC Books, 1992).

Noble, Monty, *Fight for the Ashes, 1928-29* (London: Harrap, 1929).

Oldfield, W.A., *Behind the Wicket* (London: Hutchinson, 1938).

O'Reilly, Bill, *Tiger: Sixty Years in Cricket* (Sydney: Collins, 1985).

Pawle, Gerald, *R.E.S. Wyatt: Fighting Cricketer* (London: Allen and Unwin, 1985).

Pearson, Harry, *Connie: The Marvellous Life of Learie Constantine* (Abacus, 2017).

Peebles, Ian, *Spinners Yarn* (London: Collins, 1977).

Peel, Mark, *Playing the Game? Cricket's Tarnished Ideals from Bodyline to the Present* (Pitch Publishing, 2018).

Perkins, Kevin, *The Larwood Story* (London: W.H. Allen, 1965).

Perry, Roland, *The Don* (Sydney: Pan Macmillan, 1996).

Perry, Roland, *Bradman's Invincibles* (Sydney: Hachette, 2008).

Randall, Charles, *125 Years of Cricket: Radlett Cricket Club* (Radlett: Charles Randall and Annette Kelly, 2009).

Rendell, Brian, *Gubby Allen: Bad Boy of Bodyline?* (London: Cricket Lore, 2008).

Rendell, Brian, *Walter Robins* (Cardiff: Association of Cricket Statisticians and Historians, 2013).

Richardson, Vic, *The Vic Richardson Story* (Sydney: Angus and Robertson, 1968).

Rickson, Barry, *Duleepsinhji: Prince of Cricketers* (Manchester: Parrs Wood Press, 2005).

Robertson-Glasgow, Raymond, *Cricket Prints* (London: T. Werner Laurie, 1943).

Robertson-Glasgow, Raymond, *46 Not Out* (London: Hollis and Carter, 1948).

Robinson, Ray, *The Wildest Tests* (London: Pelham, 1972).

Rosenwater, Irving, *Sir Donald Bradman: A Biography* (London: B. T. Batsford, 1978).

Roy, David, *The Centenary History of the Arthur Dunn Cup* (Beckenham: Replay Publishing Ltd, 2003).

Sissons, Ric and Stoddart, Brian, *Cricket and the Empire* (London: Allen and Unwin, 1984).

Snow, Philip, *A Time of Renewal* (London: The Radcliffe Press, 1998).

Streeton, Richard, *P.G.H. Fender: A Biography* (London: Faber and Faber, 1981).

Sutcliffe, Herbert, *For England and Yorkshire* (London: Edward Arnold, 1935).

Swanton, E.W., *Follow On* (London: Collins, 1977).

Swanton, E.W., *Gubby Allen: Man of Cricket* (London: Hutchinson, 1985).

Travers, Ben, *94 Declared* (London: Elm Tree Books, 1981).

Warner, Pelham, *Cricket Between the Wars* (London: Chatto and Windus, 1942).

Warner, Pelham, *Long Innings* (London: Harrap, 1951).

Whitington, R.S., *Time of the Tiger: The Bill O'Reilly Story* (London: Stanley Paul, 1970).

Williams, Charles, *Bradman: An Australian Hero* (London: Little, Brown, 1997).

Wilson, Peter, *The Man They Couldn't Gag* (London: Stanley Paul, 1977).

Wilton, Iain, *C.B. Fry: King of Sport*, (London, Richard Cohen Books, 1999).

## Newspapers and Periodicals

*Adelaide Mail, Advertiser, Argus, Australasian, Birmingham Post, Brisbane Telegraph, Bulletin, Cricketer, Daily Herald, Daily Mail, Daily Telegraph, Daily Telegraph* (Sydney), *Evening Standard, Fettesian, Guardian, Hindu, Independent on Sunday, Melbourne Argus, Morning Post, Observer, Port Lincoln Times, Queensland Figaro, Referee, Scotsman, Sind, Smith's Weekly, Star, Summer Fields School Magazine, Sunday Times, Sydney Mail, Sydney Morning Herald, Sydney Sun, Times, Times of India, Truth, Wisden Cricket Monthly, Wisden Cricketers' Almanack, Wykehamist.*

# Also available at all good book stores

9781785318412

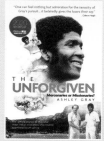

9781785315329

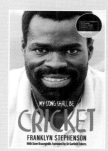

9781785315398

9781785317644

9781785318306

9781785318191

9781785317330

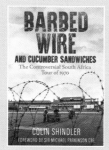

9781785316340

9781785316395